The Shocking

Miss Pilgrim

THE SHOCKING MISS PILGRIM

A Writer
in
Early Hollywood

Frederica Sagor Maas

THE UNIVERSITY PRESS OF KENTUCKY

Publication of this volume was made possible in part
by a grant from the National Endowment for the Humanities.

Published by The University Press of Kentucky

Scholarly publisher for the Commonwealth,
serving Bellarmine College, Berea College, Centre
College of Kentucky, Eastern Kentucky University,
The Filson Club Historical Society, Georgetown College,
Kentucky Historical Society, Kentucky State University,
Morehead State University, Murray State University,
Northern Kentucky University, Transylvania University,
University of Kentucky, University of Louisville,
and Western Kentucky University.

Editorial and Sales Offices: The University Press of Kentucky
663 South Limestone Street, Lexington, Kentucky 40508-4008

03 02 01 00 99   5 4 3 2

Frontispiece: Frederica Sagor in 1924 while story editor for Universal Pictures' New
York office.

"Death, the Last Visit" by Marie Howe originally appeared in *Atlantic Monthly* in 1984.
Reprinted by permission.

Library of Congress Cataloging-in-Publication Data
Maas, Frederica Sagor, 1900-
     The shocking Miss Pilgrim : a writer in early Hollywood / Frederica Sagor Maas.
     p.   cm.
     Includes index.
     ISBN 0-8131-2122-1 (alk. paper)
     1. Maas, Frederica Sagor, 1900-   . 2. Hollywood (Los Angeles, Calif.)—Social
life and customs. 3. Motion picture industry—California—Los Angeles. 4. Women
screenwriters—United States—Biography. 5. Motion picture authorship. I. Title.
     PS3525.A1122Z474   1999
     812'.52—dc21
     [B]   98-49980

This book is printed on acid-free recycled paper meeting the requirements of the
American National Standard for Permanence of Paper for Printed Library Materials.

Manufactured in the United States of America

To the "Swell Fish" that my husband,
Ernest, and I parented—
creative works that never saw the light of day.

Contents

Illustrations follow page 114

Foreword

THIS IS A HARD INTRODUCTION TO WRITE. Thirty years ago, when I started as a film historian, early Hollywood was dismissed as a place of sin and sacrifice, a modern Sodom and Gomorrah. One author called it Hollywood Babylon. I thought this obsession with the lurid overshadowed the important and often remarkable work being done at the time. In my first book, I tried to highlight the creative achievements of a vast number of astonishingly gifted individuals. But, as with any human endeavour, there was undeniably a dark side to the community, and Frederica Sagor experienced it to the full. Working women were not valued in the twenties and thirties to the same extent as they are today, and ambitious men often treated them disgracefully.

This is a story that will make you angry. A similar story could probably have been told by many women in many industries at the time. I know of another manuscript, written by a woman of roughly Frederica's age, that tells of her attempt to become an art director. She was allowed to design an important set for Clarence Brown's *The Signal Tower* (1924). She showed such flair that she was chased back to the ranks and spent the next four decades as a script girl.

Coincidentally, it was Clarence Brown's career that Frederica Sagor did so much to promote. Brown is celebrated for the films he made for Garbo and for *The Yearling* (1947). His silent films were among the finest of the period. When Frederica heard Universal was going to let him go—and he was by far their best director—she fought the decision and bought a story ideal for his talents, *The Goose Woman*, by Rex Beach.

The title may mean nothing to you, but it means everything to me. Forty years ago, when I had just started out as a film collector, I saw this title on a list from a film library in Coventry. I bought the eight reels on 16mm for twelve pounds, sight unseen. When I carried the parcel to my parents in the country and showed it for the first time, it confirmed all my hopes for the era I had adopted with such enthusiasm. Here was a picture with a first-class story, made with an innate sense of cinema, an intelligent pictorialism, and it was totally unknown. I considered it far superior to some of the accepted "classics."

When I first met Frederica, I had no idea she was the film's godmother. But then I had no idea whatsoever about her career. I was drawn to her because she had worked in silent pictures, and I could not have known that she had been given such a rough time. Nevertheless, what you are about to read is authentic. I may not agree with some of her opinions, but there can be no doubt that her story is important and should be as firmly on the record as the more traditional tales of triumph and achievement. This story is as fascinating as any tale of Academy Awards and million-dollar grosses, and it is all the more significant because of its rarity.

Frederica takes us through a turbulent era—"the best of times, the worst of times." She had great courage and was a staunch supporter of unpopular causes. Could one say, after all the evidence of this book, that the only cause she failed to support with the same implacable determination was her own?

Kevin Brownlow
London

Acknowledgments

I WOULD LIKE TO THANK these family members, friends, and professional acquaintances for their gracious and very helpful support: my nieces, Roberta Torrance Tovar and Phoebe Torrance Simpson; my great-nephew Tony Tovar; my nephew Louis Maas; and my friend Margaret Lemky; Grace Houghton, director of Emprise Publishing, Inc.; Kevin Brownlow, film historian and producer/director of Photoplay Productions Ltd.; Anthony Slide, editor of Scarecrow Press, Inc.; Thomas Stempel, professor of film history at Los Angeles City College; and Ozzie Roberts, feature writer for the *San Diego Union Tribune*. I would also like to thank the Glendale Public Library and its research staff.

Prologue

AT A HOUSE PARTY IN NOVEMBER 1988, I happened to meet an eager young writer named Sidney D. Kirkpatrick. Fascinated by Hollywood's lurid past, especially the silent era, he had just written a bestseller, *The Cast Killers*. I met him again a few weeks later, at Dutton's Bookstore in Beverly Hills, where the youthful author-celebrity was enjoying his first book launching and where I stood in line (something I had never done before) with the rest of the autograph seekers. When it came my turn, he wrote on the flyleaf of my book: "To Frederica: who paused a few moments to teach a young author some new tricks. My very best, Sidney D. Kirkpatrick."

That "pause," in truth, had been an entire evening of intense interrogation. When Sidney Kirkpatrick discovered my distant past, that I had been a Hollywood screenwriter during the twenties, thirties, and forties, he completely monopolized me for the rest of the evening, ferreting out every last detail of that almost forgotten time.

It so happened that *The Cast Killers* was about King Vidor and how he had solved the murder, after sixty years, of another great film director, William Desmond Taylor. In 1922, when the murder was committed, I was a tenderfoot in Universal's New York story department. The murder was a juicy scandal, and the newspapers had a field day. There were rumors of coverups. The head of Paramount Studios was said to have burned a bundle of Taylor's papers in the fireplace, as the police looked the other way; a well-known actress reputedly searched his house for letters she claimed were hers. The cast of suspects included the actress Mabel Normand, a possible drug addict; the beautiful ingenue Mary Miles Minter; and Mary's domineering mother, Charlotte Shelby. All were thought to have had clandestine affairs with the slain director, a philanderer and playboy of the silent era, and it was generally believed that he received his just deserts when he was shot to death in his Los Angeles bungalow by an unknown assailant. Back in 1922, this had been heady, titillating stuff for an impressionable neophyte in the film business, and I remembered it well. And, as Sidney Kirkpatrick learned in the course of our discussion, I remembered a lot of other things well, too.

"Do you know Kevin Brownlow?" he asked me suddenly, as if everyone connected with the film business knew Kevin Brownlow. I had never heard of him. Since I had been removed from the celluloid scene for over forty years, Hollywood film historians or Hollywood anything were of little interest to me. "No," I replied, "who is he?"

I soon learned all about Kevin Brownlow. Within weeks of my meeting Sidney, Kevin set himself on my trail and insisted I grant him an interview. This man was responsible for well-known documentaries on Charlie Chaplin and Buster Keaton, as well as another on Harold Lloyd. His book about Hollywood, *The Parade's Gone By,* had received rave reviews.

It was Kevin Brownlow who convinced me to write this book. He felt that I knew things no one else did and that I could tell stories as no one else could—and with credentials like his, I could scarcely argue. So I took pen in hand and began to set down my life in Hollywood as I remember it.

Now, when you reach the august age that I have and try to remember what has happened in your life, you have a lot of ground to cover. I lived through two World Wars, the Great Depression, the McCarthy era, and eighteen different presidencies. Later, when I was well into my eighties, and after the death of my husband, I made two long, searching trips to Russia to visit the homeland of my parents. In all, this story deals with frustration, disillusionment, and heartache—times perhaps best left to lie fallow or not remembered at all. Certainly that is how I felt in 1950 when at last I bid farewell, without tears, to the Hollywood screen industry that had so entangled and entrapped me in its web of promises. I was determined then to forget and go on to other pursuits. I did, and never looked back—until now.

Chapter 1

FAMILY ROOTS

MY MOTHER WAS A GRADUATE of Moscow University in the early 1880s. She had also been a piano student at the Moscow Conservatory of Music and aspired to be a concert pianist until Anton Rubinstein, who was head of the conservatory and one of her teachers, told her that her hands were too chubby, her fingers too short, for her to hope for a soloist career. Another of her teachers, just beginning his career, was Peter Ilyich Tchaikovsky. Mama treasured two small autographed pictures of these great artists, and they alone adorned her bedroom bureau until I fell heir to them.

My ever-practical mother turned, instead, to the profession of midwifery, a highly respected profession then. She received her training in Germany and later boasted that, in fifteen years of practice, she never lost a patient.

In addition to her native Russian, Mama spoke fluent German and French. When she later came to America, she learned to speak Yiddish from living in Jewish neighborhoods and shopping in Yiddish butcher and grocery stores. But English was another matter. She never mastered it, although she tried very hard.

"Your devilish language," she would say in Russian, "the spelling never makes sense. In Russian, a word is spelled the way it sounds and has one meaning. In English, a word is seldom spelled the way it sounds and has so many different meanings." In later years, when miles separated us and we had to correspond, she wrote her weekly letters phonetically, and I cherished every misspelled word.

In the 1880s in Russia, the Romanov dynasty was flourishing with the backing of the decadent Greek Orthodox Church. Revolution was in the air but successfully controlled by the powerful regime. My father had come to Moscow to meet with university students engaged in revolutionary activities. One of the students was my mother, and that is how they met. She was twenty-five years old then and considered herself an old maid. But my handsome six-foot, two-inch father changed her mind, even though he was a Jew and she was not.

Papa came from a provincial town called Zagorsk, not far from Moscow. His name was Zagorsky (son of Zagorsk). It was anglicized to "Sagor" when he came to the United States. After marriage, my mother and father lived in Moscow with her parents. Her father raised and trained horses for the nobility and military. He was also an opera buff and loved music. (One of his sons, Sasha Litvinoff, was an outstanding violinist—among the first to play the Tchaikovsky Violin Concerto in concert. He later became a conductor and, after the revolution in 1917, left for Denmark to become head of the Danish orchestra.)

While living in Russia, my parents, Arnold and Agnessa Zagorsky, had three daughters: Vera, Sonya (Sophie), and Luba (Lilly). Then one fine day, Russian officials decided that, because my father was a Jew (and a revolutionary), he and his family could no longer live in Moscow. My mother, faced with the prospect of leaving her beloved Moscow and moving to a small town in a Jewish settlement, stoically refused. If they couldn't live in Moscow, then they would live in America—where there was freedom to live anywhere you wanted, without fear of the secret police watching your every move. And she dispatched my father posthaste to New York to find a new life for us.

And so it was, three years later, that Ellis Island witnessed the reunion of my mother, my three sisters (ages four, seven, and nine), and my father. Papa was now in the curtain business and "making a living," as they put it in those difficult days of struggle. He had an apartment ready on the lower East Side. It was on the top floor of a run-down three-story walkup. My intrepid mother took one look around and would not allow her children to sleep there until she had washed down the walls and floors with carbolic acid.

After one week in America, she donned her palerina (a heavy, lined, blue cape with a hood made for Russian winters) and resumed her career as a midwife. In those days, for the munificent sum of ten dollars, a midwife attended her patient during the birth of the baby and provided one week's postnatal care. Mama always claimed that she knew more about childbearing than the average doctor—especially when it came to hygiene. American doctors, she said, arriving in their horse-drawn buggies, came to the bedside of patients without a thought of washing their hands. Only my diminutive mother, all four feet, six inches of her, arms akimbo, defied them. She had a pot of boiling water and soap ready, and they had to scrub to the elbows and then don a white gown that she had sewn for the purpose.

Mama's practice mushroomed, and she soon had more work than she could handle. In addition to working, she sewed all her children's clothes and never failed to have a hot lunch on the stove waiting for them to heat up when they came home from school. Dear Papa was never a moneymaker, and household expenses were barely met until my sisters began to teach, years later. The first thing my mother saved for was a piano—a secondhand upright Knabe that she bought for twenty-five dollars. The piano lessons for Vera and Sophie were twenty-five cents each, twice a month. The teacher was a dapper young Russian immigrant, a Mr. Danielson. Later, when he came up in the musical world, Jacques Danielson achieved the distinction of becoming the husband of Fannie Hurst, the famous novelist and short story writer. Mr. Danielson (he was always Mr. Danielson to us) was especially proud to have been the teacher of my gifted sister, Sophie, who he turned over to the noted Rafael Joseffy for launching as a performing artist. Yes, my mother was a terror in what she was able to accomplish. I like to think that her only daughter to be born under the American flag and christened Frederica Alexandrina (Freddie for short) inherited some of her extraordinary get-up-and-go.

I was born in a coldwater railroad flat on 101st Street near Madison Avenue on July 6, 1900. My mother was her own midwife with the help of my oldest sister, Vera, who was then seventeen. It was early afternoon; Papa, of course, was at business. There was no time to call the doctor, so Mama delivered me herself.

"Another girl," she said softly, shaking her head. "Your Papa will not like that. He wanted a son."

Dear Papa, how he had hoped for a son when I came along! Four daughters. But as I grew up and became more interesting to be with, he tried to reconcile his disappointment because he recognized almost from the start that I was different from my matriarch-dominated sisters. As I grew older, I was ever ready to challenge and defy my austere mother, who would never listen to the other side of the story and whose favorite word was "Nyet."

It was Papa who bought my Easter and school outfits downtown at Hester and Grand Streets on the lower East Side. Jewish merchants had their retail stores there, one next to another, and often stood in the doorway with a long hooked pole to pull in a passing customer. When finally I found the coat or dress I wanted, the haggling began. And they haggled to the last penny over the price of the garment I wanted so much. Those were moments of genuine terror for me as Papa and the merchant argued back and forth. Finally Papa, taking me by the hand, would prepare to leave the store. I was always sure he would lose the battle and I would lose the coat or dress I wanted. But Papa always won, for the merchant was sure to come running after us before we could enter another store.

On these expeditions, always made by the "elevated," Papa would give me a penny, which I inserted into a vending machine on the platform. The inserted penny would bring the magic return of a neatly wrapped stick of chewing gum. "Don't tell your Mama," Papa would laughingly caution. Another secret we shared was my first visit to a nickelodeon. There was one at the corner of 110th Street and Fifth Avenue. We had to stand in the back, for the place was packed. Papa posed me on his shoulders so that I could see. The picture? Hazily, I recall it was *Sampson and Delilah*. We came in at the end, as Sampson was tearing down the temple. Of course, I was too young to know what I was looking at. After *Sampson*, we saw a picture about Indians fighting the white men on the western plains. This was a subject to which I could better relate. Again, there was the admonishment from Papa: "Don't tell Mama." And I never did. It was nice having secrets from your Mama with your Papa.

During the summertime, my father and I would go for rides on the open-air electric streetcars, which had replaced the horse-drawn cars I could only vaguely remember. On a sultry summer day, it was a luxury to cool off, and, for a nickel, you could escape from the heat of the city and experience the wind running through your hair. You could breathe and not gasp for breath the way you would if you were still in your apartment in the city. We'd go to the end of the line, wherever it would take us. Few people got on or off because most people were on for the same reason we were, for a summer excursion, not every week, just once in a while. My mother never went along because she didn't like that sort of thing and she always had "other things" to do around the house.

In addition to the streetcars, my father would take me on the train to places outside of New York such as New Rochelle and Mamaroneck and Peekskill. We'd go various places where he had his tailor customers, and he'd show me off to them; one client was Mr. Resnick. Good God, how does that name still stick in my memory? I was always so proud of my father. I was small for my years, and he was tall, dark, and handsome (and bald-headed; he went bald when he was nineteen). I was his pet. In later years, I would take the same trains alone, to New Rochelle in particular, and lose myself in the countryside, reading and writing in my journal. I was a loner then.

In 1900, there was no electricity, only gas and kerosene lamps. No telephones. No automobiles. We had no steam heat, no hot water. We had to heat the water for our baths, which we took in the kitchen in a big tub near the pot-bellied stove. It was called a railroad flat because it was all in a line—one room leading into another: kitchen, bedroom, bedroom, water closet (no bathroom), dining room, and parlor, which was the only room that looked out on the street and got some sunlight.

But the Sagors soon changed all that. They came up in the world and moved to 1480 Madison Avenue at 102nd Street, a modern apartment in every sense of the word. It had three airy bedrooms (one facing the street), a bathroom with a bathtub, a kitchen with a gas stove, a dining room with a dumbwaiter, and a large parlor big enough for the Knabe concert grand we now acquired. It wasn't long before the gas lamps were turned into electric globe fixtures, and we experienced the marvels of having electricity. "A miracle," Mama called it. In time, too, we acquired a wall telephone that had to be cranked and that Mama, brave soul that she was, mistrusted and was afraid to use.

Central Park was practically at our back door. Every day when I was little, weather permitting, my mother would wheel my carriage to Ninety-first Street and Fifth Avenue, to the Carnegie mansion. The big iron gates would open as the splendid carriage with its black, prancing horses drove out for the millionaire's morning ride in the park.

Sometimes Mrs. Carnegie was with him, but mostly he was alone. And, do you know, he never failed to tip his hat to my mother and wave to me. Recently, I spent several weeks in New York at a bed-and-breakfast apartment on Ninety-first Street right off Fifth Avenue. Mr. Carnegie is long gone. My mother is long gone. But the Carnegie mansion is still there in all its glory—copper fittings on the pipes in the basement and the faucets in the bathrooms. All I had to do was close my eyes and remember . . .

Besides the Sagors, there were two other tenants on the fourth and top floor of 1480 Madison Avenue: Mr. Gallagher the policeman (Mama liked that, for it meant security) and the Siebels from Odessa—from Russia. The Siebels were really two families—three Rubins and five Siebels, all adults. Rose Rubin was also a fine pianist, a scholarship student of the eminent Lambert. When I was eight and confined to my bedroom with scarlet fever, Rose would treat me to a Bach-Scarlatti concert every day because she knew that I listened through the walls, and Bach and Scarlatti were my favorites. Mrs. Siebel was something else. She liked to visit and talk across the air shaft. Even though she spoke good Russian, she was the bane of Mama's life because Mama had no time for idle gossip—in Russian or otherwise. If Mama had a spare hour, she cherished it to read one of the Russian magazines to which she still subscribed. One of these was *The Neva*. The magazine serialized a novel by Gogol, and Mama could hardly wait for the next installment to arrive. Mrs. Siebel was the first women I ever saw smoking. She was never without a cigarette dangling out of the corner of her mouth. Her fingers were stained with nicotine. I thought her very decadent. Nice women did not smoke openly then.

Fourteen-eighty Madison Avenue boasted one tenant who became famous. Two floors below us lived Alma Gluck and her husband Barney. The lovely songstress from Rumania was just beginning her vocal career but was already achieving rave notices for her beautiful soprano. When finally she reached the top, she divorced Barney and married Russian concert violinist Efrem Zimbalist. The press made much of the love match and the acrimonious divorce (Barney was a bad loser).

Many of my childhood memories involve music and musicians, undoubtedly because I was immersed in it almost from birth. My sister Sophie, in particular, shared my passion. The family liked to recount how, as a six-year-old, I attended a recital she was giving and called out from our box, "Mistake!" when she happened to make one. My first piano teacher, Sophie took me to all her favorite keyboard concerts from the time I was five years old—Carnegie Lyceum, Steinway Hall, Carnegie Hall. I heard such famous women pianists as Fanny Bloomfield-Zeisler, Theresa Carreño, Guiomar Navaes, Myra Hess, as well as male greats such as Sergie Rachmaninoff, Josef Levinne, Vladimir de Pachman, Paderewski, Ossip Gabrolowitsch, Harold Bauer—and greatest of them all, Josef Hofmann. After the last encore, with the palms of our hands still tingling from the ardor of applause, the lights would dim and the appearance of the piano movers on stage would finally convince us that the concert was over. Sophie and I would dash over to Schirmer's Music Store to buy the music, especially the concertos: Schumann, Grieg, McDowell, Brahms. At home on our Knabe grand, we would duet, with Sophie playing the orchestral part and her little sister carrying the piano solo. What a time that was!

My oldest sister, Vera, had her wedding at 1480 Madison Avenue. The only thing I remember about that occasion was the terrible disaster that befell a huge platter of prunes rolled in powdered sugar and stuffed with nuts and dried apricots. I had been impatiently waiting to taste them all day. Right before dessert was to be served, however, the chandelier in the dining room started swinging wildly back and forth, and plaster began raining down on the table. The stamping feet on the roof were those of our irate neighbors from below us, giving notice that it was midnight and we were interfering with their slumber. The prunes were ruined and had to be trashed. I was only seven then, but to this day I still lament those luscious, untasted—and discarded—prunes.

Our oldest friends in New York City were the Joffes. Mama had delivered three of their children. We didn't have many friends, but the Joffes were particularly close to our family and we to them. We celebrated birthdays together and visited frequently. Solomon Joffe, an actuary at a life insurance company, and his wife had four children, a boy, Julian, who was in college, two daughters who were schoolteachers, and one little daughter, Sonochika, who was five years old when tragedy struck their family.

Sonichika was the apple of her parents' eye. In 1918, when the Spanish influenza struck, the family took every precaution to keep her safe, to keep her from falling victim. Whenever family members reentered the house, they would change their clothing, shower, and completely sanitize themselves to keep from bringing in any infection from the outside. They worried constantly and did everything they could to protect the little girl. Despite all their precautions, she was stricken, as were many others in that dreadful epidemic. Mrs. Joffe never completely recovered from the loss of little Sonichika. Though the influenza did not touch my family personally, I have vivid memories of that tragedy.

Come spring—every spring—I came down with chills and high fever. Malaria. In delirium I was always floating on a cake of ice, crying out, "Mama, Mama, save me, save me!" It was the opinion of our Russian family doctor, Dr. Eva Dembo, that the cause of the malaria was the mosquitoes breeding in the man-made lake of Central Park.

Dr. Dembo was most impressive. A large woman, she wore a high-necked shirtwaist with a man's tie and a mannish suit and hat. Her hair was cropped short. She had a deep voice. She and another lady doctor, Dr. Fanny Abramovitz, had been living under one roof and practicing medicine together for ten years or more. At the time, Dr. Eva Dembo was my role model and clinched my decision to become a doctor when I grew up. This conviction was sidetracked, but only temporarily, by seeing Max Reinhardt's spectacular production of *The Miracle*, a great play about a novice entering a convent to devote her life to being a bride of Christ. I was overwhelmed with the moving religiosity of the play and decided to become a nun instead of a doctor. As I garbed myself in white raiment and viewed my reflection in the mirror, I rather liked the role and, positive that I would make a very good nun, began attending Mass with a Catholic friend. My agnostic mother did not approve of my new aspirations, but I went anyway until I became suspicious of a young priest who liked to hold us on his lap and fondle us a little too intimately for comfort. I didn't dare tell my mother, but I lost my determination to give myself to Christ, and I returned to my goal of a medical career, which I stuck to until I went to college.

When I was nine years old, the family decided to move way out into the country—the Bronx! And in 1909, it was the country. Open fields, clean fresh air, sparsely populated. Large ads in the papers touted the advantages of getting away from the overcrowded city of Manhattan into the big, open spaces. Housing developments offered playgrounds with swings and sandboxes for smaller children and tennis courts and croquet for grown-ups as a lure. Today the same area, the very same area where we lived, Southern Boulevard and 165th Street, is the worst slum area of the borough of the Bronx, full of crumbling, rat-infested tenements, burned-out stores and buildings, gang warfare, and drugs. Through the years, I have seen election campaigners from Bobby Kennedy on down all promise to clean it up; but campaigners, long on promises, unfortunately have short memories once elections are over. It remains an eyesore.

It was while living on Southern Boulevard in the Bronx, in the apartment we occupied over Streng's Millinery shop, that my sister Sophie met her husband-to-be, Dr. Joseph Smith. My future brother-in-law's life was a Horatio Alger tale, if ever there was one. At fifteen he had stowed away on a big ocean liner to come to America. Discovered and certain to be returned to Poland, he had been befriended by a young Dr. Lichtenstein on board ship, who took him under his wing and eventually helped educate the boy in his own profession. As the boy's Polish name was long and unpronounceable, an immigration officer arbitrarily christened him "Smith." It suited him. A graduate of Johns Hopkins and an early disciple of Freud, Dr. Smith was one of our first practicing psychiatrists. President Roosevelt later commended him for his outstanding war efforts.

I could think of nothing more wonderful—a doctor in the Sagor family! Without my sister knowing it, I managed to read every one of the ardent, beautifully scripted love letters this young doctor sent her, and I prevailed upon her to discard another suitor, a lawyer from Detroit, in Joe's favor. "Marry him, please marry him!" I implored.

The wedding took place in our home on Southern Boulevard. I remember it well. I was thirteen years old. My cousin Eugenia Schiffrin was visiting us from St. Petersburg at the time. She played and sang a Chopin etude in Russian to the words of Pushkin. In the middle of the song she broke down. She had been recently divorced after an unhappy marriage. Whenever I hear Chopin's Etude No. 3 in E Major, Opus 10, I am reminded of that scene.

We had a priest and a rabbi officiate. Sophie was told that if she succeeded in stepping on the groom's foot as the words "love and obey" were uttered to tie the knot, she would not have to obey. She did not succeed. Try as she would, Joe was too clever for her. Little did I dream that shortly after their marriage, this young doctor would make a brutal, if honest, confession that he really did not care much about the piano and that he much preferred the violin. My shocked and foolish sister closed her Steinway Grand and did not open it again until after her husband's death, she tearfully confessed to me some twenty years later. "You never know," she wept softly.

We moved from Southern Boulevard to East 165th Street shortly after Sophie's marriage. We no longer needed as large an apartment. My sister Lilly and I always shared a bedroom. Our new abode had five rooms, only one flight up. After eight years on the top floor of 1480 Madison Avenue, my mother had had enough of climbing stairs. This was one of those developments with playgrounds and tennis courts. I became a crack tennis player after this early exposure to the game and won many trophies. I attended P.S. 20, an all-girls school that was a good mile away. In winter, we plowed through snowdrifts that seemed as high as we were to get to school, but what fun! We sledded tobog-gan-style down five hills into the New York Railroad tracks at the bot-tom of 165th Street. In summer, we walked or took the trolley to Clauson Point or Pelham Bay. I used to wander out there alone, sit out on the rocks until the tide came in, and write poetry or read: George Eliot, Dickens, Thackeray, Victor Hugo, Balzac, Dumas, Zola, de Maupassant, Thomas Hardy, and of course, the Russians Chekov, Turgenov, Tolstoy, and Dostoevsky.

P.S. 20 was a good school—so good, I believe, that it spoiled me for high school and even college. The quality of the teachers and the education we received at P.S. 20 simply could not be duplicated. My teachers? Miss Priscilla Zoble for arithmetic, Miss Imogene Ash for grammar, and Miss Brooks for English literature. I can still remember that queenly Canadian blonde reciting Longfellow's *Evangeline*, dra-matizing those beautiful lines and making the poem real for us:

This is the forest primeval
The murmuring pines and hemlocks
Bearded with moss and in garments green,
Indistinct in the twilight. . . .

Then there was pretty Geraldine O'Connor for gym, even prettier Betty Smith for domestic science, and old Miss Baxter, who had a touch of St. Vitas Dance (we call it Parkinson's Disease now), for sewing and hygiene. And "66"—our name for our drawing and music instructor,

Miss Ehlers, so dubbed because her two curls in the middle of her forehead made a perfect number 66. When she conducted the Glee Club and sang with us in her cracked alto voice, those two curls would bob up and down in perfect time. P.S. 20 came out at the top in all State Regents examinations. Mrs. Veronica M. Curtis was our venerable principal, and Miss Cora McKinley was her shadowy assistant. The teaching staff was predominantly Catholic even though most students were not.

But the greatest teacher of them all was Miss Lillian Vion, whom I had for history. She especially stands out in my memory because she taught me so much more than historical dates. Lillian Vion told it like it was, and when you realize that this was 1913—before World War I—it is all the more remarkable. She did not mince words about our shameful treatment of the native Indians, the mob hysteria of the Salem witch hunts, our shortchanging of Mexico in the War of 1848, the true facts about slavery and the Civil War, our cycles of booms and busts. She taught us how to appreciate cartoons, especially political ones. She taught us how to read the newspaper from the first page to the editorials and even through the business section.

She took five of us to see D.W. Griffith's *The Birth of a Nation* when it played the Liberty Theater in New York. We sat in the front row of the balcony, and it is a wonder I did not land in the orchestra. The picture had me on the edge of my seat in riveted attention, leaning perilously over the railing from start to finish. Our assignment was to write our opinion, our reaction to the film. After we did this, she gave us the lowdown. She told us that, while it was a great film depicting the horrors of the Civil War, it was not an accurate picture of slavery. I learned from that lecture that concessions often have to be made in the interest of box-office receipts and prevailing public opinion on slavery, including the opinion of D.W. Griffith, who still wavered on the subject. There were no good slavemasters, she claimed, only better ones, for slavery was totally evil. What a teacher!

"Accept nothing," Miss Vion would say. "Examine, challenge, think it out for yourself." Small wonder no teacher could approach her, either in high school or college. I owe so much to that great woman who taught me to think for myself. It was this skill, more than any other, that helped me navigate the rocks and rapids of my future life in Hollywood and live to tell the tale.

Chapter 2

FROM COLUMBIA
TO UNIVERSAL

WHEN I WAS SEVENTEEN, I was a freshman at Columbia University, on 110th Street near Broadway in New York City. All the boys I knew were either Over There or about to go Over There to fight Huns and save the world for democracy. Woodrow Wilson, whom I idolized, was president of the United States and was being blamed for getting us into the war by German sympathizers both in and outside Congress. It was not an easy time to be seventeen.

My being a journalism student was a compromise and very much a second choice. From grammar school on, it had been my resolve to become a doctor. I triumphed over four years of Latin, three years of chemistry, two years of German—all requirements for medical school entrance. But, alas, it was not meant to be. Upon graduation from high school, the family—Mama, Papa, and three imperious older sisters—held a council and decreed that I was much too comely and too good a candidate for marriage for them to back me for six years of medical training. It was a shock. I rebelled. If the family would not support me, then I would take a business course and earn my own tuition.

A business course! A job in a business office! That caused real consternation in the Sagor family, especially with Mama, who was the head of that family. Agnessa Litvinoff's opinion of the American business world was very low, indeed. My three sisters had all gracefully graduated from dreamy, wisteria-vine-covered Hunter College (or Normal College as it was known then) as schoolteachers. Mama was devastated when her youngest, maverick daughter vociferously refused to follow in their footsteps. I was not going to be a rubber stamp, another schoolmarm, no matter how prestigious a profession my mother deemed it to be. And so it was that the family, realizing how adamant I was, offered me a second choice. If not a doctor, what then would I want to be? Since it was unthinkable that I would not go to college and since English had always been my great love, I opted for journalism. It was an acceptable compromise.

I was disappointed, however, with Columbia's journalism course. I had looked forward to college, expecting it to be an exhilarating learning experience. But, as in high school, the teachers were just average. One excelled, a handsome man whom we later learned was homosexual and with whom all of us innocent maidens thought we were madly in love. His name was John Melville Weaver, and he was writing a definitive work on the life of Herman Melville. He was one of those rare birds—an inspirational teacher.

There was another factor that mitigated against my enjoyment of Columbia. I was an outside student, a student who commuted to and from college and did not live in a dormitory or partake of college-life activities, as one should in college. I left home every weekday morning around eight, at the height of business traffic, took the elevated subway at Freeman Station in the Bronx where we lived at the time, changed to the underground subway going to the west side, and exited at 116th Street and Broadway. I was loaded with schoolbooks and a bagged lunch and had to stand and hold onto a strap most of the way. I then repeated the performance at five o'clock. After classes I worked for pin money in the Columbia library, and that extended my day into rush hour going home. College was no fun for me. In fact, I came close to having a first-class nervous breakdown—and would have if my perceptive mother had not recognized that something was wrong. The tears started coursing down my cheeks every day as soon as I came up for air from the underground at 116th Street and Broadway. As the university buildings came into view, I would feel physically sick at the thought of entering and attending classes. I was one miserable, frustrated, confused novitiate, let me tell you. I can still remember the nauseating smell when I opened up my bagged lunch in the Barnard cafeteria. It inevitably ended up in the trash bin after one tiny bite. I was really in a bad way.

"Whatever is wrong with you?" Mama demanded. "You are not yourself. What is bothering you?"

I welcomed her invitation to unload. "I hate Columbia! It's as bad as high school. Even worse. I'm not learning anything. Here you are spending so much money to educate me—money I know you and Papa need for yourselves—and I'm going to let you down. I'm going to fail! I should go to work, earn money."

For once, my fantastic Mama understood—it was one of the few times in our lives together she heard me through. "Fredusha," she said, putting her comforting arms around me, "there's nothing for you to cry about. Your Papa and I would not be sending you to college if we did not have the money. So don't worry about it, foolish child. College is new to you now. You're a little frightened. You'll see. You'll study hard and get to like it."

Mama was right. But not for the reasons she set forth so tenderly that day. Her Fredusha met a red-headed football player from Boise, Idaho, who was also a journalism student. He lived on campus. When he graduated, he would be a reporter on an Idaho paper. Now when I left the subway at 116th Street and Broadway, I had something to look forward to. Mark Baker carried my books. He even rode the subway partway when I was going home, just to be with me. It was his first big crush and mine, too. It was puppy love and all it entailed: secret meetings, holding hands, stolen kisses.

I soon discovered that one was not likely to learn to be a newspaper reporter by reading textbooks and listening to professors. So, during our second summer vacation, I hired out to the *New York Globe* as an errand- or copygirl—the first female to be so engaged on that venerable paper. At the *Globe*, I learned how a paper is put to bed, how editorials are written, and how reporters run themselves ragged chasing stories and then rushing back from the field and knocking out their copy—in short, the inner workings, from A to Z, of a big, highly esteemed newspaper. And how I loved being a girl—to paraphrase a song by Rodgers and Hammerstein—even if I was often the butt of sly male humor aimed at making me blush, as I was wont to do then. I was petite with long, dark brown tresses worn in a bun at the nape of my neck, a piquant small nose, and large, brown eyes that missed nothing.

It was that same summer that the *Daily News* came into being— a tabloid that was the talk of New York because of its radical format aimed at subway-riding readers and others who enjoyed abbreviated, sensational journalism with heavy emphasis on sports. To attract attention, the paper launched a short-story contest; the story selected as best each week won a prize of a hundred dollars. The contest lasted only a few months. On the final day for entry, having some free time in the office, I borrowed a typewriter, knocked out my masterpiece, and got it in the mail by the deadline. The story eludes me now—something about a poor cobbler who falls asleep praying for a miracle and awakens to find the miracle realized. Anyway, it had the required number of words for a short-short story. The incredible happened. I won and received a hundred-dollar check, which I waved around the office before the eyes of impressed colleagues. They carried me around on their shoulders and hailed me as Miss Chekhov of 1918!

But at the Sagor domicile, it was a different story. My literary success elicited outrage, chagrin, and contempt. How could I have lowered my standards so far as to appear in print in a rag like the *Daily News?* Both my autocratic mother and superior sisters considered it a monumental disgrace, and no amount of reasoning on my part could change their minds. Only my father furtively (because he always deferred to mother) relished the fact that I had earned a hundred dollars so handily.

My last year in college found me more bored and unfulfilled than ever. Two summers of newspaper exposure had not convinced me that this was the field I wanted to pursue, even if I could find employment as a reporter. This was before radio and television, and women reporters were still rare. I had exalted dreams of writing a novel someday. Raised on classics read to me in Russian, I had decidedly caviar tastes in literature.

An advertisement in the *New York Times* Business Opportunity column caught my attention. The position offered was "Assistant to Story Editor" at Universal Pictures' New York offices. It had the intriguing ring of promise, importance, and novelty. The next day, I skipped classes at Columbia. I put in an appearance at 1600 Broadway, rode up in the rickety elevator to the fourth floor, and was interviewed for the job of assistant to the story editor of Universal. The editor's name was John Charles Brownell. He was a dead ringer for John Barrymore, with the same great profile. Fortyish and gentlemanly, he had once been an actor and, in his salad days, had shared diggings with the great Barrymore. He patiently outlined my duties, partly as a secretary, partly as a script reader. I was to assist him in general and would have as much latitude as I wanted to turn the job into anything I wanted it to be. I was hooked. It was a chance to develop, to reach out in a new field. Motion pictures! Fantastic! I took the job knowing full well I would have to leave Columbia before I graduated. I would have to face the fierce Sagor family again.

The fact that my salary was a whopping one hundred dollars a week may have influenced my sisters and father somewhat. A hundred dollars a week was more than my sisters were earning as pedagogues and certainly more than Papa was bringing home. The big salary did not impress Mama, however. Mama did not believe in big salaries, big anything. I do believe Mama was a fervent socialist at heart, and her beliefs rubbed off on me later in life, although I resisted her old-fashioned ideas when I was growing up. In later life I could see where she was right in so many areas, especially her creed that money corrupts and that all one really needs in life is to earn enough for shelter, food, and medical bills. She scorned luxury as such, and all her life she shared what little she had with others who were worse off than herself. The Widow Crockmayer comes to mind—the tea lady who sold tea and coffee door-to-door and had seven children to feed. I bet Mama had more tea and coffee on her shelves than she could have used in two lifetimes.

Since there was no stopping me, the family relented and permitted me to drop out of Columbia. My career in motion pictures had begun. I fell asleep that night with my heart pounding, all my senses aroused in anticipation of becoming assistant to John C. Brownell, story editor of Universal Pictures. The attraction to this handsome man was instantaneous. Up to that time, I had dated boys my own age and found them immature and uninteresting, even if one or two were brilliant scholastically. But now that I was becoming a woman of the world, things would change for me.

Universal proved a faster school of learning in six months than Columbia School of Journalism had in three years. In addition to John Brownell and myself, our department consisted of two full-time and several outside readers. The senior reader was a fiftyish former newspaperman named Bob Rodin, who at one time had been employed by J.P. Morgan and spent several years abroad selecting and buying rare books to fill the Morgan mansion. Bob Rodin was a veritable encyclopedia of literature, motion picture history, and development—almost any subject you could name. He became my mentor and teacher. These men vied with each other, I believe, to fill my personal library with gifts of books: a handsome set of Chekhov short stories and notebooks, a rare edition of Walt Whitman, beautiful editions of Shakespeare's plays.

These were still the days of silent films. Universal was not yet on a par with Paramount (then known as Famous Players–Lasky) or First National; both had more standing as filmmakers, and both were hot competitors for material suitable for the silver screen. Both paid handsome sums, for those days, for good stories, but Universal was considered chintzy when buying material. There were, of course, literary and motion picture agents handling outstanding authors and their work. The great prize was the galley proof. The company that first got its hot hands on the galleys from the book publishing house stole the march on the others and could buy the coveted property before anyone else had a chance to bid on it. There was much secret under-the-table maneuvering going on with the underpaid publishers' readers.

I had my own office leading into that of John Brownell. One of the nice things about our offices was that they faced the roof of the Roxy Palace, home of the famous Rockettes. Weather permitting, the Rockettes often practiced their drilled dance routines atop that roof, and we would watch them. One of the annoyances, however, was a friend of John's who would always barge in, without acknowledging my authority to protect my boss. I complained about him to John, but he dismissed it. He said he was a clever young man, a documentary film writer, who John liked to talk to. So I forgot about it.

I threw myself into my job with boundless enthusiasm, energy, and commitment. Though I was just a secretary, I took home scripts, manuscripts, and other readers' synopses and read them way past the midnight hours. I even threw fifty dollars of good money away and sent for a manual of *How to Become a Screen Writer.* Put out by the Palmer School of Hollywood and dubbed "The Palmer Method," it was heralded in full-page ads in the film journals and newspapers and had enough credited sponsors to make it look impressive and authentic. June Mathis was one of the sponsors. That was enough for me. I venerated her for credits on such pictures as *The Four Horsemen of the Apocalypse* with Rudolph Valentino. The Palmer school promised to read and correct your film scenarios. John Brownell gave me the facts when he learned what I had done—too late, alas, to save my fifty dollars. When the alleged textbook of "The Palmer Method" arrived in the mail, it was an obvious moneymaking scheme from start to finish, a fraud, a false come-on for novices like myself.

"If you want to learn film technique," John Brownell advised, "watch and study motion pictures."

He accompanied me to the theaters and explained camera shots and techniques of telling a story economically and dramatically. The Strand, the Rialto, the Rivoli, the Capital, the Roxy—they were my schools. I saw every new picture that came out—not once, but again and again. I might see a good picture as many as three or four times, analyzing it, making stenographic notes of sequences, frame by frame; that was the way I learned the techniques to screenwriting.

My favorites were nearly all made by William DeMille, the artistic brother of the showman pretender Cecil B. DeMille, whose spectaculars were all box-office shekel smashes, while William's fine sensitive pictures just got by. In particular there were *What Every Woman Knows* (from the play by Sir James Barrie, starring Lois Wilson and J. Warren Kerrigan) and *Miss Lulu Betts* (from Zona Gale's fine novel, starring Lois Wilson and Milton Sills and with a sterling script by Clara Beringer). Others included Frank Borzage's *Humoresque* from a short story by Fannie Hurst; *Deception,* with Pola Negri and Emil Jannings, which Ernst Lubitsch directed; a story about Henry VIII and Ann Boleyn, *Bluebeard's Eighth Wife,* starring Gloria Swanson and directed by Sam Wood; and finally, *The Covered Wagon,* again starring Lois Wilson and J. Warren Kerrigan, and directed by James Cruze. These were but a few of my "textbooks." Films today may be more sophisticated, come in color, and talk, but when it comes to quality, the 1920s produced some of the best fare in the history of motion pictures.

I was fierce in my passion for this new medium that utterly fascinated me with its possibilities, its potential to entertain so vast a hungry public, its beautiful canvases, its opportunities for excellence. I even found time to collaborate, working at night in the office on an original story based on an idea of Bob Rodin's called *The Orchid Lady*—a melodrama and a murder mystery that Bob and I sold for the magnificent sum of fifteen hundred dollars. It was bought by Broadway producer S.J. Selwyn but never made into a film, although Selwyn did fool around with a dramatization for the stage.

I quickly spent my share—$750—on a handsome brown caracal fur coat, purchased on the spur of the moment one lunch hour at a posh furrier's on Fifth Avenue. I also invested seventy-five dollars on a beauty kit at the newly opened beauty salon of Helena Rubenstein on Fifty-seventh Street near Fifth Avenue. Why I felt I needed those cosmetics, at that age, is a good question, but they seemed crucial to me at the time; and for one week I slathered them on my face, conscientiously following directions as given. After a week, I developed a beautiful rash, and all seventy-five dollars' worth of Helena Rubenstien were summarily dumped into my office trash basket. Since then, this old girl has never used anything but Pond's cleansing cream, a good facial soap, and water.

On the same floor with our offices were the film cutting rooms. Daily I encountered a gaunt figure, Erich von Stroheim, who was editing his film *Foolish Wives*. I would often sit in the cutting room and make suggestions to the half-crazed man, who felt that every foot of film he shot was sacred. He lacked the courage and judgment to part with any of it. Autocratic, unreasonable, and imperious as he was on the set and in the front office, he was simple, sweet, kind, and—yes—even modest, in the extreme, when he talked to the eager young woman with the big, hungry eyes from the story department, who was avidly interested in what he was doing. He had directorial genius—no doubt about that— and he was no mean actor himself, but he over-developed his films and lacked the ability to tell a story economically and dramatically. Hence, the cutting room floor was strewn with thousands of feet of film that never saw the light of day. Von Stroheim always shot enough footage for three pictures, not one. Executives in the downstairs offices tore their thinning hair in desperation—pleading, threatening, exhorting this genius to cut down his masterpiece to size so that it would be acceptable for release in movie houses. Although I recognized the wasteful extravagance of von Stroheim, I also recognized the fierce intensity he had to tell a story in every detail. He was deeply involved in character delineation. Anything that detracted from the full emergence of character development was plain sacrilege to him. The flaws I saw in the man had to do with his basic values. He had cheap ideas about men and women and their relationships. What good does it do to pay attention to detail and character development when your characters are trite and stereotyped to start with? It could be that the trashy stories on which he lavished such effort reflected what he believed to be the taste of the American public. Once cut down to practical release size, his pictures were always box-office successes. So he could have been right. Later he made a film called *Greed,* from the novel by Frank Norris, that was a classic.

I have already admitted my attraction to the story editor of Universal, who hired me to be his assistant. Working with him in close proximity only added fuel to my infatuation. Unfortunately, the attraction became mutual. John Brownell was middle-aged and quietly set in his ways. He had a good marriage of some fifteen years. To have a young, intelligent girl who obviously adored him suddenly enter his ordered life must have been quite flattering. It awakened dormant feelings associated with his wild youth and manhood, when he and John Barrymore had lived together and were deemed the ladykillers of the Broadway theater. We confined our forbidden romance to the office. We did not meet on the outside, except occasionally to take on a matinee picture or play. This was a very decent man, John Charles Brownell, and he fought valiantly to contain this situation that could bring nothing but unhappiness to everyone concerned. I must confess I was the aggressor, the predatory *femme fatale.*

Thanksgiving came. John invited me to his lovely home in Mamaroneck. I did not want to go, but he insisted that I come. He arranged for one of the men in the publicity department, Tom Bates, to pick me up at 8:00 A.M. in his Ford. We arrived about 10:00 A.M. Estelle, John's wife, accompanied John as he came out to greet us. Estelle was chic, a statuesque natural blonde about ten years younger than John. It was obvious that she adored him, too; I sensed that immediately. John had told me that they had met when both were touring with a troupe of Shakespearean players. John had swept her off her feet, even though she was a staunch Catholic from Cleveland, Ohio, and he was a staunch Yankee Protestant from Stocksboro, Vermont. Jokingly, he introduced me to her as the young woman he had been telling her about and whom he thought the Brownells should adopt into their family. They were childless.

"Not quite that age, John," was Estelle's careful response, sensing the inherent danger with a woman's intuition, especially a woman who loved her "Johnny Boy," as she called him, as much as I thought I loved him. For the first time, I suddenly realized that John was not mine to love, that he had a wife who loved him, too. It was like having a mirror held up in front of me, and the image in that mirror did not please me at all.

It was an incredible day. John owned a boat. Mrs. Brownell, Tom Bates, John, and I went sailing. We picnicked on the boat but returned to the house about three o'clock. Their maid had set a festive table, and other guests were beginning to arrive. After cocktails, we sat down to a sumptuous feast. Estelle, a superb cook, had made the assortment of pies, the candied marshmallowed yams, the cranberry sauce, the chestnut-mushroom dressing, and the turkey itself. Everything was perfection.

I thought to myself, "And you don't even know how to boil an egg." My mother, despising the kitchen herself, would never allow any of her daughters into her private preserve. "Enough I have to do it," was her excuse. She was a good cook, too.

Estelle Brownell had other accomplishments. She had a god-given, well-trained soprano voice. Her husband gently held it against her for having so readily given up a promising career in opera and the musical stage for marriage. But she was blissfully content in the role of a Mamaroneck housewife—content until a dark-haired young woman became assistant to her husband. John insisted that she sing for me, knowing how much I loved music. She had to be coaxed, for she was evidently aware of the situation and in no mood to entertain her guests—any more than I was in the mood to accompany her on the Steinway grand in their living room. She chose an aria from Puccini's *La Boheme*, the rapturous song Musetta sings in the café in the second act.

Her voice was pure, resonant. I was no stranger to quality, and she had it. My trembling fingers could hardly find the ivory keys. What was I doing there, I kept asking myself. Plainly, the man I loved was not mine to have. I felt guilty and ashamed. It did not help when, suddenly, in the middle of the song, Estelle broke down and rushed upstairs in tears. Why, why had John brought me to his home? I should never have come. I had ruthlessly entered into a good man's life and turned his head, offering him nectar he found hard to refuse. Suddenly, my strong basic values of right and wrong were facing my predatory desires, and I wished that I had never been born.

Tom Bates drove me home. We didn't talk. I was sure he was aware of the triangle drama that had transpired, as were the other guests. My family and I lived at 110th Street and Riverside Drive at the time. Fortunately, they were not yet home; they had gone to Brooklyn to spend Thanksgiving with my sister Sophie and her husband, Joe, now the superintendent of Brooklyn's State Hospital. I was grateful that I was alone to face myself and the day I had spent in Mamaroneck.

When the family returned shortly before midnight, I was in bed feigning sleep so that no one would disturb me. They would be sure to question me about the day I had spent at the home of my boss, the story editor of Universal. By this time, they were impressed with my job and recognized that it was both unusual and important. Yet there I lay, trembling with guilt and remorse, desperately trying to find a solution.

The office was empty at 1600 Broadway when I went to work on Monday. Only Lawson, the mulatto cleaning porter was there. Lawson was from Bermuda, a prince of a fellow. We were good friends. "You sure don't look good, Miss Sagor. You sick?" he inquired after taking one look at me.

"Heartsick, Lawson," I felt like saying but thought better of it. I was nothing but a silly schoolgirl helplessly dramatizing herself. I went about my duties, neatly arranging John's desk as he liked it, putting the correspondence and other matters that claimed priority or attention in place. I was on the telephone in my office when he finally arrived, late. He looked tired, utterly miserable, as if he too had not slept any more than I had. He managed a "Morning" and entered his office. I prayed for courage because the decision I had come to the night before would now have to be faced. I had carefully rehearsed exactly what I was going to say. The time was at hand to go in and say it. In retrospect, it was a perfect soap opera declaration.

"John," I began, "I am giving up this job. I love you. I can't help it. I have never felt this way about anyone else before. But I have no right to come between you and your wife. I know this has been largely my fault. Last night, when I got home, I realized for the first time what I was doing. I'm so ashamed, John. I could never hurt another woman. And yet I was about to. You have a beautiful, talented wife. She loves you!"

My resolve not to lose control proved useless. I broke down. I was hoping against hope that he would take me in his arms and tell me that he loved me, too, and that he would work it out so that we could be together. If he had, I am sure all my fine, righteous reasoning would have gone out the window and we would have been exactly where we were before—in paradise. Forbidden, but paradise.

Instead, he listened to every word of my noble speech as though it was exactly what he had expected me to say. "You are a very brave young woman to have come to this decision," he said. "I know that we have both had overwhelming feelings for one another. I tried hard to suppress mine. I am so much older and should be that much wiser than you. But there are some things that know no reason. And love is one of them. When it happens, it happens."

Then he stopped and smiled before he continued. "Dear little one," he said, "it is not you who are going to resign and give up your job. I have already done it for you. You see, on Wednesday, before I left for Mamaroneck, I turned in my resignation downstairs. I have accepted a job for more money with Republic International Films as head of their literary department. You will continue working here with Bob Rodin. I recommended Bob for my job, and R.H. Cochrane and the others downstairs agreed to give him a try. You will be his assistant. They agreed to hire a secretary for the department. Now let's start packing the few things I want to take with me, because my new job starts tomorrow."

The soap opera ended there.

Now when I think back and contemplate all of the other men who would drift in and out of my life, I realized what an exceptional man this John C. Brownell really was. There was only one other man like him—the man I married.

Next morning I had a new boss, one I knew and respected as a colleague. Bob loved me, too, but his was the affection of a friend who could wish he were years younger so that he might be more than that. A good friend he was. I learned so much from him. Bob had aspired to the post of story editor for a long time and had been passed over twice when other selections for the job were made. Now, at long last, he had the chance to prove himself. The lettering on the door now read: ROBERT RODIN, STORY EDITOR.

Of course, I knew that Bob Rodin drank. John Brownell had indicated as much once or twice when, for a week, Bob failed to show up at the office. I questioned Bob about it one night when we were collaborating on *The Orchid Woman*. He kept leaving the office and returning with renewed stamina after having imbibed from a bottle hidden somewhere. This is what he told me: "I drink," he said, "to forget. When I was a young reporter my wife and I were on a train going from New York to Chicago. There was a terrible train wreck. My wife was killed. We had been married only six months. I never got over it. It started me drinking—drinking to forget."

It was, of course, not true; it was a story concocted to win my sympathy, which it did at the time. I had no experience with anyone who drank. In fact, in our home, we never saw liquor unless it was at a wedding or a religious holiday; then it was wine in strict moderation. Occasionally, my father indulged in a forbidden glass of beer on his way home. I could always tell, because his mustache gave him away. I would refuse to kiss him, announcing censoriously, "Ugh! Beer!" and Mama would scold, "You stopped at the saloon again." Poor Papa—he had no vices that I can remember except an occasional forbidden glass of beer. And yes, the horses. He had a weakness for playing the horses.

So, knowing nothing about alcoholics, I assumed that Bob Rodin, having dreamed of becoming head of the story department for so long and having achieved that objective, would forswear the bottle and perform in the job as I knew he could. Little did I know what I was going to be up against in the ensuing months.

It happened almost immediately. The first day, he did not show up at the office. There was a conference scheduled for three o'clock in the downstairs office. I knew it was important for him to attend it—his first executive conference. There was to be a discussion of the kind of pictures that Universal would be making in the coming year.

I had to find him! He lived in a shabby brownstone rooming house in the fifties off Broadway. His musty rooms were cluttered with newspapers and magazines antedating the turn of the century. The place reeked with stale liquor from the empty bottles scattered all over the place.

Bob, however, wasn't there. His landlady indicated that he had been drinking heavily and could probably be found in some tavern or saloon on Seventh or Eighth Avenue. So I went looking. I went from one saloon to another, inquiring. Always the same answer, "Yes, he was here in the morning." "He was here an hour ago." "He just left a little while ago. . . ."

Finally, I located him—by this time, deplorably plastered. I called a taxi and took him to some steam baths that the saloon keeper told me were nearby. "They'll dry him out," he said. It was twelve o' clock, and he had to be sobered up and at the office at three o'clock. He was.

I kept this up for six months, handling the department by myself, making all the decisions, signing his name, making excuses, and covering for him in the downstairs offices. I paid his landlady to cook for him and to watch him and keep me advised as to his whereabouts. She was an elderly, faded burlesque actress who was not lacking in compassion. When Bob Rodin was sober, he was a gentleman of the old school—a man you had to like.

Then came the day when I was summoned to the front office. R.H. Cochrane, vice president of Universal, sat across the conference table from me. Also there were his brother P.D. Cochrane, the treasurer; Manny Goldstein, general manager; Ed Gulick, head of the publicity department; and Al Lichtman, head of the sales department. Carl Laemmle was absent. Harry Zehner, his secretary, was there taking notes. I felt like a martyr facing the Spanish Inquisition.

"Is Mr. Rodin upstairs?" was the flat question from R.H. Cochrane.

"No, Mr. Cochrane," I replied. "He had an appointment with an agent."

"Are you sure?"

"That's what he told me." I was quaking in my black patent-leather pumps.

Then their stern countenances relaxed as though they understood my agony and felt that I had suffered enough.

"Frederica," R.H. Cochrane said, "you are a very loyal friend, but you need not cover up for Bob Rodin any longer. We know what has been going on upstairs. When Mr. Brownell recommended Rodin to replace him, he told us he had a drinking problem. Apparently, he could not control his addiction."

"We have decided to give you a hundred-dollar increase in salary and put you in charge officially," interjected Al Lichtman, one of the truly brilliant sales minds in the business. "You've been running the department by yourself, anyway. You seem to know what you are doing."

I was completely overwhelmed at this turn of events. I had expected to be fired for my presumption in trying to run the story department by myself. I also had mixed emotions. I did not particularly want to be story editor, knowing the long, hard hours it required and what a thankless job it was. You had to wade through piles and piles of material from authors, agents, and publishers, hoping against hope that you'd come across something that could be turned into a suitable motion picture with the Universal stamp, which in 1923 generally meant a Western. Our big stars were Hoot Gibson and Harry Carey. I had adapted a story that we had bought for Harry Carey not long before and, to my surprise, was given screen credit for it. But Westerns were not my cup of tea. My taste ran to short stories selected from the current magazines and labeled "best" in anthologies, and good novels with something to say. Universal was not in a class with other studios such as Famous Players–Lasky (Paramount) and First National—both of which were beginning to buy and produce more selective material. I knew, too, that a story editor had always to be on the defensive. If the material you bought did not turn out successfully, the blame was on the story chosen in the first place. If your choice turned out to be a moneymaker, Hollywood took all the credit. From the day I joined the Universal story department, I knew what I eventually wanted to do: write. I wanted to go to Hollywood and join the writing staff on the Universal lot. I wanted to become a great filmwriter like June Mathis, whose competence I held in awe.

"Mr. Cochrane," I said when I finally found my voice, "I'd like very much to be story editor, but I will only accept the job on one condition." They surely expected that my condition would be a higher salary.

"What's the condition?" Mr. Cochrane asked icily. Remember, Universal was a chintzy outfit.

"The condition, Mr. Cochrane, is that at the end of the year, I want Universal to send me to the West Coast to join the writing staff. I want to write, to work on films."

It was a condition that they found easy to meet. My five superiors readily agreed that at the end of the year, if I so wished, I would be sent to the Coast to join the writing staff. And so, I became story editor of Universal. I was not yet twenty-three.

Chapter 3

STORY EDITOR

TWO WEEKS AFTER BECOMING Universal's story editor, I had my first "downstairs" conference with the company brass. They had given me the job, and they would want to know what to expect. I had to prove that, despite my age, I had what it took to run a story department. I was equally determined to prove not only that I was qualified but that I had very definite ideas about running that department. One of my objectives was to convince these hard-boiled execs to increase their budget allowance for story material and meet the market competition of other film companies. Up to that time, Universal had considered a thousand dollars a big price for a story, and so it was for a run-of-the-mill Western. I told them frankly that they had to raise their sights; ten thousand dollars and better was more like it if they expected to improve their overall product, get away from mundane Westerns, and compete for material in the *Saturday Evening Post, Cosmopolitan, Colliers,* and other magazines that were then running good stories and serializing novels by well-known writers.

I must say they listened closely. Up to that time, no story editor had ever presumed to address them with such candor. Here was this young woman lecturing them, pointing the way to the future, asking for a mandate to go forth into the marketplace and bid for the best that money could buy. I must have spoken my piece convincingly because brainy, canny Al Lichtman approved my point of view; indeed, he championed it. He said that, as sales head of Universal, he had long realized that Universal was falling behind and would have to improve the quality of its output. University-educated, suave R.H. Cochrane agreed. Carl Laemmle, back from Laupheim, Germany, sat gloomily, chewing on the end of his pencil, glowering at me. Having control of the purse strings, he clearly did not enjoy the prospect of throwing thousands of dollars away on stories when, up to now, Universal had prospered on moneymaking pictures where the story outlay was negligible, yet the pictures made millions. But, like other pioneers—Zukor, Mayer, and the rest of the German and Russian immigrants who fell into the golden picture business—Carl Laemmle had that same instinct to defer to more educated, cleverer minds in areas where he lacked expertise and judgment. He reluctantly agreed.

Having won tentative approval for increasing the story budget, I plunged courageously ahead. They would also have to increase the size and quality of the story department. I asked for four full-time readers. They granted me two. I hired Adele Commandini, a clever writer, full-time at seventy-five dollars a week; she was to remain my loyal friend until she fell under the influence of fascism. I also hired Phil Hurn at seventy-five dollars a week, for half days, because they would not meet his demand for one hundred dollars a week full time. What they did not know was that when Phil had discussed his joining the story department, he needed only seventy-five dollars a week for living expenses and wanted to work only half days; he got what he wanted. Phil had been one of Universal's successful scenario writers on the West Coast. We had met when John Brownell was head of the department. Now that Phil was married to a charming wife, Jane (granddaughter of the novelist Gertrude Atherton), and had a baby daughter, he had come to New York to try his hand at playwriting.

I needed him for a special purpose. Part of my job was to cover all Broadway play productions and catch tryouts out of town in Boston, Atlantic City, and Philadelphia. I knew Phil was the man I needed to accompany me to the Broadway openings and synopsize the plays so that I could present them immediately for company consideration if they contained film possibilities. Edward de Witt also assisted me. I knew that both of these readers had good judgment. I could trust them. The out-of-town plays I covered by myself.

I well remember a motion picture ball on New Year's Eve at the Hotel Astor on Forty-second Street and Broadway. I wanted so much to attend, but I had a tryout play in Philadelphia—a play that never saw the lights of Broadway and closed ignominiously in the colonial city on the Delaware. By missing the last act, I was able to catch a train back to New York and arrive at the Astor shortly before midnight.

The highlight of the evening's entertainment was the young comedian Jimmy Durante and his incomparable stooges, who helped him demolish the upright piano at which he had been performing. It was a hilarious act, and I arrived just in time to catch it.

Instead of a ball gown, I wore a trim business suit, and I had no escort. But I had the best time of my young life. At 3:00 A.M., I was still dancing. Hotel personnel were cleaning up, and the orchestra was gone; but on a Victrola, to the strains of Strauss's "Vienna Woods," my partner and I whirled in a Merry Widow fantasy on the deserted ballroom floor. Never since have I experienced the exhilaration and intoxication of being lifted and whirled through the air by so exquisite a terpsichorean as my partner, a professional dancer who had been part of the program on that memorable night.

The most interesting experience I had in covering out-of-town plays took place in Atlantic City one cold wintry day in January. Edmund Goulding was trying out his play *Dancing Mothers*. I rode the train down from New York. It was snowing, and I barely made the opening.

Dancing Mothers was a fair play—light, frothy entertainment but full of holes. In that condition, I knew it would flop on Broadway. Still I could see a film in it—and a good one, too. Back in my Atlantic City hotel room, I reached for the phone book. It was eleven o'clock, but I began to call all of the hotels in search of Edmund Goulding. I figured he had to be staying at one of them.

Sure enough, I located him. It was past midnight. I introduced myself, told him that I had seen his play and liked it, but that it needed work if it were to make the big time. Since it was so late and the weather was so foul, we agreed to meet at my hotel for breakfast and talk.

Edmund Goulding was not entirely a stranger to me. He had barged into my office with his literary agent, Cora Wilkening, some months back. A dapper, dashing man in his forties, he recounted and acted out the wonderful plot he had for a smash motion picture. It was one of the most delicious experiences I can recall—watching and listening to this talented rascal ad-libbing, creating plot and characters as he went along. Of course, I had to dash his hopes and turn him down. I could not buy a story unless it was down on paper. He promised to do this and get the story to me in a few days. I never saw it and doubt that he remembered a word of the yarn he had spun in my office. While this technique failed with the hard-boiled story editors in the East, Hollywood later bought this off-the-cuff fantasizing of Edmund Goulding after he became a success. He walked into the office of any producer, rattled off the top of his head a plot and story line, and walked away with an assignment. Very often, the next day, he later confided to me, he could not recollect what he had said. So my hunch about why I never received a synopsis of the story he concocted in my office that day was correct. He didn't remember what he had told me.

But it has to be said that Edmund Goulding did sit down and write a play in three acts with good dialogue, characters, and a plot that worked. I respect and applaud him for that.

At breakfast the next morning, I told Goulding of the changes that I envisioned in his play. As we rode the train back to New York, Goulding made copious notes. I exacted only one condition from this appreciative would-be playwright: when his play opened on Broadway, Universal was to get first crack at buying the picture rights. He agreed and lived up to his promise. The play was a resounding success and put Edmund Goulding on the map in New York and in Hollywood.

Unfortunately, when *Dancing Mothers* opened on Broadway to glowing reviews, Universal would not meet its price, and another company bought it and made a very good film. This, alas, was to be the repetitive gratitude for my labors as story editor at Universal. I would time and again best my competitors in conniving to get my hands on galley proofs or catch plays out of town but would unhappily lose out because Universal would not part with the moolah.

It soon became apparent that I needed more help in the office, and I hired a second secretary, Edith Cohen. She was eighteen and fresh out of business school. This was her first job, but she was a whiz. She had initiative and incisive judgment about people, and she handled telephone calls as adroitly as if she had years of experience. Most important of all was the fact that this young Jewish girl with three years of high school education (she came from a poor family and had to drop out of school to get a job) had intuitive judgment about material. She had a nose for it. Many was the time I gave her synopses that my well-paid readers would provide me, stories they had rejected or recommended. Her evaluation was never faulty. She knew every time when they were wrong. She was a remarkable young woman. Tragically, she contracted tuberculosis when I was in Hollywood and died in a sanitarium in the Adirondacks before she turned twenty.

One day, Edith informed me that two young men were waiting to see me. They had been sent up from Carl Laemmle's office. Their names were Willie Wyler and Paul Kohner. It had been a particularly stressful day. I was going to attend a play opening that night and was pressed for time. It was nearing five o'clock—quitting time. Why do visitors always descend on you when the business day is almost over and you are attending to myriads of details before you leave? This meant shortening my dinner hour if I were to catch the opening curtain. Rush, rush, rush—the story of my young life.

"Show them in," I said. After all, Papa Laemmle had sent them upstairs.

A shy, short fellow with a pimply, sensitive face entered. He was Willie Wyler. His companion, Paul Kohner, was taller and good-looking in a Teutonic way. He did the talking, and his command of English was really good, if heavily accented. Willie sat there and nodded passively, agreeing with his friend.

"Ve vant to vork in the story department. Mr. Laemmle vas sure you could use us."

I judged their ages to be about twenty-two. True, I was not much older myself, but I felt warmly maternal toward these foreign fledglings who had "greenhorn" stamped on their personalities. I found they were not related to Carl Laemmle, or to each other, but were the sons of family friends. The old man had advanced their passage money to the land of opportunity. He put them on minimum salary and deducted five dollars each week from their pay for their passage. They both had a schoolboy interest in films. The forward, rather demanding young Kohner refuted all of my reasons for not engaging them on the spot to become readers. They did not know that a story department was where we read and purchased material to be made into motion pictures but thought it was where ideas were born, stories were written. When I explained our procedure and that I did not see how, with their limited English, they could function, they were disappointed. Paul Kohner left, convinced that I had underestimated them and that they could learn how to become readers in no time at all. They were smart, fast learners, he assured me. Indeed, he was al-

most insulting in his response to my tempered rejection of their prof-
fered services. Willie said nothing. Unlike his aggressive colleague, he
was a timid soul.

It was nearly seven o'clock when they left my office. I felt that I
had given them kind and honest consideration. I suggested to Paul
that, with his knowledge of languages, he should seek employment in
the foreign department—which he did later. As for Willie, since he
seemed eager to get into film production, I suggested the cutting room
was a good place to start—advice he followed later as well.

Hurriedly now, I headed for Schraft's for a bit of supper. I was a
regular there, and my favorite waitress knew exactly what I wanted: a
tall glass of milk with two raw eggs whipped up with cream and sherry.
I never ate heavily before going to the theater, for two reasons: to keep
awake and to avoid indigestion. It was a regimen that paid off and is
partly responsible, I think, for my good health today.

Several weeks later, I crossed the path of Willie Wyler again. It
was a Sunday, and my sister Lillian was entertaining two old friends,
Renee and Ella Gross. Lillian had gone to college with Renee. Now
they were both schoolmarms. Ella, a regal woman, was a school principal with "authority" written all over her. I recounted the amusing story
of the two young protégées of my boss who had descended on me.

"Willie Wyler!" Ella responded. "Why, he and his brother are
boarding with Essie." Essie—Mrs. Kline—was their widowed sister
raising two daughters, who supplemented her income by taking in
boarders.

"Essie told us all about them," said Renee. "She has been moth-
ering them. They have been terribly homesick."

"Yes, and Willie wets his bed," put in Ella. "Essie has to change
his sheets every day. I told her to give him notice. She has enough to
do."

"But, Ella," put in the more charitable Renee, "the doctor says he
can't help it. It's something that will go away. Besides, you know he
helps Essie with the laundry, and she doesn't mind. She really likes
the two boys. She says they have such good manners, and are always
bringing her candy and flowers to show their appreciation."

Perhaps it is uncharitable to mention this gossipy tidbit about
Willie Wyler. But I mean no disrespect. It only proves that from humble
beginnings can come genius. Willie became an outstanding director,

winning Oscars and making such great pictures as *Wuthering Heights, Jezebel, Roman Holiday, Ben Hur, and Funny Girl.* As for Paul, he headed the foreign department of Universal Films abroad and wound up as a film agent representing such important clients as Walter Huston, John Huston, Yul Brynner, Dolores del Rio, Jeanne Moreau, David Niven, Lana Turner, Charles Bronson, Ingmar Bergman, Willie Wyler, Maurice Chevalier, his own brother (Frederick Kohner), and Ernest and Frederica Maas.

Early in my duties as story editor, Universal sent me to the West Coast to confer with their story editor and other studio executives. In those days before one-day plane flights from coast to coast, we suffered three long days and interminable nights in steam locomotive trains. In summer it was insufferably hot. Air-conditioning had not yet been invented. For me, though, this first journey to the Coast was an incredible adventure. In the daytime, I sat in the smoking lounge (I smoked then, like a chimney), conversing with a coterie of businessmen of all ages and importance, drinking scotch on the rocks. I never bought a drink or a single meal, including breakfast. On this journey, I ate my first avocado and my first artichoke—neither of which I knew existed—and instantly became addicted to both for the rest of my life. In the evening, for recreation, I learned to shoot dice with the Negro porters and dining personnel and drink Mexican tequila. I had beginner's luck, always managing to break even or come out ahead. I am afraid that the ladies on the train—for there were a few—had a very low opinion of me because of this open fraternization with Pullman union workers and also because of my popularity with the opposite sex, both black and white. But I was not in the least bothered. I was having far too good a time.

    After crossing the Mojave Desert on the fourth day and passing through sleepy Pasadena, we finally reached Los Angeles. I was met by Burl Armstrong, who was then western story editor of Universal. Burl took me in tow and delivered me to the Ambassador Hotel, where I was to stay for the next seven days. I was captivated by the impressive layout of the Ambassador: its groomed grounds, banks of flowers growing everywhere, and neat, private bungalows uniting the elegant, four-story Spanish edifice. The first thing I did was to patronize the beautiful luxury shops that fringed the lobby. One of the things I bought was a hand-painted silk Spanish shawl to be worn over an evening gown; it set me back a neat one hundred dollars. I also bought a stunning amber Spanish comb to be worn in my hair.

And wear them I did, on the second night, feeling like a Spanish fandango dancer when I was taken to the Montmartre Restaurant, a rendezvous spot for anyone who was anyone (or even aspired to be anyone) in the motion picture industry. Lily Shadur (nee Silver), executive secretary to Julius Bernstein, who was head of the studio and a nephew of Carl Laemmle, squired me around. This evening we were a party of five: Lily; her husband, Arthur, who also worked at the studio; Clarence Brown, then an unknown assistant director; and his fantastic wife, Ona.

Ona Brown was the ex-mistress of Cornelius Vanderbilt, who had picked her out of the Ziegfeld chorus and decked her with diamond bracelets from wrist to elbow on both arms. These trophies she proudly displayed and gave full credit for them to the elderly millionaire who had sought her favors and brought her West in a private railroad car. What Vanderbilt had not counted on was that his young mistress would meet a good-looking engineer who had forsaken his profession to become an assistant to Maurice Tourneur and be completely captivated by him. Pretty Ona ditched Vanderbilt and all his millions forthwith for the young man who was aspiring to become a great director. Ona married for love, but Clarence Brown, cold, calculating hombre that he was, married Ona for other reasons: Ona was aggressive, fearless, and could open doors to make way for his future—none of which he could do himself. He was innately shy and did not know how to sell himself. I would hazard a guess that Ona Brown manipulated every man of importance (and some who were not important) on the Universal lot to further her husband's ambition. Eventually, the clever Follies girl prevailed. Clarence Brown became a full-fledged director and climbed the ladder of success because he was good and had what it takes.

I had told the Browns that I wanted to meet June Mathis, and that memorable night at Montmartre she joined us at our table. This, as you can well understand, made the evening for me—meeting this seasoned, talented writer, who was flattered by my unconcealed admiration for her craft and for the pictures that she had been associated with. There was dancing at the Montmartre, but, while the others at the table moved on to the dance floor, June Mathis and I remained to talk and talk—and eat raw hamburger sandwiches. It was the first time (and the last) that I downed a raw meat sandwich. But that is what June Mathis ordered—with lots of Bermuda onions on top. How I managed to get that sandwich down I will never know. The very thought makes me ill to this day.

The Montmartre was located on Hollywood Boulevard, one block east of Highland Avenue on the north side of the street in a two-story Spanish-tiled building. It had handsome, Mexican wrought-iron grilled doors at its entrance. An individual by the name of Eddie Brandstatter ran it—and when I say "ran," I mean "Ran." Eddie B. was a restaurateur without parallel. He supervised everything from kitchen to table—no detail was too insignificant to warrant his attention. When he slept was anybody's guess, for he did all of the marketing at dawn in the produce markets downtown. He was a supremely happy, proud little man. Montmartre was a great success, and Eddie Brandstatter was solely responsible.

You could not get into the Montmartre during the lunch hours of eleven to two unless you were well known or with someone who was. The tourists lined up early in the morning for the best vantage place to see their favorites. Stars such as Mary Astor (still in her teens and undiscovered) got exposure there, circulating as models in fashion shows, good-humoredly tolerating the quips and ignoring the insults when their derrieres were caressed or pinched while passing executive tables. After all, executives were privileged, and to be noticed by them might lead to a screen test.

To be seen at the Montmartre was a must in order to remain in the swim, in the glare of the klieg lights. The trade papers, newspapers, and fan magazines sent reporters and cameramen to capture shots of those going in and coming out. If your name was mentioned in a column, you felt you were "in," going places; or you hired a press agent to make sure it was mentioned. The Montmartre was The Place to go. The Place to be seen. There was no other.

Then one fine day, the Trocadero happened and changed all that. I tell this story because it reveals like nothing else the tinsel of the Hollywood scene, its basic insincerity, its hypocrisy, its cruelty, its shabby neglect of the worthy and deserving—the desertion at the drop of a hat of the old for anything new and in the groove. Wherever the Hollywood picture people went, that is where you, if you were in the motion picture business, wanted to be seen and written about.

The Trocadero replaced the Montmartre. It also spelled the doom of Eddie Brandstatter. A group of directors and producers had pooled some capital and opened it on Sunset Strip in a stunning location overlooking the panorama of a growing Los Angeles. Almost overnight, the Trocadero became The Place. Almost overnight, in a general exodus, the Montmartre became a ghostly spot of empty tables, and the illustrious patronage were no longer waiting. Everyone flocked to the Trocadero, the new place to be seen—if you were to be counted.

Eddie Brandstatter was in a state of bewilderment. Poor little man—he could not understand, could not believe what was happening. Why? Why? Why? He had been too busy to be aware that, behind his back, the plot had been hatched at one of his very own tables at the Montmartre. For months, he hoped that the faithful would return, that this was only a passing nightmare.

Perhaps it is the writer in me that makes me feel this story as keenly as I do. More likely, it is that, as a human being who hates to see a wrong done to someone who does not deserve it, I have always wanted to tell this story. I feel it needs to be told: the destruction of Eddie Brandstatter, a decent man—the destruction I sadly witnessed firsthand in the ensuing months. Eventually, this brave little man closed the Montmartre and supported his family by opening a beanery. A beanery! It was just that—on Hollywood Boulevard near the intersection with Vine Street. Apparently, he had little capital. His spirit was broken. A man builds and achieves a dream, receives accolades, only to have that dream crumble like a sand castle washed back into the sea. I frequented the beanery as often as I could just to talk to Eddie, who wasn't talking much. The beanery was no big success. Face it: it was a flop. Then came the morning that they found him in his garage, dead in his car, gassed, a suicide.

To this day, I lay this little man's death at the door of Hollywood, which deserted him so shamelessly. They enticed away his maitre d', several waiters, and a chef. When they opened the Trocadero, they could have given him an interest in the place and let him run it. The Troc never matched the perfection of the Montmartre, never had the class, the elegance, the tone—that special magic that was Eddie Brandstatter.

I guess no one remembers Eddie Brandstatter today but this old-timer. In all the writing about Hollywood, if his name or the name of the Montmartre have ever been mentioned, I must have missed it. He has been completely forgotten. Yet the building that housed the Montmartre still stands, ironically enough, on Hollywood Boulevard, while so many other sacred landmarks of the early Hollywood scene have been demolished. The Hollywood Hotel, the most famous of them all, once occupied a lot near the Chinese Theater, but it had to make room for a high-rise savings-and-loan building on the corner and a parking lot adjacent to it. The great little hotel where most of the important names of filmdom once slept: Charlie Chaplin, D.W. Griffith, Mary Pickford, Rudolph Valentino, Douglas Fairbanks. This hotel was torn down for a parking lot with scarcely a murmur of protest.

Today, I rarely walk the streets of Hollywood Boulevard, now the milieu of drug addicts, pimps, and perverts. Still, tourists are drawn to the magic name of Hollywood. On those rare occasions when I do walk those streets and gaze upon the stars of the greats embedded in the sidewalk, I think there is one star missing—a star for Eddie Brandstatter, who earned and deserved one for his devotion to the greats in the fickle picture business.

It was at Universal Studios that I visited my first motion picture set, and watched the actual shooting. It was not at all as I had imagined it would be. It was a sterile atmosphere, softened by a studio trio of two violins and a cello creating atmosphere for a love scene. The place was crawling with participants in the moviemaking process—light men, makeup men, cameramen, script girls, set manager, assistants, and assistant assistants. Grips galore moved lights and furniture, and miles of cables were underfoot challenging you not to trip over them. It was nothing like a stage set—so orderly when the curtain goes up and the play begins. In the foreground sat the director, sprawled in a canvas chair designated DIRECTOR. He usually had a megaphone and was dressed in a loud, racy jacket over loose breeches or knickers. He often wore a hat or cap with visor reversed and a neck scarf.

Hours of preparation preceded the actual shooting. I found it extremely boring. In the years to come, I rarely visited a set unless something was being shot or I was a participating writer creating stories and scenes on the set as the action progressed. This first day, I watched them shoot a picture starring Norman Kerry. Kerry, a romantic lead in the film, was a dapper fellow, proud of his carefully waxed mustache, good crop of hair (he was always combing it), and good physique. The business in the scene involved lighting a cigarette while salaciously eyeing a young woman. Unfortunately, at this moment, he could not hold the cigarette between his fingers and light it without dropping it to the floor. He tried again and again. Finally, after innumerable takes, the exasperated director called him over.

"Norman," he bellowed before the whole crew, "for chrissakes, go home and sleep it off, will you? We'll try it again tomorrow if you can manage to come in sober."

"I'm perfectly sober now," Norman Kerry retaliated, trying hard to stand up straight. "One more li'l drink and I'll be f-f-fine." Norman Kerry was one of the early men lost to the ravages of alcoholism. There would be many more.

An unexpected surprise awaited me when I returned to the Ambassador. There was John Brownell, my first boss, in the lobby. He, too, was visiting the West Coast for his company, as I was representing mine. Here we were together again, far from home, staying at the same hotel. In fact, on the same floor. Yet nothing happened. We could easily have gone to bed and consummated the passion that had once consumed us, but we didn't. The magic was gone. The flame had been extinguished by time. Instead, we breakfasted together only once. Comfortably, we discovered that we were friends—good, fast friends.

My other breakfasts were dedicated to Julius Bernstein, head of Universal Studios, who lived in one of the Ambassador bungalows. Julius was a bachelor about five-foot, two inches tall, and he had a valet and chauffeur. He still spoke English with a guttural German accent and a lisp. When he talked, which he did incessantly, he was apt to spray his listener. A man in his forties, he knew less about motion pictures than anyone else I ever met in the business. But then Julius didn't have to know very much. He had a whiz of a secretary in Lily Shadur, and there were others to cover for the nephew of Carl Laemmle. It took Papa Laemmle a while to get wise to what a schlemiel his favorite nephew from Laupheim, Germany, was.

Julius had two topics of conversation during the week I was privileged to ride to the studio with him in his chauffeur-driven limousine. One topic had to do with his sartorial appearance. The small, nondescript man reveled in the projection of a good and expensive wardrobe.

To be charitable, you could say that Julius was insecure; but he was also the most arrogant, conceited individual anyone might want to encounter, despite his abysmal ignorance of everything related to living on this planet. It became my duty each morning to pass on his tie, to assure him it blended with his shirt and suit. I had to wax enthusiastic about his expensive suits. His shoes. I even had to pass on his socks.

"Feel this cloth!" he would say. "Isn't this a piece of goods? The best. This suit cost $150; that's a lot of money. It should be the best." And then the tie. "Look at it. Do you like it? Do you think it matches my suit and shirt? My valet always picks my ties. Feel the silk. Some quality! Cost fifteen dollars; that's a lot of money. The best. It should be the best. And the socks. Imported from Germany. I got French ones, too. And some from even London. Only the best is good enough for Julius Bernstein," he laughed. But he believed it.

We breakfasted in the sunlit patio of the hotel, a cheerful place with cages full of singing canaries; potted plants were everywhere. The breakfasts were fabulous, I should point out, but who could have an appetite seated opposite this obnoxious, opinionated character who showered you with spittle when he talked? I grew to dread those breakfasts and the drive to the studio from Wilshire Boulevard across to Hollywood Boulevard and then on to Cahuenga Boulevard, past the empty, parched brown hills. I could hardly wait for Universal Studios to appear so that I could shed this insufferable bore. Every day—all seven days that I stayed at the Ambassador—I had to go through the same routine and listen to tales about Laupheim, Germany—beautiful, wonderful Laupheim where Uncle Carl was born. At least this second topic was a bit more interesting than the *other* one.

"You must positively, absolutely come to Laupheim," he would lisp. "Beautiful, vonderful Laupheim, Germany, vere Uncle Carl vas born. If you come to Laupheim, I vill ask that they allow you to sleep overnight in Uncle Carl's bed. If I, Julius Bernstein, ask, they vill allow it. A great honor, no?"

He was serious about the honor of sleeping in the sacred bed of the sainted old man; as a loyal employee of Carl Laemmle, I was supposed to consider this a thrilling privilege. It was a pilgrimage Julius made every year. "Julius," I countered, tongue in cheek, "I wouldn't dream of missing Laupheim when I go to Europe."

"You vill like it. You vill see." He took me *seriously.*

I was almost glad when my seven-day visit, and my Julius Bernstein ordeal, came to an end. Once more, I found myself on the train heading back to my native city—New York, my beloved city and, for me, the center of this challenging universe. Los Angeles was a wasteland; Hollywood, a mirage. Did I really want to return? The answer was . . . yes. . . . Yes, if I wanted to write motion pictures. And I did.

Chapter 4

PURCHASE OF
THE PLASTIC AGE

SHORTLY AFTER MY RETURN from the West Coast, Universal decided to come up in the world. The company opened up spanking new offices on Fifth Avenue near Fifty-seventh Street in a brand-new thirty-some-story building where Universal occupied the ninth and tenth floors. The only flaw in this arrangement for me was that the new offices were no longer within walking distance of the Algonquin Hotel on West Forty-sixth Street.

The Algonquin was where Hortense Schorr, Virginia Morris, Regina Crew Cruickshank, Radie Harris, and I—all working gals in story and publicity departments, movie periodicals, newspaper and movie columns—had a special table right next to the famous Algonquin Round Table, where wits such as George S. Kaufman, Dorothy Parker, Robert Benchley, and Edna Ferber met every day for lunch. I had to take a taxi there and back, and that was a nuisance, especially in inclement weather when taxis were hard to nab. But I was not about to abandon the Algonquin and my cronies, most of whom had started at the bottom of the ladder a few years back and climbed to jobs of prominence in the industry. Hortense Schorr became publicity director for Columbia Pictures. Virginia Morris was publicity director for United Artists. Regina Crewe was the eastern rival of Louella Parsons of the Hearst newspapers. These women were my pals, my closest friends, and remained so through the years.

As time went by, I became less and less elated with my job as story editor. Covering plays several nights a week, both in and out of town, plus the reading I had to do while responding to the incessant telephone calls, wasn't easy. There were other irritants. I was forced to hire readers at the whim of my superiors, but the readers' judgment was so suspect that I had to review their work myself or rely on my young secretary, Edith Cohen, who took the books or galleys home and reported to me in the morning. For instance, there was Mrs. Guthrie, a widow of excellent breeding and background who, unfortunately, had no story judgment. She got the job through her sister, Alice Duer Miller, a writer for the *Saturday Evening Post* who knew R.H. Cochrane personally. Cochrane was also responsible for my hiring Richard Cobb— "Red" because of his flaming hair. He was a dropout from college with nothing but the fair sex on his mind. His father was a U.S. senator from Vermont and an old college mate of Cochrane's. Sally Morris, mistress of Al Lichtman, was also on my payroll to try to learn how to become a reader. She was attractive, but reading obviously had not been one of her favorite pastimes.

Shortly after I hired her, Lichtman called to say he had received two front-row seats from Al Jolson, a personal friend, and would like me to accompany him to opening night. It proved an interesting evening. We had dinner at the Plaza Hotel. I wore a black velvet evening gown, cut low in the front and back, and a band of sparkling rhinestones and pearls in my hair, quite an expensive piece that had set me back several hundred dollars. At dinner, Lichtman confided that he was leaving Universal and forming his own company with Ben Schulberg. Al would again be in charge of sales and distribution. The company was to be called Preferred Pictures. Lichtman had not yet broken the news to Universal but expected to do so in a day or two and then leave. I felt badly because I had always counted on his moral and intellectual support, and it would mean the loss of an important ally. I worried about working with R.H. Cochrane, who would now be the only one left to whom I could go with special material. I always felt awed and inadequate in his presence.

Al Jolson was not a singer I especially liked. He did his famous "Mammy" song, which brought down the house. Throughout the performance Mr. Lichtman, sitting beside me, kept rubbing his leg against mine. After the show, we had supper with Jolson and some of his friends and ended up in Al Lichtman's apartment near Central Park West. As expected from what had transpired in the theater, he was bent on luring me into his bedchamber.

"Why, Al," I said, feigning shock, "what about Sally?" Callously, he implied that he was through with her. She no longer interested him.

"And so you saddle me with her in my department! Thank you very much," I replied. He coaxed and used all the crummy arguments of a man on the make. When I finally convinced him that it wasn't going to work, he put me in a taxi, and I went home, becoming angrier with every mile.

An ardent feminist, I had a session with Sally Morris the next morning in my office with the door closed. I told her frankly what had happened the evening before and what Al Lichtman had said about their relationship. She broke down and cried.

"My advice to you," I told her, "is that you return to your family in Rochester and forget about New York and Al Lichtman. You are a nice Jewish girl from a small city, and you are going to find a decent man in Rochester and get married." I lent her three hundred dollars to buy herself a railroad ticket and some new clothes. Two years later, she returned the loan with a picture of herself, her husband, and their baby son. So I was gratified that I had shelled out the right advice. You never know in these matters.

It was around this time that Clarence and Ona Brown arrived from the West Coast. Clarence's contract was up for renewal. I was shocked when I learned that it would not be renewed at the increased figure he was asking. Universal, always shortsighted, was about to let him go. This would not have been good for Clarence, since he had as yet no outstanding picture to his credit. Fortunately, I had recently purchased the vehicle that would make the difference, *The Goose Woman* by Rex Beach, and it was still unassigned to any director. *The Goose Woman*, a novelette, had run in *Cosmopolitan* magazine. Universal parted with twenty thousand dollars—real money—for that one. It was a great story, which I outlined in minute detail to the fraternity downstairs. I could do as well as Eddie Goulding when I had something worthwhile to sell. The only difference was that what I offered was a genuine commodity and not a figment of the imagination. My strong pitch was leveled at R.H. and Al Lichtman, who had not yet resigned from Universal. They did not let me down. Clarence Brown had his contract renewed at a handsome figure. *The Goose Woman,* his first production when he returned to the coast, shot with the fine Broadway actress Louise Dresser in the leading role, put Clarence Brown firmly on the map as a director of quality pictures. He was beyond potboilers now.

To celebrate signing the contract, Clarence, his wife Ona, Al Lichtman, and I attended the Ziegfeld Follies. There, from the third row center orchestra, we were entertained by Will Rogers and his famous rope act, Fanny Brice singing the "Jewel Song" from Faust, Eddie Cantor introducing "If You Knew Suzie," and Ziggie's famous Follies girls in their fabulous costumes. Right next to me sat Ona Brown, still a dazzling soubrette herself, now sedately married and very much in love with the handsome husband at her side. This husband would ditch her as soon as he was established in the picture business and no longer needed her support. With a generous legal settlement, he retired her to the desert sands of Palm Springs. There, she and an older brother lived out the rest of their days in obscurity, far from the limelight of Hollywood that she had loved so very much.

It reminds me of a French short story I once read about a successful mistress who made the fateful mistake of marrying her lover and becoming a faithful, but dull, housewife, losing out to the new, younger mistress her husband takes on in his boredom. "Dear God," she weeps, "why have you forsaken me and punished me for my virtue and never for my sins?"

At about this time, one of my readers highly recommended an original story by a young writer whose name was Darryl Zanuck. It was a good story, and I was about to recommend it for purchase. I learned that Mrs. Strauss, of First National, and Ralph Block, of Paramount, were also interested in it. But the story troubled me—it kept haunting me. Something was uncomfortably familiar about it. Had I read it before? I searched my memory and read it again. Suddenly it came to me. I had read that same story in the anthology of Best Foreign Short Stories. Sure enough, when I went to the bookstore to check, I found it. There was the story, completely unchanged except that the background and the names of the characters had been Polish and now were American. Also, the locale was changed to the Western plains. Word for word, paragraph for paragraph, page for page—it had been copied almost verbatim. It was literary forgery so brazen that I could hardly believe it. The name Darryl Zanuck, of course, had no meaning for me then—this was long before he became one of the potentates of the industry, head of the Twentieth Century studio. Alerting Paramount and First National, I returned the script to his agent, requesting that it be withdrawn.

A good contact I had was Mary Scott, a reader at the Century Company publishing house. One day, Mary phoned excitedly to relay that she had just finished the galleys of a terrific novel—a novel about college life, written by an English professor by the name of Percy Marks. It was an exposé of the emphasis put on sports in colleges and universities at the expense of learning. At the time, this was to attract a lot of comment although we have grown more blasé about it since. Of course, I could hardly wait to meet Mary for lunch to get my hot little hands on those galleys. I read them that night after getting home around midnight from another play opening. It was after 3:00 A.M. when I finished and nearly hit the ceiling. I knew immediately that *The Plastic Age* would be a bestseller, a hot property, and here I had the precious galleys before any other company even knew of its existence.

Next day I rushed to R.H. Cochrane with my find, telling him the story in detail, hoping to buy it before bidding in the marketplace began. I estimated we could buy it for thirty thousand dollars if we acted promptly.

The purchase was achieved. I was proud as a peacock at my being able to outfox my fellow editors, who were furious when they learned what I had done. But my triumph was short-lived. The next morning, I was summoned to the office of Carl Laemmle. Son Junior, a sallow-faced, neurotic, undersized boy of seventeen, was seated at Papa's desk, his feet sprawled on top. In his hands, he held the precious galleys of *The Plastic Age*. Papa Laemmle, obviously very upset, was pacing the office. In his heavy German accent, he demanded to know why I had bought the book. "For why," he glowered at me. "For why you buy dis book?" he asked, pointing to the galleys in Junior's hands. "My son here tells me dis is a very dirty book." He wagged his finger at me in disapproval.

"Mr. Laemmle," I replied, as yet unintimidated, "this is not a dirty book, I assure you. It is an exposé of college life written by a professor, and it will make a great moneymaking picture."

"Junior here, he tells me it is a dirty book and reads me the dirty words. I cannot make such a picture. I cannot have my name on such a picture. You must sell it—sell at once."

It dawned on me why Carl Laemmle was so concerned. He had just been appointed head of the Clean Picture Campaign inaugurated by the Will Hays office. It was a new office set up to monitor the morals of the "decadent" film industry—decadent in the eyes of complaining churchmen and women and of moralists in general. The picture business was going to monitor its own morals, and Carl Laemmle took his augmented position seriously.

I knew I was licked and had no argument that would alter his decision. "Mr. Laemmle," I said, "please don't upset yourself about it." He looked agitated enough to have a heart attack. "I'll have no trouble getting rid of *The Plastic Age*. I bought it before the other companies had copies and could bid on it. Now it's hot property."

"Sell, sell at once," was his directive again, while Junior sat grinning behind his desk. I could have throttled that kid for his immature influence on his father. I wouldn't have been so hard on Junior had I known then the price he would pay one day for being his father's son and heir—and not being up to it. Before he was thirty, the Universal prince would be in a wheelchair being pushed by his sister, Rosabelle. Saddled with the job of production chief at Universal during the Depression, Junior wound up a total mess, mentally and physically.

I left my boss's office that day disappointed and disheartened. This was my thanks for beating my brains to outsmart the competition. When I reached my own office, I was fit to be tied, ready to throw in the sponge and tell them where they could take their cotton-pickin' job. One of the calls that had come in while I was downstairs was from Al Lichtman. He had resigned from Universal the week before and was now occupying new offices nearby. Al Lichtman—that name was an electric light. Of course! Al Lichtman had a brand-new production company, Preferred Pictures. They would be looking for material.

I got Al on the phone. "Al," I told him, "you're in luck. I've just bought your first production. I bought it from galleys. Got in on the ground floor. Paid thirty thousand dollars for it, and now the old man wants me to sell it because Junior read it and told him it was a dirty book. And, since he is head of the Clean Picture Campaign, he feels his reputation is at stake. It's a terrific story and a great opportunity for Preferred. Paramount and First National haven't even had a crack at it."

His answer was, "Come right over and tell me the story." An hour later, Lichtman cabled B.P. Schulberg in Hollywood a synopsis of *The Plastic Age*. After another hour, we received a cabled reply. "Buy at once. Great vehicle for Clara Bow. Signed B.P. Schulberg."

My scheme had worked, and I was sitting in the driver's seat. I told Lichtman the price would have to be forty thousand dollars because that would be the least it would bring if I put it in the open market.

I came back to Universal with a check for forty thousand dollars. I could hardly wait to face Papa Laemmle. I fully expected that he would be delighted that I had saved his reputation and he could now serve as head of the Clean Picture Campaign with impunity. And, of course, there was the little matter of ten thousand dollars' profit. A neat bonus. Surely nothing to sneeze at.

"Mr. Laemmle," I said, "I have a nice surprise for you. I sold *The Plastic Age*," and I handed him the forty-thousand-dollar check. He neither thanked me, praised me, or in any other way acknowledged appreciation for what I had done. Instead, he wordlessly pocketed the check and glowered me out of his imperial presence.

I had not seen or heard from Bob Rodin, my second boss, since the day he had emptied his desk and gathered together his few possessions, mostly books. Like a whipped dog that knows it is guilty and being punished, he left with no goodbye. I was not without concern or interest in what was happening to him. Through the grapevine of agents and friends in the business, I learned that he had been around and borrowed money. He was, of course, drinking heavily, inconsolable about losing his job, and blaming me. One day he appeared in my office. He was unshaven, his suit crumpled—as though he had been sleeping in it. He reeked of alcohol and was obviously very drunk.

"You double-crossed me, Freddie Sagor, didn't you?" He weaved unsteadily on his feet, pointing an accusing finger at me. "You are one fine friend, young lady, taking my job away from me. I thought we were pals, but you wanted this job and turned me in."

He lunged forward in his fury. But then he lost his balance and nearly fell on the floor; I knew I had nothing to fear from this poor, lost, miserable sot. Shaking uncontrollably, and finally losing all pride, he blubbered, "I need money. I need money. They won't give me a drink anywhere unless I pay for it. Freddie, I need a drink. I have to have a drink. Help me. I didn't mean what I said about your double-crossing me. I know you did what you could to help me. But I'm sick, Freddie. I need a drink. Help me."

I opened my pocketbook. I had about fifty dollars in cash. I never felt so much pity for any human being as I did for Bob Rodin at this very moment. So utterly miserable. So helpless. So destroyed. I knew there was nothing I could do for him. I had tried, goodness knows, to save him from himself and protect his job for him. But old "John Barleycorn" had him firmly in his grip and was not about to let go. Right now, the only thing I could do for him was to give him a few dollars to satisfy his thirst. He snatched the money out of my hand and fled.

I never saw Bob Rodin alive again. Several months later, J.G. Packard, a literary agent and a crony of Bob's since their reporting days, found him unconscious in the gutter near his home. An ambulance took him to Bellevue Hospital, where he died of pneumonia. I contributed to his funeral, as did many others who respected this truly brilliant man caught in the grip of that dread disease—alcoholism.

Finally, finally, came the 365th day I had officiated as story editor for Universal Films. This was the day, the great day when Universal would get a replacement for me and send me on my way to the West Coast to join the writing staff. This is what I had been promised, what I had been looking forward to, what I expected to happen. Instead, I was hauled before a court of my peers and told in no uncertain terms that Universal felt no obligation to send me to the West Coast. Their promise to do so meant nothing, and there was no written contract. I could stay on as story editor, but if I wanted to be a writer and go to the West Coast, I would have to do it on my own. Chintzy Universal had spoken again. If they could save the railroad fare, why not?

They had been expecting me to quit and now wanted me to break in my successor, who I was introduced to the next day. Her name was Namo Sugimato, a sixtyish Japanese lady. She had been married to a Caucasian rancher in Canada and had three stunning teenage children who were blonde and fair skinned. Incongruously, they all also had oriental eyes. My heart reached out to them instantly. Sugimato was recently divorced, and it was apparent that she needed this job to support her brood. Her claim to fame was a book about her life in Canada, published obscurely there. I was told she had no association with the motion picture business and knew nothing about it. She lasted less than six months and almost wrecked the story department in that time.

It took awhile for me to get over my disappointment. I had no job, I was tired, I needed rest and a change—a complete change. So, when I picked up the *New York Times* and read about the launching of a new ship, the *Paris*, headed on her maiden voyage to France, I booked passage, first class. My wounded feelings began to recover as I excitedly contemplated my adventure, my first trip to Europe. But Bobbie Burns, the poet, was right when he penned his poem "To A Mouse": *The best laid schemes of mice and men, Gang aft a-gley.* And mine certainly did "gang a-gley."

My sister Vera's husband, Nicholas Kann, a pharmacist in Gary, Indiana, had become critically ill with a blood clot in his leg, making amputation a real possibility. There were four young nephews to be considered: James, sixteen; Alexander, fourteen; Daniel, nine; and Henry, barely four. Someone had to go to Gary to give Vera a hand. My sisters Sophie and Lillian were both teaching and could not go. My mother was too old for the task. But I was free. Reluctantly, believe me, I canceled my passage. The maiden voyage of the *Paris* would sail without a passenger by the name of Frederica Sagor, eager for new scenes, new experiences. Instead Frederica would take the Twentieth Century Limited to Chicago, change there for a milk train to Gary, Indiana, and look after four bewildered nephews and a very upset older sister.

My brother-in-law, unfortunately, died several months after my arrival in Gary. My sister decided to move to Chicago and resume teaching; she took her accreditation exams and passed with flying colors. With everything settled, the time had come for me to again take stock of my own situation. Should I return to New York and embark on the European jaunt I had abandoned months before? It was tempting. But the initial excitement was no longer there. I decided that, since Chicago was on my way to Los Angeles, I might as well keep going.

Chapter 5

MY INTRODUCTION
TO HOLLYWOOD

A TEMPERATURE OF 101 DEGREES GREETED ME when I arrived at the Los Angeles station. The year was 1924, before the beautiful Union Station of today, with its Spanish tiles and flowered patios, was built. There was no one to meet me.

Soon, my five suitcases and I were deposited in a cab. My destination was The Halifax, an apartment hotel on Ivar near Vine. My rent? An easy fifty dollars a month for a fully equipped kitchen and nicely furnished studio. The wall bed, on pulleys, was supposed to come down easily, but it defied me. It would either come down too fast and nearly kill me or not come down at all. When I arrived, the place was smotheringly hot because the apartment faced east, and the blazing morning sun streamed directly in the windows. Opening them helped some. I looked out. Empty lots all around. The Hollywood Hills—no HOLLYWOOD sign yet—made a picturesque background. The neighborhood was quiet, respectable. There were other apartment buildings all around, three and four stories tall. All were furnished, and the apartments were mostly studios or one- and two-bedrooms.

In the early days in Hollywood, unfurnished apartments or houses were a rarity. Everything was temporary. The Halifax and other dwellings around it were tenanted by aspiring directors, cameramen, film technicians, actors and actresses not yet discovered, and up-and-coming writers like myself. Today the same neighborhood is closely built—one apartment building next to another—and is disgracefully run down.

The Halifax still stands, now with threadbare carpets, plaster falling off its walls, and halls smelling of ethnic cooking—Korean, Taiwanese, Mexican, San Salvadoran, Nicaraguan, Haitian, Cuban—you name it. They are all represented here—refugees from countries all over the world, where people have to flee to secure a safer and better life for themselves and their children. Today the rents for these unfortunate have-nots in these shabby hovels is easily four times what they were when the buildings were spanking new. In 1924, if the early denizens of these houses made it in Hollywood at all, they bought homes and populated Beverly Hills. The more affluent suburbs—Bel-Air, Brentwood, and Pacific Palisades—developed later.

In my studio apartment, I felt alone and frightened. I unpacked my five suitcases and found I needed another closet since my trunk was still to come. As I unpacked, I came across my new copy of *The Plastic Age*. It had just come out in print and, as predicted, was topping the bestseller lists. I eyed it long and tenderly. In the pages of that book lay my hopes for the future.

One name in my address book came to mind: Elsie Werner. A reader at Universal, she was an intelligent, hearty, outgoing person. When we had met on my previous trip out West, she was living in one of the private bungalows at the Beverly Hills Hotel, which was impressive. The Beverly Hills Hotel, exclusive in those days, catered only to the very rich and frowned on picture people because their other clientele did not care to rub elbows with the riffraff of Hollywood.

Elsie had a new address now, and at six o'clock I called her at home. She was happy to hear my voice and to learn that I had returned to Hollywood on my own, for good. She drove over immediately and fetched me to see her new abode and meet her children, whom she picked up at a nearby boarding school. Elsie's children were darling little girls, or so it seemed at first. Florence was eight, and Dicky was seven.

I remember how impressed I was by the bungalow court where Elsie now lived. Each bungalow had its own garden of oleanders, bougainvillea, petunias, magnolias, rhododendron, fuchsia, and roses. There were even some lemon and orange trees. Being a product of a canyon city like New York, I thought this was paradise. Later, I would scorn this type of bungalow living. They were the first type of Hollywood housing to deteriorate.

Elsie's life story was an unusual one. Fresh out of college, unworldly and plain, she married at twenty into a wealthy New York family in the wholesale meat business. It was an arranged marriage, you might say. There were two Werner sons; unfortunately, she did not marry the one who turned out to be a good writer but married the ne'er-do-well, the one who was spoiled, arrogant, and adventurous. Her first daughter was barely one year old and she was pregnant again when her husband decided to go to China. There, shortly after the birth of her second daughter, he deserted her, leaving her with two babies, no money, and no friends in China, which was then very unfriendly to foreigners. A Good Samaritan at the hotel, an elderly man recently widowed, recognized her desperate plight and took over until she and the children were safely on their way back to the United States. Her family provided for the children, but Elsie, fiercely determined to earn her own way, aspired to become a Hollywood writer. She succeeded in getting a job as a reader, the first step up the ladder. Elsie's parents, ordinary Polish folk, were well-to-do. Her father and a brother in New York had made a bundle speculating in New York real estate. Affluent though they were, they kept Elsie on short rations, expecting her to earn her own way in life; but they showered their grandchildren with gifts and spoiled them outrageously. Elsie, however, was not spoiled. What she lacked in pulchritude she made up for in warmth; she was open and honest, sometimes to the point of being foolish. One thing was sure: she was not Hollywood tinsel.

I got very little sleep that first night. Mistrustful of the wall bed, I slept in a chair. At the crack of dawn, I was soaking in a hot bath, trying to overcome my anxieties. Supposing Preferred Pictures had already engaged a writer to script *The Plastic Age*? Supposing . . . supposing . . .

At one minute after 9:00 A.M., I telephoned Preferred Pictures, which had opened offices and a studio in the heart of Hollywood. The operator asked no questions and put me right through. Mr. Schulberg was extremely cordial when I introduced myself. He apologized because he could not see me that day but said for me to come in next morning at eleven.

This was my ace in the hole, *The Plastic Age*. It was a good card, and I was determined to play it to win. After all, it was all I had. I called Elsie at Universal to tell her about my appointment. She was delighted and almost as excited as I was. Later, she called to tell me she had arranged for her parents' chauffeur to pick me up and take me to my appointment. I arrived in high style at 11:00 A.M., with chauffeur and limousine, wearing my most elegant outfit, and had my first interview with B.P. Schulberg.

Schulberg listened keenly as I outlined my suggestions for the film version of *The Plastic Age*. It had been six months since I had read the book, and in the interval I had had plenty of time to think about it. I knew my ideas were sound, analytical. I had control of the characters, the basic theme, the inner relationships. Mr. Schulberg, I could see, was impressed and pleased. We must have spent three hours in that interview, and when it ended, Mr. Schulberg's secretary brought in a contract, a blank contract. He outlined the terms, but I was too excited to hear what they were. I was eager to sign my "John Hancock" to that important piece of paper—my first Hollywood contract! A bona fide Hollywood writer! I had a job—a contract to write the adaptation and screenplay of *The Plastic Age!* I was on cloud nine. How lucky could I be?

Ben Schulberg, it turned out, was one of the few literate minds in motion picture production at the time. He was a college graduate and had been a reporter for the *New York Mail.* Starting as a publicist and scenario writer for Adolph Zukor and Famous Players-Lasky at fifty dollars a week, he had advanced to head the publicity department, selling original stories on the side to augment his income. In those days, his subject matter was women's rights, the disinherited, the poor, the struggling. He had a retentive memory, read the classics, and quoted from them often. He, too, had been lured by the possibilities of the silver screen. Now here he was—head of Preferred Pictures—primed for action. He had managed to snare the bankable Katherine MacDonald for four pictures. And he had Clara Bow, an obscure beauty-contest winner from Brooklyn, who would become the famous Elinor Glyn "It" girl before life in the fast lane brought her down.

Schulberg and I never lacked for interesting, lively conversation. We sparred over the merits of this or that addition to the rolls of new published fiction. Later, when he became head of Paramount, I thought he was cheapening his reputation to attain success and overlooking promising, serious material. He admitted he knew better, but he believed that the public did not want to be educated or preached at—entertainment was the magic word.

"Give them entertainment!" How often was I to hear those words proclaimed! Eventually, I too succumbed and became proficient in the light, fluffy, and mindless. In other words, like Ben Schulberg, I too surrendered to the almighty dollar.

After some weeks passed, Schulberg sent me to an ace photographer to have stills made for publicity purposes. The pictures were sensational: they made me look gorgeous, something I'd never considered myself to be. I was not interested in good looks or sex appeal. I was interested in brains. But Schulberg kept urging me to make a screen test.

"I have a talent for picking stars," he assured me. "I could turn you into another Theda Bara." He was serious, comparing me to the aging femme fatale of the early films.

"Who wants to be a movie vamp?" I protested. "If I had to emote in one of those torrid love scenes, I would burst out laughing. I'm not an actress. I'm a writer. No, thanks, Mr. Schulberg, you can't turn me into another Theda Bara."

He was finally convinced.

It was Elsie Werner who proposed that we find a suitable house somewhere in the Hollywood Hills and try living together. She would keep the children in private school, and they would come home on weekends. We would, of course, share expenses. It sounded like a good idea. Living in a house in the hills was appealing to a city girl, a New York City girl. The three-bedroom, two-story house we found was a darling, snuggled away in the hills off of Beachwood Drive and perfect for our needs. It was Spanish, with a balcony and red-tiled roof covered with bougainvillea. It was tastefully furnished with Oriental rugs, good china, and silverware. The living room had a grand piano, which captivated me immediately. The rent was $125 a month including utilities, which meant only $62.50 as my share—an expenditure I could easily swing now that I had a sure-enough contract at $150 a week for thirty weeks, with a bonus of $2,500 when my work was completed. I was riding high and handsome.

Elsie's parents, living in a Wilshire hotel, were making their limousine and chauffeur available to me for transportation to the studio.

One day when I was being deposited at the gates of Preferred Studios, I encountered Mr. Schulberg. Eyebrows raised, he reached the inevitable conclusion—that I was somebody's well-kept dame.

"Who's the lucky man?" he inquired, his male ego immediately challenged. B.P. liked the fair sex and made no bones about it. He would make a pass, and if rejected, accept the turndown gracefully and with good humor, and never try again. This time, he figured he had been mistaken in me. He was disappointed when I told him the very uninteresting real story of the limousine and the chauffeur. It was so dull it had to be true.

I was working at home and went to the studio only for occasional consultations. Once or twice, Mr. Schulberg dropped by the house to confer with me, or he drove me home from the studio. He was very considerate. He knew I had no car.

It wasn't very long before Elsie's children decided that they hated their private school and begged to come home to live. Elsie could never deny her children anything. She and their doting grandparents indulged them in any whim they dreamed up, and she succumbed. They would attend the local public school, and Elsie would employ a governess full time—someone who, when the children were in school, would tidy up the house and perform necessary chores.

Siska was French and no beauty. She had an ugly birthmark on one side of her face. She had come to this country to visit a sister and remained to marry a house painter, who turned out to be a brute who beat her regularly. He also demanded that she earn her keep. Siska had no skills but one—she played the piano. Since the most she had been able to earn was fifty cents an hour at a ballet school, she decided to hire herself out as a governess, although she had never been a governess before. Elsie hired her because she thought the children would learn French. Little demons that they were, they soon saw that they were in control. Siska screamed helplessly at them; they did exactly as they pleased, making it difficult to concentrate as I worked on the scenario of *The Plastic Age*, the adaptation of which had already been approved. All this made our living arrangements less than idyllic, but I said nothing. I was sorry for Elsie; I felt she was doing the best she could with two obstreperous youngsters and two selfish, elderly parents who also demanded her attention.

The one nice bonus for me was Siska—she was a superb pianist.

It was she who introduced me to the music of Claude Debussy. And how she played Debussy! Concert pianists like Walter Gieseking, considered a great interpreter of the Frenchman, did not have the delicacy, the subtle understanding, the poetry of Siska. Nowadays, I never hear Debussy's early etudes, his "Clair de Lune," his "Childhood Suite," without visualizing Siska at the grand piano in the living room of that Hollywood Hills house, playing her soul away, transported to France where she longed to be but would probably never see again. Elsie knew nothing of these concerts, for she was at the studio fulfilling her distasteful duties as script reader.

During the day, the fiendish children would be at school. "Siska," I would say, taking the broom and dustcloth out of her hands, "play for me. I will dust and sweep while you play." And she would play, tears coursing down her pockmarked cheeks, her Debussy reverie transporting us both. Dear Siska, what happened to you? You poor, frightened, helpless swallow, you did not last long in our household. Elsie fired you after six weeks.

Then came Olga, a White Russian ten years older than Siska. She, too, was versed in French but had better control over the children and had good references as a governess. The children soon learned to respect her because she took their privileges away when they misbehaved. Olga came from a land-owning family in the Ukraine and had an overwhelming, but understandable, hatred for the Bolsheviks who had taken over the family farms and collectivized them for the peasants to run. Her parents, relatives, and friends were shot when they organized a resistance. She was withdrawn, bitter, and very religious. Her husband, Alyosha, was employed in the household of one of California's U.S. senators, who lived in Pasadena in a three-story mansion. Alyosha doubled as butler and chauffeur for the senator's wife and children and for the senator when he was in town.

Olga and Alyosha had no apartment of their own. His wages were meager but included bed and board, as did hers; so on Alyosha's and Olga's day off, they would meet at our home and, weather permitting, sit outside on the swing on the balcony outside my bedroom, talking in whispers in Russian and holding hands like young sweethearts. They never embraced, and they never kissed; they would just hold hands. They had no other place to go, for they had no car. Alyosha took three buses to reach our place. Olga diffidently inquired if I would mind if she served him lunch; she would buy the food. She explained that the senator's wife kept her retinue of servants on short rations, feeding them three sparse meals a day, barely enough to satisfy the pangs of hunger. Every piece of bread was parceled out. This high lady held the keys to the icebox, so there could be no filching by the hired help. Only the cook had access—no one else. Of course, I told Olga that our kitchen was hers, that she and Alyosha could eat whatever we had on hand; and I always saw to it that we had plenty. After a while, I could not bear to see those two restrained, resigned human beings, who loved each other so deeply, compelled by circumstances to suppress their love, their natural desires to be together as man and wife. I turned my bedroom over to them on Alyosha's visiting day and moved my trusty typewriter elsewhere.

I never let Elsie know what I was doing; she was, I discovered, completely oblivious to the problems of others. She had all she could do to handle her own. During this time, Elsie was very much into Marcel Proust but he was over her head. She had little capacity for deep thinking. Unfortunately, too, she had poor judgment of people. She was susceptible to flattery—and sex-starved—but she had more discrimination and control than I did. I'd wanted to know what made the "big" men tick but only learned that sex was a chase for them and nothing more. Their career success was due more to luck, being in the right place and recognizing the opportunity, than it was to something special in their character. Meanwhile, I had come to regard sex as a part of life, as humdrum as washing your face or cleaning your teeth. When it was over, it was over. I was no longer romantic about it. Elsie, on the other hand, looked askance at casual sex. She had to be in love before she would consent to sleeping with someone.

Charles Brabin was an erstwhile Universal director now glad to serve as assistant to any director who would have him. But to Elsie Werner, he was the greatest, and they were carrying on a torrid affair. All she could talk about was Charles Brabin, how he adored her, how fascinating he found her—a woman of the world—how much they had in common—their interest and understanding of Proust. I "had to" meet him.

I met him. Several nights later, at seven o'clock, he came to dinner. He was a tall, spare man, very dapper, wearing a velour hat (jauntily askew) and carrying a gold-knobbed cane. A colorful kerchief was draped around his neck—I'm sure to hide the wrinkles. He was doused with feminine perfume—the same scent I used, and one which I never used afterward. He dyed his thinning hair red. I suspected, too, that he wore a corset. He was a man past sixty trying to look forty. Artificial all the way. A flatterer, a woman chaser, and not to be taken seriously. It was obvious he was trying hard to make a favorable impression on me, confirming my worst suspicions; he was not in love with Elsie.

After he left, my fluttery roommate asked excitedly, "What do you think? How do you like him? Isn't he wonderful!" I didn't have the heart to disillusion her. I knew she would find out sooner or later that her lover was a has-been whose chief claim to fame was being the husband of Theda Bara. Yes, the same Theda Bara dear Ben Schulberg had wanted me to emulate!

That was not the end of Charles Brabin. The next day, he came a-calling, wearing carefully selected sports clothes—natty gray tweed plus fours with a cashmere jacket, a Tyrolean hat with a wisp of a feather, white shoes, the gold-knobbed cane, and another scarf cleverly tucked around his neck. He was a fast manipulator, wanting me to know he had not slept a wink for thinking of me. Yes, he had fallen instantly in love with me. And he was sure, because he could feel the vibrations, that I returned the attraction.

"What about Elsie?" I asked him incredulously, knowing the line he had been feeding her and also recalling Al Lichtman's indifferent dismissal of his amante. Like the villain in a barroom melodrama, he laughed scornfully and would have twirled his mustache if he had had one.

"That silly goose!" was his reply. My hand reached out, made perfect contact with his cheek, and nearly knocked him off balance. I never told poor Elsie what had happened. I knew her well enough to know she would not have believed me. She wept for days when he did not return her calls. Exit Charles Brabin.

Mr. Schulberg was immensely pleased with my finished script of *The Plastic Age*. All those hours I had spent studying finished films in movie theaters had paid off. John Brownell had given me sage advice. I developed a cutting eye for telling a story economically and dramatically building it, much like a musical symphony.

Now that *The Plastic Age* was finished, what was my next goal?

Metro-Goldwyn-Mayer (MGM), of course, newly established under that name. It had a reputation for making pictures of distinction. They had wooed the young genius Irving Thalberg away from Universal, and he was now distinguishing himself as a man of ideas and taste. He was the talk of the industry, and MGM had plans for him.

Edmund Goulding was a writer and director at MGM now. I figured that this gentleman owed me a favor for the assistance I had given him (gratis) in straightening out his play before its successful Broadway opening. He remembered me instantly when I called him and invited me to come right over to see what he could do for me. The MGM studios, located in Culver City, were a considerable distance from Hollywood, especially since there was no direct transportation to get there. So Edmund Goulding had an MGM limousine pick me up. Again I arrived in style at yet another studio, the prestigious Metro-Goldwyn Studios, far larger and grander than Preferred Pictures, and was directed to the bungalow of Edmund Goulding.

That very day, I found myself ushered into the almighty presence of Louis B. Mayer. Edmund Goulding delivered a spiel, as only he could, on my talents and background. Mayer was particularly interested in the fact that I had just finished Ben Schulberg's first picture under the banner of Preferred Pictures. He also asked many questions, few of which I could answer, about the inner workings of the company. He was curious, too, about Al Lichtman's affiliation with Ben Schulberg. It struck me as odd that he should be so nosy about the establishment of Preferred Pictures. I learned later that Mayer and Schulberg had started out as cronies in the business and gone into partnership as Selig-Mayer-Schulberg Studios on Mission Road east of Main Street— an alliance that dissolved not too amicably. Oddly enough, when he offered to sign me to a three-year contract, renewed annually, at $350 a week and increasing to $500 the second year, I had the peculiar feeling that wily Louis B. was less interested in my writing ability than in signing someone who had worked for Ben Schulberg and Al Lichtman. It mattered little to me; I was on Cloud Nine again. My phenomenal luck was holding out. I was secure for a year. Maybe three! As I was driven home in the Metro-Goldwyn limousine, I actually pinched myself, it was so hard to believe. But it was true. I was to be on the writing staff of prestigious MGM!

Now set securely for a year, I had to supplement my wardrobe with clothes more suitable to eighty-degree weather. Before coming to Hollywood, I had bought two new outfits in Chicago—one was a beige wool dress with a hand-crocheted neckline and jabot in a rose-colored yarn, with a full-length coat to match, bordered with a band of handsome badger fur. A trifle theatrical, perhaps, but noticeable; I wore it to my first interview with Ben Schulberg. The other outfit was more subdued—a grass-green wool dress with plaid collar and cuffs and a three-quarter-length cape of the same green material with matching plaid lining. Let me tell you, those two outfits earned me a lot of attention on the MGM lot—especially from the opposite sex. I soon learned, however, that people dressed much more casually in the West, so I followed suit. But I never abandoned my tailored Madison Avenue image.

In Los Angeles, Hollywood Boulevard was the Mecca of fashion as well as fine restaurants. It was then what it should be today—glamorous, with stores like I. Magnin; specialty shops galore, some of them with home bases in San Francisco, New York's Fifth Avenue, and Paris; expensive shoe stores; fine millinery shops; jewelry stores; sweater and lingerie shops. The best there was, was there—starting at Vine and ending at La Brea Boulevard. People walked at night then, unafraid, attending pictures at the famous Egyptian Theater.

I opened a number of charge accounts and felt very guilty doing it. My dear mother would have been outraged, having ingrained in our psyches that you bought only what you could afford, never on credit. But I was my own woman now. What did I have to worry about? I had a job, a good salary, a brilliant future. Established credit was a status symbol, adding to my importance and to my image of myself as a successful Hollywood writer.

Also, I knew I had to buy a car. There was no getting anywhere without a car. Not knowing anything about automobiles—not even enough to differentiate one make from another—I bought a Moon for twelve hundred dollars cash, largely because the salesman, Earl Daley, was a super salesman and undertook to teach me to drive. He also moved in easily on my sexual favors. He was young, good-looking, entertaining. His parents had been early comics in vaudeville, and he had a good sense of comedy—no doubt inherited from growing up listening to their comic routines. Not that he was corny. He was quite sophisticated, and I took full advantage of his company while it lasted.

I was not mechanically inclined. Learning the mechanics of the typewriter had been an ordeal for me, so imagine what learning the mechanics of the automobile was like. Earl patiently taught me how to shift gears, but I could not get the hang of it. I was pretty shamefaced about it. One morning, I took the blasted car in hand and practiced shifting gears for hours until I finally got it down pat. By the time I had been driving several months, I considered myself proficient in every respect but one—I still panicked whenever I reached the top of a hill and had to make a stop, shift gears, and gun forward. Inevitably, I stalled the motor.

In the early days you went downtown only when it was impera-tive. One day an elderly neighbor of ours, Edward Wayne, who had once been editor of *Collier's* magazine, and I had important business to transact downtown. Downtown was a dreary place of neglected of-fice buildings, a few department stores, lots of empty store spaces, and plenty of parking space. After a tasty lunch at Robinson's Department Store and having transacted the business that had brought us down-town, we returned to my trusty Moon parked on a side street and started home.

It was almost five o'clock, and traffic was heavy. We came to a hill that had to be negotiated. Just as we got to the top, the traffic light turned red, and I had to stop. When the light greened again, I pan-icked—as always. I gunned the car, and it sprang forward, knocking the traffic cop in the middle of the intersection off his pedestal.

"What do you think you're doing, young lady?" he inquired, saun-tering over and asking for my license. I thought surely I would receive a traffic ticket for reckless driving, or worse, endangering the life of a police officer. But beside my driver's license was a parking permit for the MGM lot that I had just received. He saw that.

"You work in the studios?"

"Yes," I quavered, "in Culver City at the MGM studios. I'm a writer." Of course, I had yet to start there, but he didn't know that.

"I should give you a ticket, you know, for nearly killing me, but I won't. I'll settle for some movie passes and for my wife and kid to visit the studios some time."

At that moment, I hadn't the faintest idea of where to get movie passes or whether I could obtain permission for anyone to visit the studios, but I assured him as convincingly as I could that if he gave me his name and address, his wishes would be fulfilled. As we proceeded on our way to the Hollywood Hills, Ed Wayne and I had a good chuckle over my narrow escape.

What's more, I kept my word to traffic cop Mike Grogan. I sent him some movie passes and arranged for his wife and child to come to the studios. I gave them a personally conducted tour of the sets and took them to lunch in the commissary, where they saw movie extras in costume and even a star or two—a trip I am certain they never forgot.

My office was a cubbyhole in one of the many one-story bungalows on the MGM lot. Half of the bungalow was used by new writers under contract, and half of it was given over to the Publicity Department. The construction of the bungalow was shoddy. The building needed painting. It was now several shades of streaked, dirty gray. The ceilings and walls inside needed plastering. Rain leaked through the roof, sometimes into buckets if it rained hard and long enough. In summer or winter (and in southern California, summer can return as a Christmas present), the place was a furnace, with no escape from the heat. On rainy or cold days, it was a drafty Siberian cell. No matter if you wore sweaters and underwear, the damp and cold got to you so that you could hardly hold a pen or pencil, much less type. This was the atmosphere provided for those knocking their creative brains out to provide suitable fodder for the movie gins.

A few writers were ensconced in better offices in the executive building. But these were the exceptions. They had achieved this distinction through the consistent creation of box-office winners. I paid an informal call on one of them one day. His name was Waldemar Young, and I knew his work and admired his craftsmanship.

"How long will it take for me to earn a layout like this?" I asked, looking around the office. It had a couch on which to relax and piped-in steam heat. It was a raw day, and I was chilled to the bone from working away in my bungalow icebox.

"It took me five years," he laughed. "But don't feel too bad. There are only two writers in this building—Carey Wilson and myself."

Waldemar Young was in his early fifties and about fifty pounds overweight. He was prematurely grey and looked physically worn out. He admitted, in the course of our conversation, that he hadn't had a vacation in two years, not even a full weekend.

"Then why don't you buy yourself a railroad ticket or book a Panama cruise or go to Europe?" I asked innocently.

"If I did," he said, "I'd lose my seniority and be relegated to the back lot." He meant it. Mind you, these were the words of a successful studio writer on the MGM lot—one who hadn't missed a paycheck in five years. I later found out that he wasn't as *non compos mentes* as I thought he was. Whether you were a writer, producer, director, cameraman, actor, or actress—it was very easy to be forgotten in filmland with so much available talent to replace you. Hard work and good credits were often not enough. Even if you were an old pro like Waldemar Young, if you stepped too far beyond the men's room, you could return and find someone else in your chair. Five years was a long, long time for a writer to be at one studio.

Our writers' bungalow was shared by several writers. One of these was a young man named Ray Doyle, who had been lured away from a newspaper desk to work on a story about Zapata, a hero of the Mexican Revolution. He had submitted a brief outline form to MGM two years before. He was promptly given a contract at seventy-five dollars a week and put to work to develop the story. The production was to be under the supervision of the hallowed producer Irving Thalberg. In two full years on the job, however, he had had only two story conferences with Mr. Thalberg—the first when they signed him to a contract and one more after that.

Every day, Ray telephoned the Thalberg office to find out his chances for an interview with his producer. The reply was always the same: "I'm sorry, Mr. Doyle, not a chance today. Mr. Thalberg's schedule is full."

This became a joke with Ray and me because I, too, was similarly stymied in having a conference with my producer, Harry Rapf. It was on these days that Ray and I would pack our papers and pencils and hie ourselves to the Santa Monica beach, only a fifteen-minute drive away. There, on sunny days, we could escape, breathe, and go for a swim. We even took my portable phonograph along with us.

Ray was a decent fellow with a dry sense of humor and was very attached to his wife. "My woman," he called her. They had no children. She, too, worked at the same newspaper where he had been. When we weren't working (and who in his right mind ever works at the beach?), we took long walks, discussed politics (Ray was of the same persuasion as I—liberal Democrat), and read aloud from our favorite authors—Sherwood Anderson, Hemingway, Maugham, Sinclair Lewis, Dreiser.

Those were pleasant days we spent at Santa Monica away from the bungalow oven. I was really sorry when, one day, he got the pink slip and left. They never made Ray Doyle's story of the Mexican revolutionary hero—another effort charged off to profit and loss.

This situation was not unusual. Metro was full of writers—novices and pros, playwrights and novelists—working on "ideas," most of which never realized production. A word is in order here about the extravagance that existed on the Metro-Goldwyn lot as opposed to all other studios, where one had to strictly adhere to a budget and a time schedule. I have always felt the appellation "genius" has been loosely applied to Irving Thalberg, whom I consider the worst perpetrator of waste in the business. His creed was, "If at first you don't succeed, try, try again." Money and time were never a consideration—only perfection. With such latitude, it was almost impossible to fail to come forth with a good picture. But then, "genius" has its privileges, and Thalberg certainly had his.

Another writer in the bungalow was blowsy "Fred" De Gresac, allegedly a Hungarian countess. Sixtyish with short, cropped, flaming red hair, she wore pants and men's shirts and ties. She apparently knew the right people in the front office, for what she wrote when she wrote (if she wrote), Ray and I never found out. Soon enough, I discovered that she had designs on females younger than herself, and she aimed her guile in my direction. Since this was my first encounter with a lesbian, I didn't at first understand what was going on. I found mysterious little gifts on my desk when I came in, with beguiling notes—"Your liquid brown eyes sear my soul" or "We have so much in common, dear Frederica. Will you have lunch with me today? My house is not far from the studio, and my housekeeper is a wonderful cook."

I told Ray about it, and he looked as if he couldn't believe that a sophisticated writer like me, who knew her way around, was that naive. So, Ray said, "That woman is a les, stupid. Shake her and tell her to go fly a kite."

I never had lunch at the home of Countess De Gresac.

Another innocent, and a writer in our bungalow, was Ruth Cummings. But since she was a niece of Louis B. Mayer and the sister of Jack Cummings, who was being groomed for producership, the countess knew better than to venture in her direction. Ruth's specialty was writing the titles accompanying silent movies.

I did not hobnob with any of them, other than my good buddy Ray. For laughs and relaxation, I preferred the rowdy bunch in the publicity department. Bill Conselman was there, earning fifty dollars a week. While on that job, he created a comic strip called "Ella Cinders," which became very popular. He later sold the motion picture rights to that strip for a princely sum. But not to MGM—they spurned it. First National bought it and made a moneymaking picture out of it with Colleen Moore. Bill Conselman became a producer at the Fox studios. But poor Bill never did know much about motion pictures and ended up a successful alcoholic, dying before he was forty-five years old.

When I came on the MGM lot, I was assigned to the unit of Harry Rapf, though I would have preferred to be under the wing of Thalberg. Eddie Goulding escorted and introduced me to Mr. Rapf and his secretary, Madeleine Ruthvin. Madeleine and I became great friends, a friendship that lasted through the years, including the McCarthy era and long after MGM, Harry Rapf, and I had all parted company.

Harry Rapf was no man to win a beauty contest. He was short with an unfortunate nose that dominated his face. The man himself was ordinary: devoid of charm and, underneath, mean-spirited. Mr. Rapf eyed me suspiciously, wondering, I suppose, what my association was to the popular Goulding. I had not yet learned that Eddie had earned the reputation of being the rake of the MGM lot.

Mr. Rapf handed me a script called *Dance Madness*. "Read it right away," he directed, "and give me your opinion. We're not satisfied with it and feel it can be improved. The story is scheduled for immediate production and already cast. Conrad Nagel and Claire Windsor are going to star. Bob Leonard will direct."

I flew back on wings to my bungalow, nearly knocking down Clark Gable as I left the executive building; he was just a visitor at the MGM lot then, and not yet a star. I had the script of *Dance Madness* in my hand, and I was cocksure that, with my construction expertise, I would discover glaring flaws and get an opportunity to shine.

Dance Madness was based on an original story by S. Jay Kaufman. As I read the script, I realized that Mr. Kaufman's "original" story was not so original but was patently a rewrite of a famous Ferenc Molnar farce, *The Guardsman*.

But no matter. The script was brilliantly written by a writer named Alice D.G. Miller (unrelated to the magazine writer). It was hard to find much wrong with it. It was a farce with a small cast of characters and many bedrooms. Conrad Nagel is a gay young blade who woos and wins Claire Windsor, a teacher of esthetic dancing. In Paris, a year later, his fancy strays to a French actress played by Hedda Hopper (before she abandoned her acting career to rival gossip columnist Louella Parsons). When Claire Windsor goes to denounce Hedda Hopper as a husband stealer, she finds that Hedda is married to her own former dancing teacher and is not at all charmed by Nagel's pursuit, so the two women decide to discipline Nagel. There is a masked ball where Claire Windsor pretends to be Hedda, and husband Nagel makes ardent love to his own wife. It was the light, fluffy bedroom stuff that entertainment was made of in 1925.

I read the script several times; each time, I liked it better than before. However, nothing is written that some scheming writer cannot improve. I could see where the characters could be strengthened here and there and situations further developed or cut for better impact. I managed to find flaws, but it wasn't easy.

In less than two hours, I was back in Mr. Rapf's office and was granted immediate entrance.

Had I read the script?

Yes, I had.

What did I think?

"It's an excellent script . . . ," I said.

Mr. Rapf was not in the least happy about that reaction. So I added the famous "but"—"an excellent script, but. . . ." And I proceeded to enumerate my changes to strengthen the story line. Film writers develop a language of their own when talking to producers, blithely spinning off high-sounding generalities that deal with the intricacies of good film writing. The process usually worked in the early days because most producers knew nothing or nearly nothing of the writing process; the more erudite it sounded, the more they were convinced that they were getting their money's worth.

Mr. Rapf was enormously pleased with my suggestions. He ordered me to do a complete "rewrite," incorporating my changes. I finished the job in less than a week.

"A fine job, Miss Sagor," Mr. Rapf complimented. "You saved the story." He sent my script off to the Script Department to have copies made for himself, the director, and all others who would need one.

As I started to walk back to my bungalow, floating on air over my first triumph, I ran into Madeleine Ruthvin. She had a tall, ungainly young woman in tow behind her. "Frederica, this is Alice Miller," she said. "Alice, Frederica has been assigned to rewrite *Dance Madness.*"

"Oh," she said, eyeing me with undisguised bitterness. While I professed being glad to meet her, Alice Miller was patently not pleased to meet me and quite rightly resented having her baby rewritten.

I was honest. "You did a super job," I told her. "There really was very little I could offer to improve your work." I meant every word.

She softened, seemed to understand, smiled, and spoke—one writer to another. "You know, Frederica, Mr. Rapf never liked me. Right from the start. I don't know why. I got along with Bob Leonard but not Mr. Rapf. He seemed to find fault with everything I said and wrote." She was on the verge of tears, and I felt like a heel.

I learned more later about Mr. Rapf's likes and dislikes, especially for writers. Alice D.G. Miller did not even get honorable mention for the writing job she had done on *Dance Madness* when it was released. Instead, I, Frederica Sagor, was given full credit for the adaptation and script.

Writers in those days had little redress. The Writers Guild was new and not powerful. If you had a valid grievance, the guild would mildly protest for you—write a polite letter. But a writer had to be chary about protesting because the word quickly got around from studio to studio, executive to executive, that you were a troublemaker. If you wanted to stay in the business, you learned the hard truth about credits on the screen. Producers had budgets. One way to enhance those budgets was to swell the costs for preparing scripts. Also, the first script to be written might be a perfect one—and often was. But if the date of production was months off, the first script had to be rejected. New writers had to be hired and another script written. And then another and another until, finally, the day of actual production was at hand. At that juncture, the last writer to be hired to do a rewrite got the credit.

Once in a while, there might be a sharing of credit with one of the previous writers, providing he or she had sufficient clout to demand it. Otherwise, the last writer hired snatched the merry-go-round gold ring—as I had with *Dance Madness.*

It wasn't right, and it wasn't fair—but that was how Hollywood operated.

Chapter 6

HOLLYWOOD PARTIES

NOT KNOWING WHAT BEING A SCREENWRITER in films was going to be like, I had high aspirations and expectations. For weeks after I turned in my script on *Dance Madness*, I was deluged with stories, plays, and scripts and asked to read them. Most were garbage, plain garbage, and I said so. One or two had possibilities, but I never heard any more about them after they reached Mr. Rapf's desk. Meanwhile, I waited with bated breath for my next assignment.

The big talk about MGM was something called *The Big Parade*, in production with John Gilbert and Renée Adorée, directed by King Vidor. Light, fluffy *Dance Madness* was not the kind of story I wanted to do again. *The Big Parade* was, and I was overjoyed to be connected with the studio making it. At last, a talented young director, King Vidor, who dreamed, too, of making better fare, had persuaded an equally young producer named Irving Thalberg that art and box office could mix profitably. They would make a picture depicting war as it really was.

The daily rushes of *The Big Parade* drew ecstatic praise from all quarters. I sneaked in and was overwhelmed by what I saw. Soldiers with dirty, haunted faces. Strong stuff, my kind of stuff—realism. How I ached to work on a great story with a meaningful theme warranting the production that *The Big Parade* was getting. Later, when Vidor and I met and discovered that we shared the same dreams, he outlined an original story he had written and wanted me to work on. But my Pinocchio-nosed producer would not release me. Seven years later,

King Vidor made that story. It was called *Our Daily Bread* and was a critical depiction of the living conditions of working-class people.

I was finally happily assigned to the newly formed Norma Shearer unit, to be supervised by Carey Wilson, who, in turn, would work under the supervision of Father Rapf. Norma was a budding actress, deemed worthy of stardom after a succession of light, low-budget films had proven to be moneymakers. Norma was a plain-looking gal, really, with a cast in one eye that was the bane of cameramen. Plain though she was in person, she had a magic quality under the klieg lights. She was absolutely transformed by camera magic. Not a brainy girl, she had good common sense and a fine family background. Her widowed mother had come from Canada and entered her two daughters as extras to work under D.W. Griffith at Mamaroneck in the East. Norma's sister dropped out of pictures, but Norma had that something extra and kept on working. There was a brother, too—Douglas, who later became head of the MGM sound department.

Norma and I, and other writers, stars, and studio personnel, had a special table in the MGM commissary adjacent to the private dining room of Louis B. Mayer. He often shared his favorite homemade chicken soup and potato latkas with us. At that table, also, were the private secretaries of the executive producers: Madeleine Ruthvin, secretary to Mr. Rapf, and Margaret Bennett, secretary to Louis B. Mayer. I single out these two women now because they were a vital part of MGM and yet, in another sense, not a part of it at all. While they knew about everything that was going on, they were aloof from their tinsel surroundings—this petty, competitive business. Both could have become independently wealthy if they had listened to their bosses and purchased the stock and real estate recommended as surefire investments. They had the inner ear, and through them, so did I. "We" were told to invest in Beverly Hills real estate—back then just a cow pasture. They were urged to invest in Palm Springs real estate—then unpopulated desert but later the winter playground of the wealthy. Speculation was not in their genes or mine. We were too critical of our so-called betters, did not respect them, and therefore did not emulate them. The studio waste, dirty politics, devious schemes, head-chopping, ruthless ambition, greed, power out of control, debauchery so prevalent in this girlie business—in our young political eyes these were all manifest consequences of unleashed capitalism. Here were three socialists, longing for a better, fairer, more disciplined world than the one in which we were earning our daily bread. Nor did we stray from these ideas. They only became stronger through the years.

At that commissary table, Erich von Stroheim occasionally joined us. He had finished *The Merry Widow*, with Mae Murray, and was now involved in cutting down the miles of footage he had shot. He recognized me from the New York/Universal days, when I used to join him in the film cutting rooms next to my office. Once again, he was miserably unhappy because of pressures from the front office and would end up behind the eight-ball once more, with the picture taken out of his hands. Incorrigible Erich von Stroheim.

Greta Garbo and Mauritz Stiller sometimes ate at our table. New to the lot, they were lonely and anxious. Stiller had made an outstanding picture in Sweden that Louis B. Mayer saw and liked. He promptly sought to bring him to the MGM lot. Stiller, however, had his young protégée Garbo under his wing and was grooming her for stardom. He refused to sign the contract unless it would include Garbo. Mayer reluctantly agreed. Now here were the two of them in America on the big picture lot of MGM, and the tables were reversed. Garbo had some screen tests, and now rumor had it that Garbo was "in" and Stiller was "out." He returned to Sweden and died there at an early age.

Then there was Marion Davies. She often joined us in the commissary—sometimes with William Randolph Hearst and once with two apple-cheeked, identical twin boys of about twelve in military uniforms. Gossip had it that they were the offspring of this winter-and-spring attachment. What a buzzing there was in the commissary on that day!

The name of Ruth Harriet Louise is not known today, but it should be because she was a superb portrait artist. A young woman of about twenty-two, she was the studio photographer at MGM and photographed all the top stars and also the not-too-top stars, the writers, directors, producers—just about everybody who was anybody on the lot during 1925, 1926, and 1927. She was self-effacing and had no idea of her worth. But she was great. I have samples of her work amongst my souvenirs to prove it. She used to pressure me to sit for her.

"Come on, Freddie," she would coax. "I have some free time this afternoon." I would sneak out to her studio on the lot, and she would pose me to her heart's content. She claimed that I was as photogenic as Greta Garbo. But, thank heaven, unlike Ben Schulberg, she did not see me as another Theda Bara. Ruth, too, ate at our table in the commissary.

Joan Crawford was another regular at our commissary table. I had been on the lot only a few weeks when Eddie Goulding called me one morning and asked if I would like to join the welcome party going downtown to meet the Santa Fe train, which was bringing yet another young hopeful to the MGM roster of starlets. This one had been discovered and signed by Harry Rapf, who had picked her out of the chorus at the Winter Garden in New York. Not having anything better to do, I went along. The name of the starlet was Lucille LeSueur.

When the train pulled in, I couldn't believe what I saw. My first thought was that the name "LeSueur" (pronounced "sewer") was certainly applicable. She was a gum-chewing dame, heavily made up, skirts up to her belly button, wildly frizzed hair. An obvious strumpet. I was introduced.

"You a writer, huh?" She looked me over, her gray eyes cold and calculating. Restless ambition was written all over her. Crude as she was, everything about her seemed to say, "Look out. I'm in a hurry. Make room!" We kidded among ourselves about Harry Rapf's choice and forgot about it.

A week later, she looked me up. She had remembered my name from among the others she had met that first day. "They've given me a new name," she told me. "From now on, I'm gonna be Joan Crawford, see? Lucille LeSueur, I'm burying her. For good. I was thinkin' I oughta change-like and kinda live up to being Joan Crawford. Because Joan Crawford is gonna be a Hollywood star—that's why she came out here." Her determination was fierce.

I wondered where I entered the picture, since she had sought me out. "How can I help you . . . Joan?" I asked.

"You're a writer, right?"

I nodded.

"I like the way you dress. You dress like a lady. I need that. I want to be dressed right. Smart. I figured you could help." How could anyone turn down an ambitious young person like that? I took her on. Next day, Saturday, my Moon and I picked her up at a nondescript hotel where she was staying in Hollywood, and we went shopping.

The studio had given her a sweet advance, so she had money. The wardrobe we bought toned her down: navy blues, grays, browns, blacks; suits, dresses, coats with coordinating accessories. Tailored clothes, good materials, solid colors augmented with colorful scarves and sedate jewelry. She had a good figure, though she was a little over-weight—something she would correct in a few weeks, with the same alacrity and determination she put into everything else connected with her Joan Crawford transformation.

Trying on the new clothes in the stores, the image in the mirror bespoke a new personality—a personality you could not ignore. Her head was high, her carriage straight and tall. She had class, even if it showed only in her wardrobe. She worked on the rest to suit her new clothes. She studied French. She studied diction. She went to dancing school. She read good books and used a dictionary. And she married men like Franchot Tone and Douglas Fairbanks Jr., who were edu-cated and sophisticated and helped with the final polish. By the time she had become a real star, Joan Crawford had almost become a genu-ine lady, but not quite; her earlier leanings somehow always showed through.

Joan was welcomed at our commissary table. But she was a loner and did not make friends easily, especially women friends. She was distrustful of everyone, including herself. She preferred to keep her distance so that she could easily withdraw before becoming too deeply involved. She had only two interests, two obsessions: her goals of star-dom and of becoming a good actress. At considerable cost, she achieved both. What she could not achieve was tranquility, either in her mar-riages, her adopted children, or—most important—in herself. She never learned to give or receive love. So, in the end, she died a lonely victim of too many sleeping potions and too much alcohol.

Almost from the first day that they met in the commissary, Joan Crawford disliked Norma Shearer. They were complete opposites. As warm and outgoing as Norma was, Joan was cold and reserved. Norma was generous in spirit; Joan was calculating. She remained envious of Norma Shearer as their careers progressed. Joan saw Norma as a pet of the front office—in the good graces of Louis B. Mayer and Irving Thalberg, cushioned and protected, winning all the best roles, the best pictures. The budgets on Shearer pictures were usually two or three times the budgets for Joan Crawford B quickies. But Joan's B quickies became better and better because she tried harder and harder. She was not to be put down. Harry Rapf didn't know when he picked Lucille LeSueur out of the chorus of the Winter Garden that she would have the fight, will, ambition, and talent to become an authentic star. It happens sometimes.

I call Carey Wilson a writer manipulator. No writer himself, he milked the brains of writers and used their ideas as his own. He was a dapper fellow with a waxed mustache and an aloofness that hid his inadequacies but impressed those who paid his handsome salary. They did not recognize his superficiality. To my dismay, I now found myself under the wing of this Svengali, this writer vampire.

One morning, I was given a title to write: *His Secretary.* There was no story. Just a title: *His Secretary.* I was to concoct a story—characters and plot. Norma Shearer was to star.

I came up with a plot and characters: boss meets secretary. Conflict: boss hates secretary, secretary hates boss. Development: boss falls in love with secretary, secretary falls in love with boss. Happy ending: boss and secretary became man and wife.

Sound familiar? Been done before? Of course. Over and over. Dozens of times but always foolproof. The trick is in the development—clever business, innovative situations, scintillating direction with a good script, sparkling performances, and—voila!—you have a box-office smash.

I had a brainstorm and quickly wrote a twenty-page outline for a fast-moving comedy. Carey Wilson read it and made no comment. He sent it to the script department for retyping. I was not a good typist, especially when I did creative writing directly on the typewriter. It came back without either my name or his on it. Just the title: *His Secretary.* He lost no time taking it in to Mr. Rapf.

Soon he returned with the good news: "Harry thought it was super. Wants it developed into a script." Still in Never-Never Land, I was overjoyed and eager to get to work. I worked hard in the studio and at home, into the wee hours of the morning. I gave it my best shot. When I turned the finished script in to Carey Wilson, the title page read: "His Secretary, Adaptation and Scenario by Frederica Sagor."

Carey Wilson said, "It's a fine job, Frederica. I'm sure Harry will love it. It's funny. It's clever. I'll read it to him myself. Harry hates reading scripts." The script, one hundred pages, was sent to the script department for re-typing. When it came back, I picked it up eagerly. The title page now read: "His Secretary, Adaptation and Scenario by Carey Wilson."

Adaptation and Scenario by Carey Wilson?! There it was, in black and white. By Carey Wilson—he who had not contributed a comma, a single idea. It was mine! All mine! I could not believe it, yet there it was: Adaptation and Scenario by Carey Wilson. My anguish showed.

"If you don't see your name, Frederica," he said, "don't worry about it. You'll get screen credit in the end." Oh yeah? I never did— Carey Wilson did. This was the way I was used for a series of early Norma Shearer pictures. All moneymakers. I wrote every one of them, practically from scratch, and received credit for none. None. The worst part was that there wasn't a blasted thing I could do about it.

I became totally disillusioned with my work, my sex life, and the whole motion picture business because of what I saw going on all around me—it was a bacchanal. The master of ceremonies was my depraved friend, Edmund Goulding, with Marshall Neilan, another director, a close second in command.

These two men initiated more young women—and men—into more kinds of kinky sexual practices than one can possibly imagine. The carrot stick that they dangled was the promise of a screen test, a good part in some picture in which they were involved, or that they would use their clout with some other director shooting a picture on the lot. Few, if any, of these seductions bore fruit. The sexual route was definitely not the way to go for anyone seeking to climb the ladder of success. It would, if anything, work against you unless you had talent that could not be denied and the gumption and iron will to win recognition. Joan Crawford was a shining example.

Oh, yes, Edmund Goulding tried to induct me into his seamy, lecherous world. But once he was convinced that I was not made of putty and after I had rebelled in disgust at what was going on, he seemed to enjoy using me as a mother confessor to ease his troubled conscience. He claimed to be an ardent Christian Scientist who read his Bible every morning when he got up and every night before he fell asleep.

"Eddie," I warned him countless times, "one day you are going to be caught up in a terrible scandal that is going to make Fatty Arbuckle's fall from grace look like a pink tea."

He laughed with amusement and continued with his jollies. Somehow, he got away with it and died in his bed. His lifestyle was no secret. Everyone from the grips to the executives knew what he up to. Sexual excesses were rampant everywhere but particularly at MGM. If anything went wrong, MGM managed to save itself from notoriety, all the while being permissive with dissolutes like Eddie Goulding.

Actually Eddie's interests were primarily in males—women were the preserve of fun-loving, libertine, inebriate Mickey Neilan. Morally, Mickey was a shade above the hedonist Goulding, but he was louder and cruder than that smooth master of the revels. Goulding had polish and suaveness that covered his sick mind; Mickey was brash, just honest. I suppose it really would be difficult to choose between them. Neilan's weakness was pretty virgins, if there were any around (and there were a few). His most notorious victim was actress Sally O'Neil, a pretty Irish girl from the streets of New York City. When I first met Sally, she was in her teens, fresh as an Irish shamrock and full of spring laughter. When Mickey Neilan got through with her, she was in her twenties and had become a narcotics user and a whiskey swiller. Tears welled up in her eyes when you spoke to her kindly. The virgin Sally was mesmerized by this old man, her lover and mentor, who was easily thirty years her senior. She had a career of sorts, but it was brief. When Mickey Neilan and MGM dropped her, she vanished from the limelight.

With two such debauchees in charge of revels at MGM and others like them on other lots, wild parties were commonplace events. The first one that I attended, before I was at MGM, was at the home of Clara Bow, shortly after I began to work on *The Plastic Age*. I can't remember how I got there. Clara Bow herself had invited me, and I believe I took a taxi, not yet having bought my Moon.

"We're gonna have a ball tonight," Clara giggled when she asked me to come. She giggled a lot. She was such a child—love-starved and over-sexed. Everybody took advantage of her as she climbed to stardom. With Clara, a good-looking grip was as welcome in bed as some big-time director or producer. She later married an actor by the name of Rex Bell and had two children. But respectability and responsibility were too much for her, and she ended up a mental cripple, in the hands of a psychiatrist and a private nurse.

Ben Schulberg counseled me not to go. "You'll be bored and disgusted," he warned. But I went, curious to see for myself.

I got there intending to have a look-see and leave. Everyone was drunk or on the way to getting drunk. I am not much of a drinker. One good highball and I am on top of the world; two, I become very quiet, pedantic, and suspicious—no fun at all; three drinks, and I am out.

The last thing I remember was seeing Clara atop a table, shimmying her clothes off and dancing in the nude to the hoots of her appreciative and inebriated audience. I must have passed out because the next thing I knew I was home in my own bed with a horrible hangover. Elsie told me that a Negro chauffeur had brought me home at 3:00 A.M. (Ben Schulberg, bless his heart, told me later that he had given instructions to Clara Bow's chauffeur to keep an eye on me.)

This experience scared me. I resolved there and then never to indulge in more than one or two drinks at any party I attended. It was a resolution that I did not break. I believe that I have watered more house plants with cocktails and highballs than any female living. That way you could have a drink in your hand until the next round, and nobody was the wiser.

Another party I wish I had not attended was one given by MGM for Ray Long, editor-in-chief of *Cosmopolitan* magazine or, really, head of Hearst Publications. He was an important hombre; when he came to the Coast, he was royally wined, dined, and entertained. The party took place at the Ambassador Hotel in a row of bungalows reserved for the high jinks. This was one party that Eddie Goulding and Marshall Neilan somehow missed.

First, there was a sumptuous dinner in the main dining room of the hotel with French champagne flowing freely. Ray Long, a short, corpulent, balding man already three sheets to the wind made a slurred speech. Irving Thalberg and Harry Rapf reciprocated in like manner.

My escort was Max Marcin, a well-known playwright whose forte was melodramas. His most recent play, set in a courtroom, had been cleaning up on Broadway. Max and I had been assigned to cooperate on a story (again, just a title, really) called *Flesh and the Devil.* Max was in his middle sixties, a wizened, wiry little fellow with keen, cunning eyes. Selfish and opinionated, he spoke the language of the executive elite.

With the dessert, a group of starlets, nightclub belly dancers, and ladies of the evening made their entrance. They were greeted by halloos of drunken delight, and room was made for them at the table, one girl to each unescorted male. The party got merrier and merrier, with the popping of champagne corks. Pretty soon, the men started disappearing with one or two girls, heading for the bungalows. Max Marcin disappeared along with the rest.

I was cold sober, having emptied my wine glass under the table every time it was filled by attentive waiters looking for tips. I found myself left to my own devices and should have called a taxi and gone home. But I was curious about what was going on in those bungalows. Several drunken men tried to entice me there, but I shook them off. I finally got to where the action was and saw more than I had bargained for. Undressed, tousled men chased naked women, shrieking with laughter. Included in this orgy was Ray Long, Mr. Hearst's representative; Harry Rapf, my own producer; and even the immaculate Irving Thalberg—all drunk, drunk, drunk.

What had I gotten myself into? My one thought was to vanish from the scene as quickly as I could, grateful that everyone was too drunk to take any notice. Heading for the nearest exit, I came face to face with the shocker of the evening.

Antoinette! My dressmaker!

Pretty, thirtyish, Parisian Antoinette, who had her dressmaker shop in a small Hollywood Boulevard apartment that doubled as her home. A wonderful seamstress, she could copy any costume you wanted with taste and detailed precision. Using my charge accounts, I would take out expensive designer clothes and have her reproduce them, then send the originals back. It saved me hundreds of dollars. She had made some exquisite outfits for me and for many others. I was wearing one of her evening gowns that night—a flared, delicate, multi-colored chiffon as lovely as a rainbow.

Yet here she was. Antoinette, a call girl—half-naked, lying across a chair, her hand stretched out to receive the hundred-dollar bill being pressed into it by Eddie Mannix—gross, ugly, hairy, vulgar Eddie Mannix, Louis B. Mayer's bodyguard.

The rest of what I had witnessed of this stupid, nauseating evening hardly mattered to me; but Antoinette did matter. Gifted, hardworking Antoinette, stitching her fingers away past midnight, ruining her eyes, fighting to make a living—now selling her favors at a film orgy! That really hit me where I lived. I fled the scene, got a taxi, and sobbed all the way home. Antoinette never sewed any more costumes for this Hollywood writer. I did not judge her or fault her; I simply could not face her, knowing what I knew about her secret life.

But one positive thing came out of that experience: my blinders came off for good. I'd seen firsthand how Hollywood can bring you down if you allow it to do so, and I—unlike Antoinette and so many others—had enough basic self-respect not to let that happen to me. Not long afterwards, my friend and literary agent Ruth Collier phoned to invite me to a housewarming party at Lew Cody's. Cody, I knew, was an important client of Ruth's; she was a talent agent as well as a literary agent—most agents were in those early days. He had established himself as one of filmdom's most successful villains: the man who suavely steals the other man's wife; the man you love to hate. I didn't much want to go, but I knew that Ruth, as Cody's agent, had to put in an appearance at the shindig. "We won't stay long," Ruth promised.

We arrived at ten o'clock at the Tudor-English mansion in Beverly Hills. Our host, remarkably sober despite his usual heavy drinking, gave us a grand tour. There was an enormous swimming pool, a rock and cactus garden, a rose garden, plus extensive wooded grounds. The house had two stories, twenty rooms (ten of these were master-sized bedrooms on the upper floor), and ten bathrooms.

Ten bathrooms! Each was almost as large as the adjoining bedroom, and all were luxurious, with sunken tubs; Spanish-tiled showers as large as the dressing rooms; tiled mirrors everywhere, even on the ceilings; exquisite, individually monogrammed bathrobes; powders, creams, and perfumes—everything the most expensive. I had never imagined anything like those bathrooms; what an incredible emphasis on the *chambre du bain!*

The rest of the house, in contrast, was nondescript—comfortable but garish, representing the taste of its thespian owner, an actor with more money than he knew what to do with. Large sofas, lounging chairs, hassocks, lamps, dining table, and chairs. The key word was "large." No art on the walls, no antiques, no library.

As I said, the party was well under way when Ruth and I got there. Among the guests were the famous Orsatti brothers, recently elevated into the agency business with the rumored backing of Louis B. Mayer. They had the inside track at MGM, where rumors connected them to the Mafia racetrack and gambling interests. Frank Orsatti immediately attached himself to Ruth, who was not a pretty woman but had a way with the opposite sex. Fatty Arbuckle decided to pursue me, his bold, uninhibited advances indicating that he had learned little caution from his scandalous ordeal. He was an unappealing specimen of the human race, and I got tired of his persistent efforts to entice me upstairs to one of the ten bedrooms or *chambres du bain*.

Around eleven o'clock, Ruth and I decided to quit the party, but how? We couldn't just walk out the front door. Ruth had a client relationship with the host and could not afford to offend him. So we withdrew to one of the bathrooms and held counsel.

Then Ruth discovered that the bedroom adjacent to that bathroom had a balcony with a heavy post covered with ivy alongside it. Midway down was a marble projection. If we could lower ourselves from the balcony via the ivy-covered post to this projection, we had it made; it was an easy jump to the ground.

Our scheme successfully accomplished, we sped away in Ruth's roadster and chuckled all the way home. We could picture Frank Orsatti and Fatty Arbuckle hunting all over the place for us and not being able to figure out where we had vanished. We knew they would both be too drunk to remember anything the next morning.

On another occasion, Ruth and I went sailing in a yacht belonging to Alvin Frank, son of the "Frank" of Harris & Frank, a well-known clothier. Ruth later married Alvin. The yacht dropped anchor at Catalina Island and, as we came ashore, we were greeted by the ruddy-faced mayor of Catalina, happily in his cups. Then we all headed for the beachhouse home of Marian Bailey, who was the cousin of Mary Ford, director John Ford's wife.

Marian was an attractive divorcee with lots of money, an alcohol problem, and an ugly disposition when she got drunk. During the early part of the evening, we had a steak barbecue and then danced on the veranda under a full moon. The evening was soft and warm, and we were all having a good time. Charles Farrell was there and so was Richard Arlen—two decent, personable chaps. They were yet to emerge into full bloom but were both well on their way. Suddenly, we were alerted to a commotion emanating from the kitchen. Then we saw the red-carnationed mayor (he always wore a red carnation and full tails when he greeted important guests to the island) running as fast as he could. Right behind him, brandishing a butcher knife, came Marian

Bailey, murder in her eye and heart. She had nothing on but bra and panties. Ruth, Charlie, Richard, and I looked at each other with the thought that if someone was going to get hurt, even murdered, we wanted no part of it. We repaired to our respective rooms and locked the doors. Next morning, we were told that it took three of Marian's servants to hold her down and take the butcher knife away. Then they managed to get her into the shower and cool her off. Apparently, this was a routine they were used to. As for the mayor, he took off when they grabbed Marian. Accustomed to bearing the brunt of Marian Bailey's drunken furies, he would be back another time. There is no telling how some of us get our kicks in this life.

I received an invitation to go to the Hearst Castle in San Simeon one weekend. The invitation came from Marion Davies herself. Norma Shearer and I were to share a bungalow, and I was looking forward to it. Then came a telephone call from the wife of Pete Smith, head of the short subject department at MGM.

"Frederica," she pleaded, "Pete is in Riverside with Harry Wilson. They have both been on a binge for three days. Pete was in the hospital with a gallbladder attack, Harry came to see him, and they both took off for Riverside. I'm worried sick."

Harry Wilson was head of the publicity department of newly formed United Artists. I had met him through Bill Conselman, a fellow alcoholic. Unlike Bill, though, Harry could stay sober for months on end. He always had plenty of liquor in his office, which he offered to others but would not drink himself. But when he went off the deep end, he was a total dropout. Still, I liked Harry. He was friendly and fun to be with when he was sober.

"Can you come with me?" Pete's wife asked. "I could handle one of them, but not two."

She sounded so desperate that I felt I couldn't refuse. I thought, "Well, I'll get another invitation to San Simeon" (which I never did), "so why not help the poor woman out?"

It was over a hundred degrees when we reached Riverside. We found the two culprits in a stifling, box-sized room at the famous Riverside Inn, dead drunk. They were so drunk that at first they did not know who we were. When it sank in, they were relieved that we were there, for Pete was in a bad way, experiencing a lot of pain from his gallbladder.

The drive back to Los Angeles was a nightmare. I drove Harry's roadster, and Pete's wife took Pete in her car. At every town, Harry insisted on getting out, having a drink, and buying a bottle for the road. Finally, we reached his house in Laurel Canyon, where his housekeeper helped me get him out of his car and into bed immediately. We emptied all the liquor we could find into the kitchen sink. But he had squirreled more away in the wooden beams of his living room ceiling, in the closet, in the garage. It was hopeless.

What was this strange predilection I had for attracting and befriending alcoholics? I think it was because I sensed that it was a serious disease, as yet unrecognized, over which its victims had no control—and it was so common in Hollywood, then as now. Bob Rodin, Bill Conselman, Harry Wilson: all were lost causes because of their drinking.

Meanwhile, my living arrangements with Elsie Werner were falling apart and rapidly nearing a climax. The truth of the matter was that Elsie was jealous and resentful of the progress I had made: screen credit for *The Plastic Age*, screen credit for *Dance Madness*, a writing contract at MGM. She attributed my success to my being more attractive than she was and felt it was my personality, not my ability, that was responsible. She never took into account the training I had had before I came to the West Coast and my talent for writing films. Instead, she had convinced herself that she had much more to offer the film business as a writer than I did. After all, she was a devotee of Marcel Proust, a heavyweight, while I was not. A little knowledge in the wrong brain can be a dangerous thing.

Her inflated ego encouraged her to seize upon an advertisement in the *Herald Examiner*. It was a blurb that some nondescript film company was about to enter production and was looking for talent: writers, directors, cameramen, technicians, and (of course) actors and actresses. The ad offered exciting participation in film production for a fee of five hundred dollars. The ad was clearly targeted at the rejectniks knocking on Hollywood doors who were unable to gain a foothold.

Elsie had her interview and came home flushed, excited, triumphant with an assignment. She had been given a one-page synopsis of a murder mystery plot—for which she had blithely parted with five hundred dollars—to be returned when she handed in her full treatment. Then she would be put on a weekly salary of a hundred dollars a week to complete the screenplay. There were many such come-ons in the early days—swindlers conniving to get some easy money from the naive desperates striving for recognition.

"Elsie," I cautioned, "this sounds like a setup to me. You can still stop your check."

"You would say that," she replied. "Of course, I know this company isn't the great MGM. But it's a start. The man who interviewed me was no phony. I can tell a phony as well as you can. This man and I clicked. We saw eye to eye on everything. That's why I got the assignment."

She believed every word. Poor Elsie. She lost her five hundred dollars and, of course, was never remunerated for her hard work on the extended development she turned in. The mythical producing company simply disappeared from the scene one morning when they had collected all that it was safe for them to collect before the investigation of their activities began. None of this endeared me to Elsie.

I was not surprised when, shortly thereafter, Elsie informed me that she and the children were leaving Hollywood and going back to New York. Having been rejected as a writer by Hollywood, she was going to try her hand at playwriting.

Her father had bought a large tract of land in the San Fernando Valley and was going to realize a lifelong dream of becoming a farmer. Alfalfa was the crop. Sad to relate, it proved a disaster. Then came the Panic of 1929, and he was completely ruined financially.

As for Elsie, I saw her once again years later in a New York department store—Macy's. She had been married in the interim to an English actor and toured abroad with the stock company of which he was a part. They divorced eventually. Elsie was now hoping to make a million dollars in the cosmetic business. One of the girls was in college; the youngest had run off, married at age sixteen, and made Elsie a grandmother. That was the last I saw or heard of Elsie Werner.

It was a relief to be living alone after Elsie and the children departed. But my tranquility was interrupted by the calamity that befell my trusty Moon chariot that had been so faithfully transporting me back and forth from the Hollywood Hills to the studio at Culver City. It just stopped breathing, and no amount of coaxing would induce it to change its mind. Luckily, there was a gas station nearby, and I was able to roll it there.

"You ever put oil into this car, get it lubricated?" asked the station attendant suspiciously.

"No," I replied innocently. "Nobody told me I had to."

"Well, lady," he informed me, "you've completely burned out your engine, and that's going to cost you plenty. My advice to you is that you'd be better off buying another car."

How was I to know? Earl Daley had sold me a car and taught me to drive it, but he had neglected to instruct me about taking care of it. I knew nothing about automobiles. I was the first in the Sagor family to own one. Blithely, I had assumed that all you had to do was feed it gas. Ignorance may be bliss, but it can be mighty costly. I hung on to my Moon, but my pocketbook paid the price.

As the days passed and I continued to work on Norma Shearer stories (that Carey Wilson continued to appropriate), I grew increasingly restless and unhappy. Then, at last, came the day when Bob Leonard phoned to tell me that *Dance Madness* would be previewing at the newly opened palatial Alexander Theater in Glendale, and he would pick me up. As I watched the picture unfold, my head was reeling. There on the screen in large letters was my first MGM screen credit: ADAPTED TO THE SCREEN BY FREDERICA SAGOR. Somehow this credit meant more to my vanity than did the writing credit I received for *The Plastic Age*. But it shouldn't have, because *The Plastic Age* was to endure and be pronounced a classic.

Forty-nine years later, in 1974, *The Plastic Age* was shown at the Silent Movie Theater in Fairfax. That same year, *The Great Gatsby*, a remake of the famous F. Scott Fitzgerald novel about the Roaring Twenties and starring Robert Redford, was bombing at the box office. The *Los Angeles Times* had this to say about "my" movie:

> Popular movies reflect values and aspirations current when they were made and consequently [are] never so revealing as when viewed years later.
>
> Therefore, *The Plastic Age*, this week's attraction at the Silent Movie on Fairfax, is fascinating not only as a terrific showcase for "It Girl" Clara Bow, but also as a document of the Flapper era. Above all, this 1925 Paramount production, filmed largely on the Pomona College campus, is still just plain enjoyable to watch. . . .

The Plastic Age reverberates with the very quality of Roaring Twenties desperate gaiety, so perfectly embodied by Miss Bow, that *The Great Gatsby* tried so hard to recapture.

Dance Madness was a big moneymaker, and Bob Leonard was once more in the good graces of Louis B. Mayer. Before *Dance Madness*, the studio had seriously considered canning him as a has-been, merely the ex-husband of Mae Murray. Now they were entrusting him with the next Norma Shearer picture, *The Waning Sex*. Bob Leonard asked that I be assigned the writing job. Finally, I had an ally with enough influence to liberate me (I hoped) from the tentacles of Carey Wilson.

Chapter 7

MY FRIEND, RIZA

About this time, I received a letter from my dear friend Virginia Morris in New York, who was now handling publicity for Preferred Pictures. It referred to a young woman, Riza Royce, who had appeared in a New York play on Broadway and drawn the attention of J.G. Bachman, treasurer of Preferred Pictures. He had signed her to a three-month contract at a nominal salary, subject to the approval of B.P. Schulberg. Would I meet her at the station when she arrived, take her under my wing, and help her to get settled? Any request from my friend Virginia was a mandate.

I was not disappointed when I laid eyes on the lovely young woman alighting from the train. I knew at once it was Riza Royce. Royce was her stage name. Her real last name was Marks; she was the youngest daughter of the Rivoli orchestra conductor, Otto Marks. The mother was Catholic and had raised her six daughters in the Catholic faith, but she felt increasingly sinful for having married a Jew. Her husband took up with their German housekeeper, who had more to do with the up-bringing of the children than did their mother.

Riza had natural auburn hair, beautiful skin that needed very little makeup, and gray-blue, almond-shaped eyes. But I thought her most outstanding feature was her nose—a patrician, Viennese nose with a classical bump that gave her character. She was not quite twenty-one years old.

I could see at once she was as frightened as a rabbit; she was trembling and very near tears. "Where are you staying?" I asked, certain the studio had made arrangements for her. But they had not. "I have an extra bedroom waiting for you," I found myself saying. Having three sisters so much older, my childhood had been very lonely. I'd longed for a younger sister when I was growing up. And here she was.

Riza had been given three months' salary in advance—fifty dollars a week for three months, six hundred dollars in all. She needed a car immediately. She came home with a new Buick that took all her money as a down payment; further payments were $125 a month. That Buick cost twice as much as my trusty Moon, but Riza "had to have" a Buick. Studio pictures were made by the best photographer in Hollywood, and that cost a considerable amount, too. Riza also needed new clothes desperately. Her wardrobe was spare, to say the least. Much taller than I, she could not wear my clothes. Until then, she had been sewing her own clothes, and they looked it. I financed the career of Riza Royce, believing in her future. For eight months, I paid all her bills and fed and nurtured her. When I subscribed to concerts or bought theater tickets, I bought some for her, too. Wherever I went, Riza was included. After all, she was my baby sister, wasn't she? I had to look after her, especially since my Riza was a virgin and resolute about saving herself for the man she loved. Secretly, I thought, "Gal, you're in the wrong business."

The first big disappointment came when Ben Schulberg did not pick up the option of my protégée. From the start, he disagreed with his treasurer in the East, J.G. Bachman. Riza Royce was not his idea of star material for the box office. To put it plainly, he thought there was not enough sex appeal; she looked too much like plain Norma Shearer (and, in truth, they were look-alikes). In Schulberg's estimation, one Norma Shearer on the screen was enough. Besides, while Norma Shearer clearly had a cast in one eye, it was something a cameraman could deal with.

What they could not deal with was a prominent nose on either male or female faces. Riza's aristocratic nose with its classical bump was a no-no. B.P. Schulberg's advice to Riza was to have plastic surgery. If she expected to get anywhere in Hollywood, she had to get her nose fixed. Hollywood's film noses had to be inconspicuous. That was the rule of thumb for noses. No one knows how many beautiful noses have been unmercifully bobbed and sacrificed by inexpert Hollywood plastic surgeons over the years, with the owner finding stardom elusive even after the sacrifice.

I discounted the judgment of Schulberg about her nose. After all, his was only one man's opinion (I was to learn differently). I talked my friend and agent, Ruth Collier, into taking Riza on and representing her. Ruth may have been good at taking me to parties, but she was a cold fish when it came to pushing talent. She pushed a commodity—be it actress or writer—only so far. If the response was less than positive, the client was dropped like a hot potato. Agents sell only what they find easy to sell. They are all cautious to a fine point about selling anything too hard. If they did not operate that way, the welcome mat would not be there for them to come calling again. They have to keep the studio doors open. These were facts I had to learn the hard way when I too became an agent some years later.

Riza and I had some great times living together. You can be sure we did not lack for male companionship. Indeed, we had to fight hard to keep the wolves from the door; even the neighborhood patrol cops tried to move in on us. Two attractive women living alone in Hollywood were vulnerable from every quarter. When we did not capitulate, rumor spread that we were lesbians.

I must admit that, up to this point, I had not been too discriminating about my male sexual preferences. From Elsie, I had learned about the good old pessary and so felt free to play the field. There were few restraints in Hollywood about sleeping around. It was in the air like a contagious disease. I was young and exploring life, not realizing that, all the while, life was exploring me. Handsome men, particularly vainglorious actors, did not appeal to me. Men of accomplishment did, regardless of looks or age. I sought to discover what made them tick. But the more I slept around, the less I discovered. Indiscriminate sex is a matter of pursuit and conquest. The conquest accomplished, the sex act became mechanical. Men who chased indiscriminately did not make great lovers, for sex without caring is nothing. But I did not know this, and I had to learn my ABCs through experience. To be virtuous because one has never faced temptation is no proof of virtue; to be virtuous in the face of temptation is another matter.

Perhaps that is one reason I respected the virtue of Riza Royce. She faced the same temptations that I did and made the choice. My own experiences had proven increasingly disappointing. I began to realize that this was not the way to go. The answer to sex was not variety but constancy. Would I ever find a partner to whom I could be totally committed and who would be totally committed to me? Had I ruined my chances? I began to wonder seriously about these things.

A profound change was in order. I opened the windows and doors of my home in the Hollywood Hills and let in lots of fresh air. I decided that what the Hollywood scene, and I, needed was some good, old-fashioned culture.

I came from a home where music was as important as breathing. Our home was filled with pianists, singers, violinists, cellists; Fedor Ivanovich Chaliapin, the great Russian operatic bass, was a friend of Mama's. He brought his friends, other musicians. The samovar was always steaming and ready. So with this background, it was second nature for me to introduce music into my home in Hollywood.

On the studio sets, fine musicians played Bach, Brahms, and Beethoven while actors translated their feelings to the silent screen. Some of these musicians were real professionals. MGM hired the best. I put out the word that we were looking for volunteers to entertain.

Riza and I both loved to entertain. Our maid, Hannah, was a divine cook who could concoct hors d'oeuvres that would have challenged any French chef. We made good use of Hannah and her boyfriend, Martin, who butlered at our open house every Saturday night. We served no alcoholic beverages—plenty of good food but no cocktails; only coffee or tea—like it or leave it. They liked it. We soon had a houseful every Saturday night with guests such as Victor Fleming, King and Florence Vidor, Ona and Clarence Brown, Robert Florey, Sada Cowen, Arthur Lubin, William Powell, Louella Parsons, Bob Leonard, Viola Brothers Shore, Jack Gilbert. And song writers and set designers. Even lecherous Edmund Goulding dropped in and behaved. The studio musicians played solos and trios. Gathered around the piano, we sang all the hits, Foster melodies, even opera. The popular song "In a Little Spanish Town" (1925) was conceived at my house. Mabel Wayne discovered its lovely melody on the ivory keys of my piano: "In a little Spanish town, / 'Twas on a night like this, / Stars were peek-a-booing down, / 'Twas on a night like this." These extravagant evenings were a strain on my budget, but who worried about that? Perhaps I should have worried a little more.

At the studio, I continued working on *The Waning Sex*. Everything had been discarded but the title, and it was up to me to dream up a new story line. I did: girl chooses Career instead of Romance. It was an amusing comedy drama, fashioned for the talents of Norma. I was lucky, for the production date was set and imminent.

When the first draft was completed and approved, another writer was added: F. Hugh Herbert, who had been imported from England, where his first novel had just been published. He was considered a budding talent, which turned out to be true later when he turned again to fiction. This was his first exposure to the intricacies of film writing and film technology.

However, Herbert was a quick study. A bachelor in his early forties, he was devoted to a spinster sister and looked after her, just as he and his sister had looked after their parents, now deceased. Both were unworldly and stodgy.

Hugh and I had almost daily conferences with Harry Rapf as the story developed and we got into the script. It soon became apparent that we differed widely on story structure. With the unharnessed enthusiasm of a creator, Hugh could not stop adding and adding and adding more and more business—some of it good but not germane to the story line. I could foresee that all this lovely embellishment was going to end up on the cutting room floor. To my increasing dismay, Harry Rapf was mesmerized by this clown, who acted out all his fantasies. Bob Leonard also succumbed to the spell of this storyteller with the Charlie Chaplin mustache and clipped British accent. I was proven right when the superfluous material was shot; most of it was discarded, adding thousands of dollars to the cost of production. Such are the peccadilloes of great producers and directors.

To break the growing tension, Bob decided to take us to Coronado. "We need a change, Harry," he proposed. "We're getting stale working so hard. A couple of weeks working in Coronado, and we'll come back relaxed and ready to go into production."

So, Hugh, Bob, and I boarded the day train to San Diego. Bob's limousine and chauffeur were waiting for us and took us to the island. There, we set up shop in the bungalows of the famous Hotel del Coronado, long the winter resort of affluent Easterners and Europeans. It was a magnificent Spanish structure with private bungalows surrounding it; the Pacific Ocean lapped at our back doors. Each of us had a bungalow with bedroom and kitchen. Meals were brought to us if we did not care to go to the hotel dining room. The Hotel del, like the Beverly Hills Hotel in Los Angeles, looked down its nose at Hollywood. It was only then, in the mid-twenties, beginning to cater to the film industry. It was, and still is, ultra-expensive. But money was no object at MGM.

Of course, the real reason for Bob Leonard's suggesting that we go to Coronado wasn't to finish the script, but to attend the horse races in Mexico. When the racing season was on, everyone headed for dusty, forlorn Agua Caliente, whose claim to fame was its racetrack.

I had never been to a racetrack but had heard a lot about them at home because my dear father, an exemplary husband in every other respect, was addicted to the ponies. It was the one bone of contention in the married life of Agnes and Arnold Sagor. As a small child, I remember my mother in hysterics, upbraiding my penitent father for squandering the household money for the week at the racetrack. Gambling became the symbol of evil in my mind—a terrible sin. With these values ingrained in me, I found myself now at Agua Caliente, watching my colleagues betting their bankrolls.

"Aren't you going to bet on the horses?" everyone asked.

"Not a thin dime," I replied. They could not believe it, but I stuck to my guns. When it came to the horses themselves, that was a horse of a different color. They were such magnificent animals, every one of them—that I found myself hanging around the stables, admiring them, petting them, feeding them carrots and sugar. After all, my mother's father—my red-bearded grandfather—had raised horses, hadn't he? I had the love of them in my blood.

To pass the time and make things more interesting, I picked favorites—willy-nilly—to win. Bob Leonard was the first to notice that I picked nearly all the winners (win, place, and show) in the first race, as well as the second and third.

"Hey, Sagor," he asked incredulously, "how'd you know?"

"Guessed," I said. "Liked the name. Liked the horse. Just a hunch." In the third race, Bob followed my "hunches" and won. He won pretty handily in the fourth and fifth races, too, on my hunches. The rumor spread: "That Sagor dame is clairvoyant. She talks to horses. Follow her tips."

I rarely guessed wrong and must have been touched by Lady

Luck. My guesses were 90 percent accurate. Hunt Stromberg, an MGM producer, and his spouse; Joe Schenck and Norma Talmadge; Bob Leonard; Hugh Herbert—all of whom sat in our double box—came to me for tips. I enjoyed my newfound fame, even if I could not account for it, and they all profited handsomely. I should have demanded a cut of the winnings; as it was, all I got was a five-pound box of chocolates from Hunt Stromberg. I should add that, in subsequent visits to the racetrack through the years, I have never been able to repeat that phenomenal performance at Agua Caliente.

Later, I had to pinch myself to believe those two weeks in Coronado happened as they did. With so many motion picture celebrities around me, I took them for granted. Every day, I sat next to Norma Talmadge, whose films I had watched with awe and admiration in New York. I never dreamed that I would one day address her as "Norma," although Joe Schenck was always "Mr. Schenck" to me, out of deference to his importance in the industry.

Joe Schenck and Norma Talmadge—what an odd couple they were. In the two weeks we spent together, they rarely spoke or even looked at each other. Norma, in a flopping picture hat, sat there sphinx-like. The only time she came to life was when some young gigolo visiting the track came to pay her homage. Joe Schenck amused himself with the amorous sport of pinching the bottom of every female within reach, including me. I presumed that this exercise was the best he could manage at his age.

I remember the evenings at Coronado, especially the long walks along the white sandy beach with Hugh and his interminable serenades. His favorites were the Irving Berlin hits; he murdered them. He had no voice and couldn't carry a tune. But he loved to sing, hum, or whistle—all off-key—until I wanted to scream. To this day, when I hear those Irving Berlin ballads of the twenties, I cringe and want to clap my hands over my ears—as I wanted to do then to shut out the noise of F. Hugh Herbert's dysphonia. For that reason, I was glad when our two-week holiday in Coronado was over.

If being saddled with Hugh every evening was my problem, Bob Leonard had a different one. This huge (he weighed over 250 pounds), fiftyish man was in love with the intensity of a college boy. The object of Bob's affection was a young starlet recently signed by one of MGM's casting scouts. Gertrude Olmstead was thirty years younger than Bob.

No beauty, she did have youth and innocence, thanks to an ogre of a mother always at her side. Mama, a practical woman, did not frown on her daughter's taking the eye of an important director. But Mama held out for marriage. No fooling around with Mama's virginal daughter! She checked on Bob in the Who's Who of finance; he had plenty.

Believing in the old adage that absence makes the heart grow fonder, Mama removed Gertrude from the Hollywood scene and took her back to Minnesota to visit Grandma, who was "ailing." The ruse worked. Bob Leonard could do nothing else all day but sigh and pine over the girl who had won his heart. He sent flowers, jewelry, and copious telegrams declaring his love. Finally, she accepted his proposal of marriage. The date was set, Grandma made a miraculous recovery, and Gertrude and her Mama were there to greet Bob when we returned from Coronado.

The best part of the story is that it was a happy marriage, as marriages go, with Gertrude contentedly gaining weight to match her husband's. They were a perfect match of laissez-faire temperaments, and how they both loved to eat!

Two weeks in Coronado did not further the progress of our script. Since the date of production was close at hand, Hugh Herbert and I had to get down to business when we returned. We worked all day in the studio, had conferences with Harry Rapf, and continued at my home into the wee hours.

After a particularly long session one night, it was nearly 1:00 A.M., we were both groggy, and I was ready to call it quits when the most extraordinary thing happened. Suddenly, Hugh Herbert dropped to his knees at my side. "I love you! I love you!" he kept repeating, breathing heavily and clutching me desperately. "Will you marry me? Please say you will marry me, Frederica!"

What a turn of events! I felt no attraction to this pudgy Englishman. I could hardly keep from laughing. "For Pete's sake, Hugh," I said, "what do you think you're doing, proposing to me at one o'clock in the morning? You're not in love with me, and I am not in love with you. Stop being silly. Get off your knees and go home." Without another word, he did just that. The subject never came up again, but I am sure he never forgave me.

The next day was a tough one from the minute we got together to work on the script. Guess what? The darling little man had dreamed up another full reel of cute business and gone off on a tangent again. Instead of cutting, he was embroidering on a script that was already way over length.

We had a story conference with Harry Rapf and Bob Leonard. Hugh did his thing. He threw himself into the exposition of the characters he was seeking to expand. They were secondary characters—two teenagers whose exploits, if allowed to run rampant, would detract from the major story and weaken it. Hugh Herbert had yet to learn that a good, tight script was made up of choice situations economically tied to the central story line, each situation advancing the progression of the whole. One could go on endlessly inventing new business that weakened the story structure. Surely, Harry Rapf and Bob Leonard knew this. They were seasoned filmmakers. Yet they were laughing, buying Hugh Herbert's embellishments. Apparently, they were as lacking in the knowledge of good film technique as my pompous, amateur collaborator.

The Waning Sex was my story. I had given it birth. I had breathed life into its characters. I had given it plot and careful development. I simply could not sit by any longer and suffer my brainchild to be ruined.

"Mr. Rapf," I exploded, admittedly out of sensible control, "what Mr. Herbert has proposed today is going to end up on the cutting room floor. This story is not about a couple of teenagers who never belonged in the story in the first place. They are extraneous characters of Mr. Herbert's invention and detract from the comedy situations of our two principal characters. I suggest we cut them out of the story entirely."

I should have stopped right there. But, carried away, I went right on giving Rapf, Leonard, and that supercilious Englishman a lesson in filmmaking I thought they needed to learn.

"I concede," I continued, "that Mr. Herbert is an inventive writer. But he doesn't know where to stop. You don't go on and on dreaming up new business to be added to a script that is already over length."

I could see Harry Rapf and Bob Leonard both recoil at my criticism. Mr. Rapf, his reddening countenance indicating his rising blood pressure, took it personally, as I suppose he had every right to since he was the executive producer whose chief task was to keep the development of a story under control. I had gone too far. I had overreached myself. I felt it in my bones.

"Are you telling me I don't know my business?" Mr. Rapf inquired icily.

"I'm sorry, Mr. Rapf," I hastened to add. "My only interest is that we get a good, tight script."

"I believe I'm the best judge of that, Miss Sagor," Harry Rapf snapped. "I'm the producer on this picture and whether you like it or not, we are going to shoot Mr. Herbert's story, Miss Sagor, not yours."

Wow! Mr. Herbert's story! That put me in my proper place. It had implications I did not want to think about.

It was about this time that the very private Norma Shearer confided a happy secret to me. "Frederica, I want you to be the first to know. Irving proposed last night. We're engaged." She had a sparkling diamond ring to prove it. She and Irving Thalberg had been dating quietly for some time without any of the Hollywood busybodies being aware of it. I had been privileged to be one of her confidants. But happy as I was for her, because I knew how much she was in love, I could not help but be apprehensive about this strange alliance. Here was this virgin young actress with a Protestant background, closely tied to her mother, sister, and brother, marrying this Jewish wunderkind producer closely tied to his Orthodox mother and a neurotic sister. He was a mama's boy, the result of being a sickly child. Two different cultures. How would it work out? I tried desperately to warn Norma of what she was getting into, but she was too much in love to listen.

Perhaps this was why Norma turned her back on the picture scene after Irving's untimely death. Left a widow with two small children, she took herself and them far away from the scene of her triumphs—and her in-laws. She opted for the open space of Aspen, Colorado, where she fell in love again and married her handsome ski instructor, Martin Arronge. She even had her lawyers ensure that none of the pictures she had made for MGM would be run again until after her death.

When, in 1980, she was admitted to the Motion Picture and Television Country House and Hospital in Woodland Hills, she was very ill. I wanted to go and see her. But I thought better of it. We were both in our eighties. So much had happened in the intervening years. She might not even have remembered me, and then again, I might have brought up memories best forgotten. Norma died at the Woodland

Hills Hospital on Sunday, June 12, 1983. Sleep well, dear Juliet, sleep well . . .

I was finally able to arrange a screen test at MGM for my protégée, Riza Royce. I had worked on it for months, trying first one and then another of my contacts at the studio. Eddie Goulding, Bob Leonard, King Vidor, and Clarence Brown were not interested in Riza because they felt she looked too much like Norma Shearer, even if her test proved she had talent.

Finally, I prevailed on my good friend Max Marcin to arrange the test. At last, she would have something on film, something to open doors for her. I got the finest cameraman in the business, Lee Garmes, to film the test.

But I did not count on Blanca Holmes, a sometime actress and wife of Stuart Holmes, a successful character actor. They were into seances, numerology, and horoscopes, controlling half of filmdom with their occult powers and predictions. Riza was in the clutches of this seeress and would not make a move unless Blanca read in the horoscope that it was a good day in Riza's stars to venture forth. And the day chosen for Riza's screen test was not a "good" day.

"You have to postpone it, Freddie," she pleaded. "You have to make it another day."

"I can't, Riza. I can't postpone it. It's set for eleven o'clock tomorrow morning."

"Blanca Holmes says it's a bad day for me."

"You can't let Blanca Holmes run your life for you, Riza," I pleaded. "You know how hard it was for me to get you this test."

Next day, at eleven o'clock on a perfect morning, Riza Royce got her screen test. Now, a screen test at MGM was no small achievement—any aspiring actor or actress would have given their right arm for the chance. MGM, in particular, spent more money and took more time and effort to bring out the best in its hopefuls than any other studio. Having Lee Garmes making that test was another big plus. He was a superb artist. She also had a good script and a good leading man.

The result? Riza blew it. She faltered. She moved awkwardly. She couldn't remember her lines. Lee Garmes tried over and over to shoot the simple scene: two people falling in love against their better judgment after having been alienated. Lee Garmes was kind, patient, and understanding.

"Come on, Riza," he coaxed. "One more time. Give it your best this time. Loosen up. You're tied in knots."

But this was not Riza's day. Blanca Holmes had told her so. Lee Garmes gave up. The test was called off. Riza Royce had muffed her chance; Lee Garmes, Max Marcin, and I would be called in to account for wasting studio time and money.

I was mad. Furious! Everybody experiences nervousness before he or she steps before the cameras. But a good pro recovers and delivers. What Riza demonstrated was that she was a big ninny who had capitulated to the will of Blanca Holmes.

I grew more and more frustrated with Riza. She called me her "fairy godmother," but underneath, she was shallow and did not appreciate me.

The materials for a yellow chiffon nightgown lay in the bottom drawer of her bureau, hidden away for nearly eight months. I had admired a similar gown that Riza had made for herself. This was when she first came to live with me.

"Do you really like it?" she asked, flattered.

"Love it," I answered. "It's beautifully made." (It was all stitched by hand.)

"Freddie, darling," she purred, hugging me, "I'm going to make you one just like it."

I was thrilled. I would have cherished such a gift. The material was bought; the gown was cut. But somehow, Riza never found time to finish it. There it lay in that bottom drawer, untouched.

So, in my mind, it became a sort of symbol that Riza did not really care enough about her "fairy godmother" to want to please her. She had time for everything else, but none for me.

Once, Ben Schulberg and I differed in a discussion of Tolstoy's War and Peace. Riza boldly sided with Ben against me, even though she had never read the novel. Schulberg snapped (he never liked her, and he was a good judge of people), "You don't know what you're talking about. Read the book. I don't agree with Freddie, but she has read the book and knows what she's talking about."

Then there were the times when she would intrude on the story conferences between Hugh Herbert and myself, entering the fray always on the side of Hugh Herbert against any position I might hold, even though she was hardly qualified to judge. I had to put my foot down.

"Riza," I told her, "I'm having enough trouble convincing Hugh without interference from you. Where do you come off, anyway, to side with Hugh every time against me? I get the feeling, Riza, that you like putting me down. And I don't like it. After this, please either stay in your bedroom when I have a story conference or take a walk."

Flushed with embarrassment, she had nothing to say.

Now the time had come for me to make an accounting. Over the past eight months, this aspiring actress was in my debt to the tune of three thousand dollars. I did not charge her room and board. I had believed in her. At considerable price to my own self-esteem, I had managed a screen test for her. And she had let me down, blowing a once-in-a-lifetime opportunity because it was not in Blanca Holmes's galaxy!

And so, that evening when I went home from the studio, I picked up my courage. "Riza," I told her, "for your own good and mine, you've got to get out and find yourself a job. You'll never get anywhere leaning on me. And I can't afford to carry you any longer."

She started to cry. She had been expecting it, I am sure, ever since the screen test disaster. I walked out of the room, near tears myself. I felt sick, mean, heartless. It was Hannah's day off, so I decided to have dinner out and take in a movie.

I got home a little after ten, and Riza was nowhere in evidence. There was a note. "Dear Freddie. I am going to the Green Hotel. Thanks for everything. I'll send for the rest of my clothes later. Love, Riza."

I knew she had no money. Not a penny. I called the hotel. It was a small, new place, two blocks east of Vine on Hollywood Boulevard.

"What are your monthly rates?" I inquired.

"One hundred and fifty dollars," I was told.

"You have Riza Royce registered, I believe?"

Yes, they had. "She came in tonight."

"I'm a friend of hers," I told the clerk. "I'm sending you a check to cover three months' rent for her."

That done, I could sleep better than I would have. I was filled with anxiety. Despite everything, I loved that girl. I didn't know what was in store for Riza Royce. But I shouldn't have worried. It proved to be an unbelievable Cinderella story. In less than three months, Riza Royce became Mrs. Josef von Sternberg.

One block west of Vine on Hollywood Boulevard, within walking distance of the Green Hotel, was a delicatessen called "Henry's." It was famous because it was the favorite hangout of Charlie Chaplin, his family, his working crew, and his friends—a veritable private Chaplin Club. Among the regulars who ate at the Chaplin table was Josef von Sternberg, not yet the big director he was soon to become. He had just finished making a low-budget picture on his own called *The Salvation Hunters*, an arty film that was receiving a lot of favorable attention since its release in February 1925.

Into Henry's each morning, hungry for her nickel cup of coffee and doughnut, walked Riza Royce. Josef von Sternberg was there each morning, too, ordering his own cup of coffee and doughnut. Riza returned to the delicatessen at lunch time. Josef von Sternberg was there, too, at the Chaplin table. And he was there the next day and the next and the next. And so was Riza. Each had been eyeing the other and was aware of their growing interest.

"Would you permit me to buy you a cup of coffee and a doughnut?" the director asked one morning. It did not matter that this stunning, statuesque young girl was a head taller than he. From that morning on, Riza ate all her meals at the Chaplin table, and Josef von Sternberg paid for them.

It was my on my twenty-fifth birthday—July 6, 1925 (I cannot forget that day)—at seven o'clock in the morning that the telephone woke me up. It was Riza.

"How would you like to stand up for me today?" she blithely inquired. "Joe and I are getting married."

"Joe? Joe?" I returned sleepily. "Joe who?"

"Josef von Sternberg, of course," she proudly informed me.

"Who's he?" I asked. I knew nothing of the daily visits to Henry's or of the blooming romance between my ex-roommate and the director of *The Salvation Hunters*. I had heard of his movie but had not seen it.

I played hooky from the studio that day. Instead, my Moon and I headed for West Hollywood and the sheriff's office, where the wedding was scheduled to take place. In those days, West Hollywood was an unincorporated strip of territory with its own sheriff and law enforcement. The sheriff's office was in a dirty, tiny store with two roll-top desks and two swivel chairs—one for the sheriff and the other for the only working judge on the strip. A toilet in the back was in plain view. The only other furnishings were a battered broom and a large cardboard box serving as a wastebasket. This was the romantic setting for the wedding of Josef von Sternberg and Riza Royce.

"Do you take this man for your lawful wedded husband?" the old judge hiccuped. He had had "a few" and had also removed his dentures.

"I do," replied Riza almost inaudibly.

"Do you take this woman for your lawful wedded wife?" the judge hiccuped again.

"I do," replied Joe, slipping a gold band on Riza's finger.

"I now pronounce you man and wife."

The ceremony was over. The groom was reminded to kiss the bride. It was all so brief—so incredible.

"Are you two really married?" I asked. I couldn't believe it. And it proved a curious, if temporary, alliance—a marriage convenient for both participants. It lent an aura of security and respectability to an up-and-coming director who felt himself in an atmosphere he did not fully understand or belong in, but in which he was determined to be noticed. For the bride, it was an immediate and happy solution to her financial situation and a heaven-made opportunity to reach her ambition, to achieve stardom, with a talented young husband to further her career. These, rather than sexual attraction, must have been the underlying motives for the marriage; it did not hurt Joe to have a young and attractive wife at his side—any more than it hurt Riza to be married to a man regarded in the inner cerebral circles of the Charlie Chaplin coterie as a potential film genius.

Von Sternberg was not, of course, his real handle. He was plain Joe Sternberg from a poor Polish-Jewish background in New York City. The "von" was an additional flourish to enhance the image he wished to project. It remained a question as to how much was genuine talent and how much was pompousness and posturing. He had a camera eye, for certain; if there was any genius in the man, that is where it lay. But he lacked deeper appreciation and insight into other human beings. *The Salvation Hunters* proved a rare shot in the dark, holding as it did interesting sociological significance enveloped in mood photography. Nothing he did later measured up to this promising beginning. I am sure Charles Chaplin would agree. Chaplin was a realist, a penetrating analyst of what makes the rest of us mortals tick. Von Sternberg was not endowed with Chaplin's compassion and vision. Underneath the "von" veneer, he remained just plain Joe Sternberg.

Perhaps the shabby background and brevity of the marriage ceremony was an omen of the future. The marriage took on the same tacky development of two people who were mentally, spiritually, and physically unsuited. The only thing they had in common was ambition. There was a honeymoon following the murmured vows in the West Hollywood sheriff's office. When Riza von Sternberg returned to California after three months abroad and in New York City, I knew that something was seriously amiss. She had lost twenty pounds and was as nervous as a cat. She finally confessed to the incredible.

On the train trip from L.A. to New York, the honeymooners did not splurge on a compartment but had separate beds. Joe ordered his bride to the upper berth, while he slumbered below. In New York, to keep expenses down, they stayed in the small Bronx apartment of his mother, sleeping on a broken-down sofa-bed in the living room. It was there that the marriage was consummated . . . or was it? According to Riza, Josef von Sternberg's equipment was faulty.

Before they embarked for Europe, Joe ordered his wife to part with her topcoat, which he gave to his mother in payment for her hospitality. He promised to buy Riza a coat in Europe, but he never did, despite rough, cold weather at sea during their crossings and in the mountains of Bavaria. Poor Riza nearly froze to death, but he was impervious to her complaints. There was verbal abuse as well. Riza was made to understand her inferiority, ignorance, and stupidity. Her husband did not believe she had film possibilities and would do nothing to advance her career. He too considered her patrician nose a handicap.

Outraged, I confronted the idiot. "What have you done to my girlfriend, Joe?" I wanted to know. "Who do you think you are, anyway?"

He walked out of the room, not deigning to reply. Only a few weeks after their return to California, Joe was signed to a directing contract at Paramount. He did mellow a little then and even bought his wife a respectable coat. With their economic situation established, the von Sternbergs bought a modest Spanish house in the Wilshire district near Fairfax Avenue on Drexel. Riza took on the role of a good and obedient hausfrau—wife, cook, and scullery maid. She took her marital vows seriously and proved herself an exemplary consort. With a good and willing housekeeper to look after him, the ever-frugal von Sternberg allowed his wife the "princely" sum of ten dollars a week to buy the groceries. He paid the utility bills, but she was to run the house on ten smackers a week, including frequent dinner guests. Sam and Sadie Ornitz were visitors, as were Mr. and Mrs. Jack Bachman; and Jules Furthman, Joe's favorite script writer; and, later, Mr. and Mrs. Ernest Maas.

With the backing of Ben Schulberg, who was enormously impressed with *The Salvation Hunters,* Joe's career took off. When *Underworld* with George Bancroft proved an unqualified box-office success, and which elevated his career immeasurably, Joe was able to negotiate a new contract in short order at more than twice his original salary. Riza's allowance, however, did not increase.

Emil Jannings, star of the German masterpiece *The Last Laugh,* did not like Joe, and the feeling was mutual. Their tension emanated from the fact that they were both by nature dictatorial and egotistical. After directing Jannings in *The Last Command,* in which Jannings played a White Russian general who goes amok in a war film, believing it to be the real thing, Joe vowed he would never work again with the insulting, demeaning German actor. But when Jannings returned to his homeland and needed a director for *The Blue Angel,* he cabled Paramount and asked for Josef von Sternberg. Joe fell for the implied flattery (and handsome remuneration) and accepted the assignment.

Riza was ecstatic. She loved being Mrs. von Sternberg. She was almost ready to forget her own career and continue to revel happily in the shadow of a husband on the rise. She was, however, still perplexed about sex, which, in her case, appeared to be a farcical performance leading nowhere. "Is that all there is to it?" she kept asking. "I don't know what you people see in it."

Dear Riza—she was not to learn the answer until several years later when, divorced from Joe, she met Sidney Buchman, playwright and eventual head of Columbia Studios under Harry Cohn, and, still later, ostracized from Hollywood along with his brother, Harold Buchman, a writer, during the black McCarthy witch-hunt period. They met on the train while returning from New York to Los Angeles. Although Sidney

Buchman was happily married to a woman as steeped in Marxism as he was, they had a brief affair that opened Riza's eyes to what she had been missing in her marriage to the great Josef von Sternberg.

The Blue Angel was Riza's marital Waterloo; cast for a small part was an unknown (in America) actress by the name of Marlene Dietrich. She recognized her golden opportunity. Joe's sexual weakness was something that she, in her sophistication and worldly outlook on life, could handily take care of. And she did. To Dietrich, it did not matter if the attraction was man or woman. She was cognizant in all the ways of making love and enjoying sex. Once emancipated from his closet agony, Joe lost all interest in Riza and concentrated on his absorbing discovery, Marlene Dietrich. Morocco, Shanghai Express, The Scarlet Empress, The Devil Is a Woman—voila! The once-un-known bit player became a big motion-picture star, a sex symbol, with her husky voice, her languid eyes, her calculated sexy carriage, and responses so eloquently studied that they became an art form. Like Greta Garbo, Dietrich had what I call a plateau face, a cameraman's face. Also like Garbo, Dietrich was a good and fast study. She worked hard to achieve her stardom. She was no accident. She had what it takes.

It was Joe who offered Riza the divorce. The news came to me via a telephone call. Riza was staying at a nondescript apartment-hotel on Cahuenga Boulevard. "Freddie," she sobbed, "Joe has left me. He wants a divorce." And then came the real bomb-buster. "I've had my nose fixed. I just got back from surgery."

"Riza! Riza!" I managed when I had halfway recovered from the shock. "You didn't do it!"

"Yes," she replied. "I'm in a lot of pain right now, but I'll be all right in a day or two."

"Riza, why did you do it? Why? Your beautiful nose. How could you?" I sobbed.

"I had to. Blanca Holmes, everyone, said it was standing in my way," was her teary response. Blanca Holmes again! Well, no matter now. The deed was done, and after my initial outburst, my practical instincts took over. "What about your divorce?"

"Joe's attorneys are handling it," she said indifferently.

"Not if I can help it," I shot back. "Your lawyers are going to handle it, Mrs. von Sternberg. You have that husband of yours over a barrel, and he's going to pay the piper. You can name your own settlement, and you're going to."

The attorney who represented her was the best in the business and known for his successful, out-of-court divorce settlements. If memory serves me right, it was Greg Bautzer who handled Riza's divorce. The settlement was in the neighborhood of $150,000 in cash (a lot of money in those days!) plus 25 percent of an extensive art collection Joe had amassed. And he had some beauties: early Picassos, van Goghs, Monets, and Manets. He had been collecting since 1923, and his eye and taste were unquestionable. In later years, when he was broke and no studio would have him, he lived off his collection. All he needed to do was put a picture or two on the market, and it took care of his needs for a year or more.

Riza was now a woman of means. Her nose job, however, was a fiasco. The doctor, who claimed to be an experienced plastic surgeon, had left her with a wide, bumpless, flat prominence with gaping nostrils. It completely changed her aristocratic countenance, for me anyway.

The first thing Riza did when she received her alimony money was pay me back in full, every penny of the money she owed me. Later, when I needed some art in the home that my husband, Ernest, and I bought in Westwood, she let me choose from the collection she had from Joe. Partial to black-and-white prints, I chose two Zorach drawings (husband and wife) and a Lazawick drawing of the New York City skyline. They are in my proud possession today. Looking back, I regret I had not been more pragmatic and chosen a Picasso or a Monet or two. Oh, well . . . I no longer needed the money as desperately as I did at the time when Riza and Joe got married. I had been flat broke then and had to write Joe, asking him for what Riza owed me. I still have the letter in my files. This was his reply: "Dear Miss Sagor, I do not know where you get the audacity to address me about money that you claim is owing to you. When I married my wife, I did not take over any of her obligations. Josef von Sternberg."

Now, my concern was for Riza's future. I urged her to establish a trust, an annuity, so that she would be protected in later years. She turned a deaf ear to my practical advice and, instead, fell in love with Stanton McDonald Wright, a painter of some renown, an innovative colorist who was heavily influenced by oriental art. He swept her off her feet. About fifteen years her senior, he was still a handsome, virile hunk of masculinity—what did it matter that he had another mistress in Santa Barbara? They lived in a ménage à trois for awhile. Then Riza and her swain went to New York and Europe and later returned to New York and took an apartment on Park Avenue with furniture especially built to suit their taste. Riza continued to buy her lover's paintings, forking out five or ten thousand dollars, as if money grew on trees. In all this while, I never heard from the lady, not even a postcard.

Then came the day when she returned to California five years later with a three-year-old daughter—a fairy child called Linfa Wright, supposedly born in wedlock. But the painter, who had returned to his mistress in Santa Barbara, never acknowledged parenthood, and there was no wedding license in evidence. Riza rented a home near where we lived in Beverly Hills, and Ernest (the dear man I had married in the interim) and I became Linfa's family.

Riza was still under the influence of Blanca Holmes, who did more than her share to help Riza reduce her fortune. Eventually, Blanca decreed that her client needed to go to New York again (probably to rid herself of Riza's dependency), and Riza complied, "storing" all her handmade furniture, paintings, and other worldly goods with Blanca. When she finally came back to California, she did not look me up. She existed on extra work in her later years, I understand, from kind directors like George Cukor.

The last time we talked was when I was visiting my old friend Hortense Schorr at the Hollywood Roosevelt Hotel. Hortense, then head of the publicity department of Columbia Pictures, had come to L.A. for studio conferences. Riza happened to call while I was there and, learning that I was sitting beside Hortense, asked to speak to me.

"Freddie, darling," she simpered over the phone. "How are you? I'm dying to see you, darling. You wouldn't recognize me. I'm a stunning red-head now."

"Riza, darling," I replied, "I'm a stunning white-head now who's been in the phone book right along, but whom you never bothered to look up. I'm afraid I'm not dying to see you." And I handed the phone back to a bewildered Hortense.

Riza passed away not so long ago, and I regret it if I sound bitter now. I still have an affection for her and will always wish our relationship could have ended differently.

Chapter 8

THE TROUBLEMAKER

IN THE FALL OF 1926, I had a sudden and violent abdominal attack in the middle of the night. Doubled up with pain and not having a doctor of my own, I summoned Dr. James Reed, an orthopedic surgeon who ministered to the medical needs of half of filmdom. At Orthopedic Hospital, he diagnosed my distress as tubular reaction and indicated that an operation was the solution. Naturally, I was considerably upset because that meant I would not be able to bear children. To this day, I remain convinced that all I had was an old-fashioned bellyache. I was to learn later that the unprincipled Dr. Reed tended to operate whenever possible because that was where the money lay. But trusting him and in pain, I did not seek a second opinion. I slumbered blissfully under ether while the dextrous Dr. Reed removed my fallopian tubes, and, just for good measure, my perfectly healthy appendix.

When I awoke, my room was a flower shop—so many flowers, in fact, that I sent some to other patients along with baskets of fruit, perfume, candy, and even books. I recall that Theodore Dreiser's *American Tragedy,* a bestseller then, was one of them. As I recuperated, I had a portable typewriter brought in and did some writing after a conference of sorts with Bob Leonard and F. Hugh Herbert, who came to see me several times. There was a constant flow of visitors, mostly from the studio. Even a young man from the mailroom dropped in with a bouquet. It was all very touching, and I felt very special to receive so much affection from my colleagues.

After ten days of pampered invalidism, I returned to the studio, sans fallopian tubes and appendix. While I love children, I chose to regard the fact that I could never bear them as less than a major calamity. Fortunately, the dear man I would marry felt the same way.

The script of *The Waning Sex* was in production; and, as I watched some of the shooting, I could tell it was going to turn out to be a fine vehicle for Norma Shearer. She sparkled in the part because, as she told me, she could identify completely with the girl who had chosen a career in place of romance, only to find that the clinging vine methods of the "waning" sex are what gentlemen prefer. Bob Leonard, now blissfully married to his beloved Gertrude, achieved the ultimate in comedy. He knew how to exact the best performance from his actors—even from wooden Conrad Nagel, the leading man.

F. Hugh Herbert and I were working separately on other projects and hardly speaking. Then I did something extremely unwise. Eager to free myself from Harry Rapf, I went to Hunt Stromberg and asked to be assigned to his unit. How naive I was! How ignorant of studio politics! What I did was a very big no-no. Producers might steal from one another and stab each other in the back, but when it came to dealing with dissatisfied, unhappy writers, producers were fraternal brothers who stuck together—especially when some lowly writer challenged their sovereignty.

I never was transferred to Stromberg's unit, and Harry Rapf never forgave me for requesting such a change. When it came time for my studio contract to be renewed, Harry Rapf axed me for my presumption.

"She's a talented writer," he conceded to his secretary, Madeleine Ruthvin (who was my friend), while dictating the fatal memo that would seal my fate at MGM. "But she's a troublemaker."

Troublemaker! That was the worst assessment anybody could receive in those days in the picture business. A troublemaker was defined as anyone who defied (however unwittingly) the authority vested in executives and producers. The rumor spread like a contagious disease; agents picked it up—along with directors, producers, and other writers.

"Don't touch her. She's a troublemaker." And so Frederica Sagor found herself out of a job.

Initially, I was sure that Ruth Collier could find me another writing assignment. I liked her, and we were friends. But I quickly learned that her powers of persuasion were as limited as her contacts. A small agent, she did not have ready or easy access to executives, producers, or even directors. Casting directors, story departments, some editors— yes. But for a writer to get important assignments, it was necessary to deal at the top. That was how I had gotten started. A direct contact with Ben Schulberg, head of Preferred Pictures, earned me *The Plastic Age* assignment. A direct contact with Edmund Goulding, a well-entrenched director and writer at MGM, gained me entrance there. No agent, big or small, could have accomplished this.

Who else did I know at the other studios? Who else had ever heard of Frederica Sagor, aspiring screenwriter with only two screen credits to her name? And my third, *The Waning Sex*, was in perilous question. Once I was off the MGM lot, Hugh Herbert, a skillful bridge player, ingratiated himself with Harry Rapf and Bob Leonard. Carey Wilson was the fourth hand.

It was from Madeleine Ruthvin I learned that a secret preview showing of *The Waning Sex* was being held in La Jolla, north of San Diego, California. Of course I wanted to be there, so I headed my trusty Moon one hundred miles south to the snazzy seacoast resort, which seemed an ideal choice for a preview of our sophisticated offering.

Did I say *our*? As the credits unfolded on the screen, there, large as life, appeared the name of F. Hugh Herbert as the sole author of the adaptation and screenplay of *The Waning Sex*. Nowhere was there a mention of Frederica Sagor, the writer who had been handed a title, nothing more, and who had birthed the characters and story line from scratch. Apparently, that argumentative conference with Harry Rapf had cost me my credit. I shrank into my seat, praying that no one would notice me. The fact that the picture was a scintillating success, winning a standing ovation from the audience, only made the situation more poignant. As everyone gathered in the lobby to congratulate its star, Norma Shearer; producer, Harry Rapf; and director, Bob Leonard; as well as the undeserving Lilliputian writer, F. Hugh Herbert; I managed to slip out of the theater. Through tear-dimmed eyes I found my Moon in the parking lot and began the lonely, long trek back to Hollywood.

There was plenty of time to reflect and review the events that had brought about this catastrophic turn of events in my writing career. Tears were a waste of time; I had some good hard thinking to do. With every click of the flying miles, I put it all together again. My denial of credit on *The Waning Sex* was, of course, retaliation for my impudence in challenging my producer's august judgment, even though he was well aware that without my treatment he would have had nothing to work on but a title. He was also well aware that when Hugh was called into the picture the hard work of establishing the plot and characters had already been done. Hugh's contribution, it could be fairly said, was to add some extraneous characters and business that ended, as predicted, on the cutting room floor—proving me right, but ironically curtailing my sweet MGM contract.

Ruefully, I realized I had played my cards badly. One did not lightly challenge authority in the movie business. There were times when one had to button one's lip, and I had been too cocky, too sure of myself. But now, how to undo the damage of my abysmal inexperience in the world of studio politics? That was the conundrum, the "sixty-four-dollar" question! There was only one way; I had to swallow my pride and use what writer's wits I had left to appeal to Harry Rapf to reverse my punishment. There was still time before they shipped prints of *The Waning Sex* back East.

I wrote a pleading, groveling, hypocritical letter to Harry Rapf, designed to appeal to his ego. I asked him to perform the magnanimous gesture of pardoning me, his repentant supplicant, who, after all, had only been trying to do her job, her best, for the aggrandizement of the roaring King of Lions, the great MGM. The letter, still in my files, took three days to compose. It did the trick, at least as far as that one film was concerned. I was given credit with F. Hugh Herbert for *The Waning Sex*—but I was not welcomed back to MGM.

Weeks passed and even months, and Ruth Collier came up with no assignment for me. Meanwhile, there were bills to pay. I had been living on a bountiful scale with no thought of tomorrow: a full-time maid, my musical evenings, and all sorts of extravagances. All this, plus my rent, plus my horrendous doctor and hospital bills depleted my bank account to a nice round zero.

But the worst of it was that I still owed money for things I had purchased on credit. That was a lesson I richly deserved for blithely disregarding my dear mother's admonition to "Never buy on credit! Always pay in cash for what you buy or do without it." Oh, how I wished I had followed this sage advice! The embarrassment, the chagrin I suffered in those awful months was almost more than I could bear. As debts go, I did not owe much—less than a thousand dollars. But how the collecting agencies, the faithful minions of the merchants, dunned me. I dreaded the ring of the telephone. Again and again, they echoed the same refrain: "When can we expect your check, Miss Sagor?"

Miss Sagor, in reply, repeated over and over how sorry she was not to be able to make payment at the moment. As soon as she was working again, she would take care of the bill. But when a job did not materialize, it became next week and then next week. It was painfully demeaning—a nightmare for me. I knew others in the business, the successful crowd, who ran their accounts into the thousands and paid them off in pittances when pressed for payment. They were, nonetheless, considered "special" customers, to be treated with kid gloves. Unfortunately, I did not belong to that class of customer.

During this period, I was involved with a British actor named Henry Victor who spoke the King's English with a slight German accent. His father, a wounded German war prisoner, had been quartered in England and had married an English nurse. Amiable, protective, kind, and understanding, Henry was a handsome specimen well over six feet in height. He had been working in British films when he was signed to a two-year contract by a Paramount talent scout. In six months, he had played only one part at Paramount—a Prussian officer in some war film. Both of us were free and idle, and we spent much time together at Santa Monica beach. Powerful swimmers, Henry and I swam way out on calm, sunny days and played around in the water like a couple of dolphins. There was a platform out there near a buoy where we could sun ourselves. Henry had a gift for reciting Goethe in German, nearly overcoming my dislike for that guttural language in the musical resonance of his recitations.

Henry helped me get an apartment over a garage in the hills of West Hollywood, off Sunset Strip, that belonged to some English friends of his. The apartment wasn't much, but the house, high in the hills, surrounded by trees, was what struggling writers like to call a "hideaway." It was just one room with an economy kitchen. It had no bedroom, but there was a studio couch and room for my typewriter, record player, and even a bookcase. Best of all, the rent was only fifty dollars a month, and my new landlords were willing to wait for payment until I was working again. What more could I ask?

After a drought of nearly six months, while I worked like a Trojan completing a 150-page treatment on the life of the great Spanish painter Francisco de Goya—a labor of love that was rejected as being too arty—Ruth Collier finally came through with a package deal for two features to be developed from scratch for an outfit known as Tiffany Productions.

While Tiffany Productions was not in the big league, it was by no means one of the fly-by-night companies springing up everywhere and turning out spurious products labeled "quickies" in the industry. Tiffany Productions had started its existence with Mae Murray, who appeared as a star in eight productions. That made Tiffany one of the best-known independent producers and brought new fame to the star. Metro distributed these pictures, which did phenomenal business. Phil Goldstone was titular head of the company, in charge of production; and M.H. Hoffman was vice president in charge of sales and distribution. Both were still young men, in their early forties and fifties—intelligent, high-school educated, and indefatigable workers. They quickly established that they could make outstanding productions without featuring big star names. Their successful box-office product was the result of their careful choice of good writers and directors and their ability to prepare a production properly before shooting—instead of rectifying mistakes while the picture was in production or after it was made. While prestigious companies such as MGM swelled production budgets by hiring multiple writers to develop a story, Tiffany did it with one writer whose work they had analyzed and in whom they had confidence. They followed this economical procedure into every aspect of production. There was no soldiering at Tiffany. Everyone knew his job and did it—from the bottom to the top. The end result reflected the perfect combination of efficiency, good judgment, and the ability to pick the right people.

I was engaged to do two stories on the Tiffany 1925-26 production program. One was titled *That Model from Paris*, suggested by the Gouveneur Morris story *The Right to Live*. The second was to be an original farce with the alluring title of *The First Night*. The remuneration was good: five thousand dollars for a story, treatment, and script, with twenty-five hundred dollars to be paid upon commencement and twenty-five hundred dollars to be paid upon completion of the script. The total time allotted was six weeks. After that, if the writer continued to work with the director on the set throughout the shooting schedule, there would be further remuneration of three hundred dollars per week, with an additional thousand-dollar bonus at the end if the picture was brought in ahead of schedule. To a writer out of work, this sounded like manna from heaven.

My reputation had preceded me as a specialist in light, frothy entertainment. Associated with the flapper age and amusing farce comedy in *Dance Madness, The Plastic Age,* and *The Waning Sex,* I was hired for my expertise. In other words, I was "typed"—an all-too-prevalent disease in the industry, affecting writers, directors, producers, and actors. It was a malady hard to overcome; but since it offered ready money, the victim had no recourse but to accept the typing or remain unemployed and starve.

I knew that I was going to like working for Tiffany on my very first day when I met Lou Ostrow, Phil Goldstone's right-hand and good man Friday. Whereas Goldstone, under studio pressures, was often brusque and impatient (not unlike Harry Rapf), Lou was calm and encouraging, quick to praise, full of good suggestions, and sensitive to the need for that extra cup of coffee in the beanery downstairs. When I worked late, he would follow me home in his car to be sure I got there safely. His method earned him cooperation from everyone he supervised. Lou was thirtyish, over six feet tall, and good-looking, with a great smile that lit up his face. Yet, when he smiled or laughed, you felt he was crying inside, hiding some secret sorrow. The sorrow, I found out later, was the young Irish wife he adored but who was a hopeless alcoholic. Lou came from an unusual family. His brother, Senial Ostrow, was president of the Sealy Mattress Company and an ardent Democrat. His mother was an ardent Socialist, who—much to his chagrin—picketed her son Senial's factory in a labor dispute. Lou had no political leanings but was proud of his Jewish origin and of having been born in the good old U.S.A.

My job as writer on *That Model from Paris,* the first of the two stories I had been engaged to do, was to supply "the story line," as it was called. The Morris story supplied us with a plot and characters, but actually there was very little in the published story that could be used. I was given the latitude of creating my own story and developing my own characters. Having had plenty of good, hard experience at MGM in doing just that over and over, I plunged ahead and put my imagination to work, creating a story line that would lend itself to the development of good comedy situations, or comedy "business." My story line was approved the next morning in the first conference attended by director Louis Gasnier, Lou Ostrow, Phil Goldstone, and myself.

My next task was to develop the story line into a treatment—creating situations, furthering the plot, and giving life and breath to the characters. Again, my work was analyzed by Gasnier, Ostrow, and Goldstone; suggestions were made that were approved or disapproved by all present; and the new version was sent away to be typed. Each day I brought in another segment, and the same procedure followed until the story was fully developed into a full treatment approved by everyone.

The next step was the script, or continuity—breaking the treatment down into camera shots: long shots, medium shots, and closeups. This, I initially worked out and brought in for everyone to scrutinize—changing and rewriting as we went along. Finally, almost six weeks to the day after I'd begun work, the script was finished and ready for shooting. Copies were made and distributed to the producer, associate producer, actors in the cast, script girl, director, cameramen, casting director, and anyone else who would be a part of making this film. Goldstone, Ostrow, and Gasnier all expressed satisfaction with my inventiveness and the alacrity of my work—the result, I should point out, of grabbing a few hours' sleep in the early hours of the evening when I came home; working from midnight until dawn came up over the hills of Hollywoodland; wallowing in a hot bath, my mind still working away; and appearing at the studio promptly at nine, looking fresh as a daisy. But I loved what I was doing, the cooperation I was getting, and the appreciation and recognition I was receiving as a writer. I was even more thrilled when Phil Goldstone asked me to remain on the set and work along with Mr. Gasnier throughout the making of the picture.

Louis Gasnier was a top director with an impressive list of silent picture credits. He was working at Tiffany's for a fraction of his former salary because he had fallen from grace when the Hays office had had him ostracized. He had a reputation for decadence that was well-deserved—having several mistresses, giving wild parties at his home in the Hollywood Hills, and luring producers and associates to participate in the revelries.

Side by side with him, day in and day out, often into the night, I developed a high regard for his ability, his love of his work, his attention to detail, his sophistication and comedy sense. He was a pro. There was plenty of evidence of his competence as a director. He knew what he was doing, and he had the knack of cutting his film in the camera. There would be little waste on the cutting room floor with any picture Louis Gasnier made.

With a heavy French accent, he exacted sterling responses from his performers, Marceline Day and Bert Lytell.

"Marceline," he would say, "now we do it again. Only this time you look up like this into his eyes." And he demonstrated the scene with the leading lady, showing her exactly what he was after.

"Bert," he would scold the leading man, "you do this without passion. You love this girl, oui? Do you know what the amour is? I will show you." And he would show Bert Lytell how to offer his heart on the screen.

To appreciate the product that Louis Gasnier and Frederica Sagor turned out, we can read the reviews the picture received when it was released. The following appeared in the trade papers in September 1926:

> *Film Mercury: That Model from Paris* should prove good entertainment in almost any theatre. The more mature will take it with tongue-in-cheek, but will enjoy it. The romantic and gullible will leave the theatre completely satisfied.

> *Variety:* A story of a Cinderella who becomes beautiful and, after many trials, weds the fairy prince. This theme is always pleasing to movie audiences; it is impossible to fail. . . . Miss Day is charming, a very good actress and chock full of appeal. Bert Lytell excels in this one as a good comedian.

> *Telegraph:* An intriguing comedy drama of a girl who poses as a Parisian model and who was as American as Henry Ford, and the complications into which her seemingly innocent impersonations lead her. . . . The story is well plotted, the situations novel, and the picture highly entertaining. The continuity excellent.

Moving Picture World: That Model from Paris is excellent entertainment for any theater. It has spirited action, good characterizations and a human and comical story.

Since the picture was brought in ahead of schedule, Louis Gasnier and I both received our thousand-dollar bonuses. I was primed now to go to work on the second project, *The First Night*. Richard Thorpe was to be the director. I knew nothing about him except that Tiffany felt that he was an up-and-coming addition to the directorial ranks. They were willing to gamble and afford him a chance to show what he could do. He was modest in story conferences, almost self-effacing, having nothing to add and nothing to object to. Concocting a farce is a zany business. Thorpe seemed satisfied with my story line, even more pleased as the treatment matured, and eager to go to work shooting the picture when the continuity was completed and the scripts distributed to the set crew. Again, I was told that I was to continue working on the set and to give Mr. Thorpe all the support he needed.

"Don't hesitate to tell him if he falls down or is weak," Phil Goldstone counseled me aside. "This is your story, and you want to see that what you put down on paper comes out the way you wrote it. It's a fast-moving farce, very funny. Lou and I think it will make a hilarious movie. We just hope Thorpe has the light touch he needs to pull it off."

He need not have worried. Richard Thorpe may never have directed a dizzy, zany farce before, but he got the tempo right from page one to the finish. He understood the absurdities of the plot, looked to me to explain each scene as I had conceived it, and carried on from there, translating it into action. He did a yeoman job. *The First Night* became his calling card to an MGM contract. From then on, he did not have to prove himself by working for peanuts at an independent studio. He rose right to the top.

I patterned the story of *The First Night* after the Broadway successes of A.H. Woods, a master of farce. The story is somewhat complicated. Dr. Richard Bard, played by Bert Lytell, is a successful psychiatrist, a personable bachelor in his early forties. He is accustomed to having his women patients fall in love with him and is quite adept at handling them by directing their interests elsewhere. That is, until Doris Frazer, played by Dorothy Devore, comes in to see him. For the first time, the handsome doctor loses his professionalism and falls

(*Above*) Agnes and Arnold Sagor's first three daughters, (from left to right) Lillian, Vera, and Sophie, were born in Russia. Frederica (*left*) was their only child born after the family immigrated to America. She is shown here in 1913, at the age of thirteen.

Preferred Pictures sent Frederica to ace photographer Walter Frederick Seely to have publicity stills made while she was working on a screen adaptation for *The Plastic Age* in 1925.

Louis and Sophie Maas, Ernest's parents, in 1920. Louis was an early film entrepreneur and owned the third nickelodeon in New York City.

Film director John Huston and Ernest's brother Irving at a film festival in Japan. Irving worked in the foreign department at Fox and eventually became the executive vice president of the motion picture association.

Frederica while working on *The Plastic Age* in 1925. Photograph by Walter Frederick Seely.

Ernest Maas's Roycroft Productions made independent and industrial films in the early 1920s. By 1926 Ernest was a writer, director, and producer at Fox Films.

Ben Schulberg gave Freddie her first break when he hired her to write the scenario for The Plastic Age. Photograph courtesy of Sonya O'Sullivan.

Dance Madness, starring Claire Windsor and Conrad Nador, was really the child of another writer, Alice Miller. When asked to do a complete rewrite, Frederica found she could offer little to improve the already excellent script. As the last writer on the project, though, she received all the credit.

Burying Lucille LeSueur forever, the newly christened Joan Crawford engaged Freddie to help her build a wardrobe befitting a lady. Photograph by Ruth Harriet Louise.

Having had his career at MGM saved by *Dance Madness*, Bob Leonard was given the next Norma Shearer film, *The Waning Sex*. The writer he wanted and got was his and Norma's friend Frederica Sagor. Photograph by Ruth Harriet Louise.

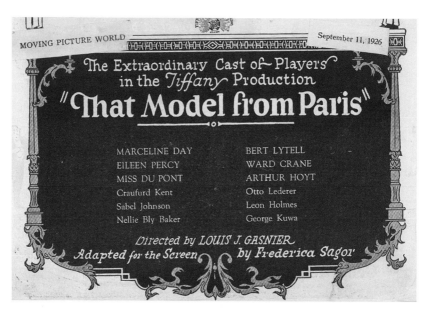

The Extraordinary Cast of Players in the Tiffany Production

"That Model from Paris"

MARCELINE DAY
EILEEN PERCY
MISS DU PONT
Craufurd Kent
Sabel Johnson
Nellie Bly Baker

BERT LYTELL
WARD CRANE
ARTHUR HOYT
Otto Lederer
Leon Holmes
George Kuwa

Directed by LOUIS J. GASNIER
Adapted for the Screen by Frederica Sagor

Typecast as a specialist in light, frothy entertainment by her success with *Dance Madness*, *The Plastic Age*, and *The Waning Sex*, Frederica was hired to work on *That Model from Paris* and *The First Night*. While not the great writing she wanted, the money was good and sorely needed.

Tiffany Productions, INC. presents

"The First Night"

by Frederica Sagor

WITH

BERT LYTELL, DOROTHY DEVORE
HARRY MYERS, FREDERIC KOVERT
WALTER HIERS,
LILA LESLIE, JAMES MACK, HAZEL KEENER
JOAN STANDING AND NELLIE BLY BAKER

Directed by RICHARD THORPE

A TIFFANY PRODUCTION

With regular studio assignments, marriage to Ernest Maas, and the sale of three original scripts, 1927 was a very good year for Frederica.

Frederica's *Free and Easy*, retitled *Silk Legs* by Fox, also made it into the MGM list–under questionable circumstances. MGM's production retained the original title.

Both ardent Democrats, Frederica and Ernest supported President Roosevelt and worked diligently in his 1944 campaign. Their efforts and leanings translated into trouble for the couple during the McCarthy era several years later.

In addition to producing and directing, Ernest Maas promoted his contest ideas to the film and television industries. Two of his best ideas were U-Spot-It and Lucky Penny.

Frederica and Ernest Maas, 1940.

'THE SHOCKING MISS PILGRIM'

"The Shocking Miss Pilgrim," Twentieth Century-Fox's new Technicolor musical, brings Betty Grable to the screen in the role of America's first distaff office worker. It all happens, according to the film, in 1874, when no really respectable girl would dare poke her nose into the exclusively man's world—the business office. But Betty takes the plunge, and the picture unfolds the hilarious and romantic story of her trials and triumphs, set to previously unpublished music by the late George Gershwin. Here are some of the highlights of Betty's relationship with her reluctant employer, Dick Haymes. (1) The "female typewriter," her heart in her mouth, reports to work. (2) Mustaches waggle and necks strain as the swish of a skirt is heard for the first time in any office. (3) But Betty's boss, Dick Haymes, seems to have his mind strictly on business. (4) Romantic business, that is. (5) And that is how the phrase "So she married her boss" was born.

Six years in the making, *The Shocking Miss Pilgrim* was a great commercial success for Frederica and Ernest.

Frederica Sagor Maas with Ozzie Roberts, feature writer for the *San Diego Union Tribune*, in 1998. Photograph by Hal Eshelman.

Frederica relaxing at home in La Jolla, California, in 1997. Photograph by Mary-Jane Wiesinger.

in love with his patient. Doris, who is engaged to Jack White, a conventional businessman played by Frederic Kovert, also falls head-over-heels in love with the doctor. He adroitly analyzes her mental distress—and the reason for seeking his help—to be caused by loving the wrong man. When Doris breaks her engagement and declares her intention to marry her doctor, her fiancé is not about to accept his rejection gracefully. He decides to manufacture a past for the physician. In the army, the fiancé had been in a musical playing a female role. To thwart the romance now, he decides to impersonate a French wife for the doctor. The doctor and patient elope to the same hotel where the fiancé-impersonator is staying. He has enlisted the cooperation of the house detective by convincing him that he is the deserted wife of the doctor and is seeking revenge on "her" faithless husband whom "she" no longer loves. There is the dangling promise that "she" is attracted to the house detective and that they will become sweethearts when "she" has taught "her" husband the lesson he has coming to him. The vulnerable detective falls in with the scheme to expose and break up the marriage of the newlyweds before it can be consummated.

What follows is sheer bedlam. The newlyweds arrive, and things begin to happen. The bride is baffled and decimated at the appearance of the doctor's "wife." The doctor, of course, protests that he has no wife, French or otherwise. But how to convince his bride on their wedding night? There are chases in the halls, mixups in rooms, and a final solution when the fiancé's wig comes off, disclosing his real identity.

Complicated? Ridiculous? Of course. The definition of "farce" in the Random House dictionary is "A light humorous play in which the plot depends upon skillfully exploited situations rather than upon a development of characters. A foolish show. A mockery." There you have it: *The First Night* in a nutshell. It was the ultimate in foolishness.

The First Night was not one of my proudest or happiest accomplishments. Secretly, I was a little ashamed of it. I knew the script was over-developed, but when working for an independent company, on a deadline, where time is of the essence, there just were not enough hours left in the day or night to streamline it. I was guilty of over-inventiveness, much unnecessary business—flaws I had accused my former collaborator, F. Hugh Herbert, of committing on *The Waning Sex*, proving that all writers are vulnerable to committing the sin of overwriting.

But social relevance or literary quality were not my producers' concern. Much to the satisfaction of Tiffany, *The First Night* received good reviews and played long runs. *Variety* said aptly, "The picture got reams of laughter and, after all, that's what counts." Plus, the picture was brought in ahead of schedule, so my remuneration included another thousand-dollar bonus. With the money earned at Tiffany (well over ten thousand dollars), I was able to clean up all my debts and have enough left over for a bank account again.

The time had come for me to do some soul-searching. I was not in love with Henry Victor, nor he with me; our relationship had grown stale. My mother and sisters, sensing from my letters that I was unhappy in my work and lonesome, urged me to come back home. I was ready to quit the picture business.

Chapter 9

MEETING ERNEST MAAS

THE THOUGHT OF SPENDING the rest of my career writing flimsy fare like *The First Night*—to say nothing of contending with studio politics and the insanity of Hollywood life—had become unbearable. Perhaps, I reflected, my true vocation lay in writing novels and short stories and not in the movie business at all.

The more I considered this possibility, the more excited I became. If I turned out short stories of quality, I thought, magazines would surely buy them. If I had something to say in a novel, how could it fail to get published? I made up my mind to pack up and quit Hollywood, go to San Francisco, get myself a secretarial job, and write in my spare time . . . nights . . . weekends. If I found out I was not a Hemingway or a Sinclair Lewis, I could always sell real estate or insurance. Or get married!

Before I turned out the light and slumbered on this momentous decision, I picked up a copy of *Variety* lying on the bed table and scanned it. Why I should have given a hoot about anything in *Variety* now that I had made up my mind to wean myself from the Hollywood scene, God only knows. It was an addiction, I suppose, to this rag of information, this Holy Bible to all who worked in films.

In *Variety,* I read that my old boss, John C. Brownell, now story editor of Republic International Film, was in town. I reached him the next morning at the studios on Gower Street. "I'm quitting the picture business, John," I informed him dramatically. "I have some plans and need your advice. Could we take lunch?"

Musso-Frank's restaurant was crowded, as usual, at lunch hour. It was popular with Hollywood entertainment people. Opened in 1919 by two young Italians, now gone to their reward, it had a reputation for first-class cuisine with a French emphasis, quiet elegance, low-key lighting, and rich mahogany accents (especially in its commodious private eating booths). Its waiters were tiptop veterans. To wait on table at Musso-Frank's was a coveted diploma in the restaurant fraternity. Busboys were willing to work for a pittance in the hope of rising one day to the status of waiter at this fine eatery.

     After a short wait, John and I were shown to a center booth by the maitre d'. I ordered a mushroom omelette soufflé, one of my Musso's favorites. Musso's provided a generous assortment of hors d'oeuvres—heavy on olives, radishes, scallions, celery, and carrot sticks—and a basket of crisp, sourdough French bread and bread sticks.

     John listened with interest to my plan to move to the Bay City. He showed sympathy and understanding but was definitely opposed to the idea, feeling strongly that I had achieved more success than I realized and that I should hang on and not throw in the sponge just yet. He made me promise to reconsider my decision seriously. While we talked, I savored my mushroom omelette soufflé and became increasingly aware of the occupants of the adjoining booth or, more correctly, conscious of one occupant who was facing me—a young man in his middle thirties. There was something unusual, distinguished, about him and, at the same time, something familiar. He could have passed as a twin of Irving Thalberg—the same olive complexion; the same sensitive, inquisitive eyes and shy smile. Short in stature like Thalberg, he too projected a tall, impressive personality. It was evident that this young man was watching our booth with special interest. In my feminine conceit, I assumed that his interest was in me. And I was glad that I had chosen my favorite outfit for this occasion: a chalk-white, elegantly tailored sharkskin dress with a full-length black velvet coat, perky black velvet bonnet, high-heeled patent pumps, and patent pocketbook. It was a chic outfit that poor Antoinette had made for me. As it turned out, I was not the attraction that brought him over to our table.

     "John," he said warmly, "what are you doing here? It's great to see you again."

     "You remember Ernest Maas," John said to me. "You always complained about the way he barged into my office without waiting to be announced." Of course! I now remembered the arrogant young man who had no respect for female assistant story editors.

"Ernest is a new producer at Fox," John explained. "If I know him, he'll be running the studio before long."

Forgetting my presence, the chauvinistic producer continued to chat with my former boss. Then, taking his leave, he bowed stiffly in my direction, perfunctorily murmuring, "So nice to see you again, Miss Sagor." He returned to his own table. How quaintly old-fashioned, I thought—bowing to a lady. Yet I rather liked it. However, since he professed no further interest in our table, I gave him no more mind.

A week later, I received a phone call from Bill Conselman, now a producer at Fox as well.

"How about dropping in to see my new office at the studio," he invited. "I'll show you around and maybe even buy you a lunch."

Bill's idea of lunch was a "drinking lunch" in one of those dark cafés where you can't read the menus or see what you are eating. He had just returned from a month's holiday in Paris and New York, his first visit to either city. All he could remember were the wonderful Bloody Marys he had consumed in Paris and the wonderful daiquiris in Twenty-One and Sardi's in New York City. If he attended the theater or visited any art galleries or ancient cathedrals, he forgot to mention it. Across the continent, across the ocean—what a long way to go just for a drink, I thought, feeling sorry that life had apparently no interest for him beyond getting stoned.

"By the way," I inquired, "do you know an Ernest Maas? He's a new producer on the lot, I believe."

"Ernie—Ernie Maas? Sure I know him; like him, too. Smart fellow. No phony. Nice little guy. You know him?"

"Not really," I replied. "Met him at Musso's last week. You wouldn't happen to know where his office is?" I found myself trying to be very casual.

We had returned to the Fox lot by now, and poor Bill was too stiff to show me around the studio as he had promised. His instructions were "Turn left when you leave my bungalow and walk straight ahead. He's in the third bungalow on the right."

I had not planned this when Bill called and invited me to visit the Fox lot.

"Why are you bothering to look up this man?" I asked my compact mirror as I powdered my nose and freshened my lipstick. The answer was simple: "It can never hurt a writer to make contact with an up-and-coming producer. Who knows? He might have in assignment up his sleeve." It was worth a try.

But the answer did not satisfy me, and as I followed Bill's instructions and neared the third bungalow on the right, I began to have second thoughts about intruding upon a man I hardly knew. He might be too busy to see me—in story conference, perhaps. Vain peacock that I was, I wished that I had worn my Frenchie-smart navy outfit—the one that had won much flattering comment. Instead, I was wearing an expensive, but somber, wool ensemble: a tailored black dress with white piqué collar and a jacket and hat trimmed with Persian lamb.

"Oh, well," I thought, "what difference does it make? Judging from the brush-off at Musso's, he'll probably never notice what I am wearing, anyway."

The door of the bungalow was partly ajar, nearly closed, so I knocked ever so lightly. No one answered. I timidly pushed the door open. He was seated at his desk, lost in concentration, reading a script. I observed that his sartorial coordination was flawless. He was wearing a blue-striped button-down shirt, British school tie, gray cashmere jacket, and light tan trousers.

"He knows how to dress," I noted. He was puffing away on a briar pipe, filling the room with the scent of fine tobacco. "Why, Miss Sagor," he exclaimed in pleasant surprise, rising and coming to meet me. I was relieved. He remembered my name, and he did not seem displeased to see me. On the contrary, he seemed to welcome the intrusion.

We talked for about an hour—shop talk, mostly. I told him what I had been doing. I could see he was impressed and genuinely interested. He told me that he had just returned from location in Jasper National Park, in Canada, where he had been supervising the production of *The Country Beyond,* a James Oliver Curwood story that Irving Cummings was directing. He and Cummings had collaborated on the script. He had only one regret, and that was that he had barely an hour to make the trip to the glacier. But he managed to reach it, see its awesome grandeur, and dash back in time to make his train. Sol Wurtzel, overall head of production at Fox, had wired him to return to work on *The City,* an original story that was floating around the studio and that Roy Neill was to direct. In fact, that was the script he had been reading when I came in.

Finally, not wanting to wear out my welcome, I got up to leave. "You have a phone number no doubt, Miss Sagor?" he teased. "Yes, Mr. Maas, I do," I assured him.

"If I promise to use it, will you give it to me?" he asked. He did not have to ask twice. He jotted it down on a pad on his desk. Two weeks passed, and he did not call. "Well, that's that. My shot in the dark didn't work," I thought. But I was premature; he did call a few days later.

"Miss Sagor," he inquired almost diffidently, "would you care to be my guest next Saturday night at a dinner-dance Fox is giving at the Ambassador? I must forewarn you, Miss Sagor, I don't dance." On Saturday, punctually at seven, my doorbell rang. My escort, looking very comfortable in his tux, stood in my doorway with a boxed corsage of white and purple orchids.

"I hope these will go with your dress," he said, eyeing the pastel chiffon evening gown I was wearing, the same Antoinette creation I had worn to that unhappy affair at the Ambassador. We had two glasses of sherry before we took off. Then he helped me into my silver brocade evening wrap and helped pin the corsage to the white fox collar.

"You'd better take a scarf for your hair; I have my top down." His car was a two-seater maroon Chrysler roadster. It was a windy evening, and I was glad he had suggested the scarf.

Unlike the MGM orgy, the Fox affair at the Ambassador was like a family get-together—good food, drinks, and music—the best bands— Gus Arnheim, Abe Lyman—heavenly to dance to. And I danced the evening through with plenty of partners. I waltzed with Sol Wurtzel, Irving Cummings, John Stone, and Jack Ford and fox-trotted with Henry Dunn (brother-in-law of William Fox) and Lou Tellegen, scheduled to make a film at Fox. I had one dance with Tom Mix, Fox's bread-and-butter Western star.

We were seated at the table of honor with Sol Wurtzel. My escort kept the ladies at the table amused while their spouses were on the dance floor. He seemed pleased that I was having a good time. He was "Ernest" now, and I was "Freddie." "Freddie suits you," he decided.

At eleven o'clock, I was dancing with Jack Ford again. "What say, Fritzie, we duck this pain-in-the-neck shindig and take in a burlesque show on Main Street?" "John, you're brilliant," I applauded. "I'll tell Ernest, and you get Mary." Mary was his wife.

It was 2:00 A.M. when the four of us left the burlesque theater, said our goodnights, and went to our cars. But it was nearly 5:00 A.M. when Ernest Maas and Frederica Sagor returned to her hideaway apartment in the hills of West Hollywood. With the top down, we had driven all the way to Malibu and back with me snugly wrapped in a car blanket to ward off the ocean breezes. And we were still talking—after talking for three hours straight from the time we left Main Street until now—when we turned the engine off. We had covered every subject—our careers, literary preferences, political points of view, evaluation of people, likes, and dislikes. In all the time I had been in Hollywood, I had encountered no one so knowledgeable, discerning, and voluble with such a span of interests so close to my own.

We were silent now as a new day began to dawn. In silence, we repaired to my kitchen to make ourselves some coffee. Although we filled the coffee pot with water and the percolator basket with coffee, we did not turn on the burner. We had something else in mind.

The next day, I wrote Henry Victor. "Dear Henry," my letter began, "I feel it only fair that you be the first to know that I have met someone else and entered into a new relationship. This, of course, means a parting of the ways for us. I wish you well and offer particular thanks for introducing me to Herr Goethe. Sincerely, Frederica."

He wrote back: "Teuer Freundin: So it is to be farewell for us. I am happy for you. You will always remain a very special memory in my life because you are a very special person. The bard said it best: parting is such sweet sorrow. Henry Victor."

I never saw Henry again. After his contract ran out, he returned to the English stage and screen. According to *Variety,* which ran his obituary in 1936, he married and returned to California, bought a house in the valley, and went into real estate with his wife. One day, while gardening, he suffered a massive heart attack. Only thirty-eight! Much, much too young . . .

I showed both letters to Ernest. He read them and smiled but had no comment. While driving to Malibu that same night, he told me about a relationship he had had of some six years duration. Her name was Ruth Sheets, and she came from the South. She was related to the famous Sheets candy family (in the Huyler, Schraft tradition). She was a successful stockbroker, a financial wiz who worshiped money. They broke up when it became plain that their relationship had nothing going for it outside the bedroom.

"It was not an easy parting," he said. "I think Ruth had second thoughts, cared more than she realized. But it was too late. I knew we had to let go; it was best for both of us."

Now having told my newfound love about Henry Victor, we were even, ready to start two clean slates.

One of the most difficult things I have ever had to do was to tell Ernest I could not bear children. One night, after we had been seeing each other for about two months, I finally summoned up the courage. After an unusually profound and meaningful intimate encounter, I felt he had to know. After he had fully digested what I had told him, he shrugged his shoulders and said, very matter-of-factly, "Well, that's that."

"And what does 'that' mean?" I asked, feeling hollow inside.

"It means that it shouldn't alter our relationship one bit, Miss Sagor." It was his habit to address me that way whenever we had a particularly serious discussion. "Children are fine, if you want them," he went on. "But if I'd wanted a family I would have married long before this. I'm thirty-six going on thirty-seven, remember. An old curmudgeon of a bachelor." Then he paused and eyed me keenly. "But what about you?"

"I'm not sure," I said. "I love children. I feel cheated and sad to be denied the wonderful experience of motherhood."

"Children are children," was his reply. "There are a lot of babies out there; why does ours have to be a biological child? I should think it would be even more meaningful if it were a chosen child that somebody else could not care for."

The subject never came up again until shortly after we had returned from our honeymoon. We spent a Sunday afternoon picnicking with friends who had two very special youngsters, ages four and six, and they had completely won me over. When it came time for us to leave, they were loath to see me walk out of their busy lives. "Please, please don't go, Aunt Freddie," they begged, having adopted me into their family.

As Ernest and I were driving home, he observed, "You're pretty fond of kids, aren't you, Miss Sagor? Maybe we should adopt some."

I knew him well enough by this time to realize he was probing. "Let's wait," I replied cautiously.

And so we waited. As it turned out, we did not need a family to be happy and fulfilled. We were self-sufficient unto ourselves. Every day we were together we grew closer, leaving less room for the intrusion of children. Today, in retrospect, now that I am alone, I whisper to myself, "A son, a daughter, some grandchildren—that would be nice." But then, I have friends and their children, attentive nephews and nieces and their children. Yes, some great-great ones too, on both Ernest's side and my own. I am pleased and proud to know I have won their devotion and love. Ernest was right. They do not have to be your own.

Inasmuch as Henry Victor's friends were my landlords, I felt it prudent to move. I found a cheerful apartment in a red-brick, four-story house south of Hollywood Boulevard between La Brea and Highland on a quiet, dead-end street lined with jacarandas. It was called "El Palacio." My apartment looked out on a garden court. The warmly furnished sitting room had a desk that would hold my typewriter where I could work facing the garden. It had a bright kitchen and a bedroom. The apartment was number 326. I had a key made for Ernest.

Mrs. Gilbert, the apartment manager, let us know right from the start that she was a church woman and would stand for no hanky-panky of any kind. So we told her we were married, and she believed us. "You're a lovely couple," was her favorite greeting whenever we ran into her.

When, a year later, the newspapers heralded the forthcoming nuptials of Frederica Sagor and Ernest Maas, we wondered what Mrs. Gilbert thought when she discovered we had been living in sin all the while under her protection.

During the year I lived at El Palacio, Ernest continued to maintain his bachelor quarters at the Mayfair Apartments on Wilcox, north of Hollywood Boulevard. The Mayfair was under the management of Lucy Carter, a Massachusetts socialite who had come upon hard times and had a young daughter to support. Lucy Carter did not run as tight a ship as Mrs. Gilbert. A sophisticate, she became aware that one of her favorite tenants, Ernie Maas, spent many of his nights away from home, but few others were aware that he spent those nights at the domicile of Frederica Sagor. No one among our friends suspected that we were serious about each other, and so Mrs. Gilbert was not the only one surprised by the announcement of our coming marriage. In fact, it could be said that we could be included in their company. Our decision to get married, we liked to claim, was prompted by our decision to make a trip back to our hometown to see our families. How to explain that we were just living together? To avoid embarrassment, we opted for holy matrimony.

As I look back through the haze of time, ours was a trusting relationship—fifty-nine years of solid marriage after one exploratory year. Past relationships did not exist, had no importance, held no curiosity or interest. It was our future together that counted. We never quarreled about money—not once. We had disagreements—mostly about our work. One thing, for sure, we never went to bed angry or without saying, "I'm sorry."

Nine years older than I, Ernest Maas was a hard taskmaster. I was undisciplined and thought the world was my oyster. One of the bones of contention between us was my profanity. For instance, "bastard" and "son of a bitch" had slipped into my everyday vocabulary.

"I don't mind your calling someone a bastard if he deserves it," my taskmaster said. "But not every man is a bastard—you have to break yourself of that habit."

It was a warning I did not take seriously enough. We were riding on Hollywood Boulevard late one afternoon. Someone cut in front of us, nearly scraping our fender.

"That bastard, that son of a bitch!" I cried out. The roadster came to a standstill against the curb.

"Now you can get out and walk home, Miss Sagor," he ordered. I got out and stood dumbfounded as the roadster sped away without me.

Luckily, my apartment was not too far away. Still, ten blocks is a long walk. With every step, every block, my fury mounted, and my blood pressure rose. When I reached my apartment, I poured myself a stiff drink of Scotch with no chaser and smoked half a pack of Lucky Strikes, all the while seething at the demeaning treatment to which I had been subjected. Suddenly I realized how hilarious it was. Frederica Sagor had to walk home because she used forbidden words once too often.

"Of course the bastard is dead right," I told myself.

The telephone rang. "Am I forgiven?" he wanted to know. He was. He was forgiven again when on another occasion he played a practical joke on me because of my excessiveness. I had a passion for large black olives, and whenever we went to Musso's I had our waiter bring me a special order of them. Imagine my shock to see our waiter wheeling a cart to our table, filled with dishes full of black olives.

"I thought I'd give you an extra treat tonight," Ernest explained with a straight face. Then we both started laughing. How could you get mad at a guy like this?

In those carefree days, both Ernest and I spent a great deal of our income on clothes; and I, being especially fashion-conscious, often sought the services of a private designer. This way I did not have to waste time shopping around in store after store. When I "lost" Antoinette, Ruth Collier steered me to Irene, an up-and-coming fashion designer then rapidly gathering a fine reputation through the film grapevine. Irene's very first shop was located in a shopping center near the University of Southern California and Vermont Avenue. It was a distinguished old neighborhood, not far from Adams, the street of resplendent mansions, but far from the hub of Hollywood fashion.

While Antoinette was primarily a dressmaker, with few designing skills, Irene was a full-fledged creative designer, rapidly building up a clientele. A handsome young woman you would not easily pass by, she was gracefully tall with a patrician carriage and a lovely head of light brown wavy hair that she wore in a bun at the nape of her neck. She didn't need makeup for she had an Irish complexion with a natural blush in her checks. Her eyes were blue-green and merry.

Irene did not remain a shopkeeper long. MGM, learning of her talents, signed her to a contract to head their wardrobe department and design clothes for their stars. She stayed there a number of years before opening her own salon and, under the "Irene" label, sold clothes to exclusive stores across the breadth of the U.S. Unfortunately, for all her success, Irene was a desperately unhappy woman. Mistress of a prominent Paramount director who was married and had several teenaged children, she longed for respectability. She and her paramour had met when Irene, just another Hollywood aspirant fresh from a university drama school, had a small part in one of his pictures. Instant attraction became permanent commitment, yet everyone involved in the unhappy triangle was devoutly Catholic, so divorce was out of the question.

I got to know Irene well; she had few friends she trusted. "I know I am a fool, Freddie," she confided, "but I can't let go. I guess I am a one-man woman." And I guess she was. After his premature death, there was never anyone else for Irene.

Not only did Irene design my trousseau, from delectable shimmery nighties to spiffy elegant evening frocks, but many of my work clothes as well. If Irene made me a successful dress or outfit, I would have it copied in different shades: blue, gray, tan. And of course, I had hats to match! Dobb's hats were my favorite. I bought these bell-like cloches by the half-dozen in different colors. Ernest liked clothes as much as I did, and he too had his shirts and suits custom-made. Looking back, this seems like an incredible period of extravagance and self-indulgence for both of us, but it would stand us in good stead. In the lean years ahead we would have plenty of good clothes to fall back on.

In preparation for marriage, I had given up my apartment. On the night of August 4, I was invited to occupy one of the twin beds in Frances Agnew's place. Frances was a writer I had met when I was at MGM. Since she had no car, I transported her back and forth to work. She lived in a small hotel on Hollywood Boulevard near Western Avenue. A spinster nearing fifty, Frances was far more excited than I was that at 11:00 A.M. the next day, on August 5, Ernest and I were to declare our commitment to each other at City Hall. She had a thousand questions.

"Frances," I pleaded, "let's call it a night. I'm bushed." Finally she was quiet, and we dropped off to sleep. But not for long. My bed was shaking, the building was groaning, the standing lamp near my bed was perilously waving back and forth, headed in my direction. Earthquake! I jumped out of bed.

The telephone. It was Ernest. "Just checking to remind you we have a date tomorrow," he said. "Good night, sleep tight," and he hung up. He didn't mention the earthquake, but of course that is why he called.

The ceremony at City Hall proved a moving experience. Henry Dunn and his handsome wife, Malvina Fox-Dunn (sister of William Fox), were our witnesses. Malvina and I both wore red and white carnation corsages. Henry and Ernest wore red carnation boutonnieres. I was clad in my Frenchie navy blue outfit, and Ernest wore a brown tweed jacket and gray flannel trousers. For "new" I carried a pair of beige Italian shorty kid gloves with embroidered cuffs, a wedding gift from Frances Agnew. For "old," a Swiss lace handkerchief that Malvina had used on her wedding day. For "borrowed," a pink garter belonging to Riza. All three still repose in my treasure box of memories. The judge, tall and graying, did not take his duties lightly. With considerable feeling, he sermonized on the meaning of holy matrimony. Ernest and I were both unexpectedly moved by his simple words and the solemnity of the occasion. How very different, I thought, from that day when Riza and Joe von Sternberg had made their vows before an inebriated judge in West Hollywood.

"I do," I whispered, trembling. As Ernest slipped the thin classic gold band onto the third finger of my left hand, his hand trembled too. We were not prepared to be so affected, either one of us. The lesson came home: marriage was not something to be taken casually.

Since our train did not leave until five, we had plenty of time after the ceremony to drive up Wilshire Boulevard to the Ambassador Hotel for a delayed lunch. What we did not expect was that Malvina and Henry had ordered champagne, a wedding cake, and a special luncheon spread. With our entrance, the musical trio played Wagner's Wedding March as we made our way to the festive table. Ruth Collier, Mary Ford, and others were there having "a girl lunch." They joined in our festivities, as did everyone else lunching there that day. Champagne corks popped, and everyone had a piece of wedding cake.

At five o'clock on the dot, last goodbyes said and rice showered upon us, the Santa Fe Chief left the station. We had a compartment and were glad to be alone. Tired but happy, neither one of us felt equal to eating a full dinner in the dining car, so we had sandwiches and coffee brought in to us. We retired early to read, Ernest in the upper berth, I in the lower, but by morning we were both sound asleep in the lower. After all, we were little people who could fit in comfortably together. We never used the upper in the remaining days of travel.

Our reservations were at the Buckingham Hotel on Fifty-seventh Street across from Carnegie Hall, a suite with a sitting room, bedroom, and kitchen. It was an old hotel but had an air about it. It was a favorite with musicians, many of whom lived there. We were made aware of this as soon as we arrived in our room. Someone was playing the piano on the floor below—a great artist, I knew at once.

"Who is that playing?" I inquired of the porter bringing in our luggage.

"Sergei Rachmaninoff," I was told.

This was a musical dividend I had not expected! The very idea— of staying in the same hotel and listening to the great composer in the throes of composition—was an unbelievable experience for me, loving music as I did. We heard him often throughout the week we stayed there. Then came the day when we entered the hotel elevator, and there he was! I was too shy to speak to him, and I imagine he would have summarily dismissed me if I had. Instead, I took notice of his famous hands. They were large, strong, and powerful, like his music.

The first thing that Ernie and I did when we arrived was call our families. I showed Ernest off first to my family—they were living on 137th Street and St. Nicholas Avenue then. When I rang the upstairs doorbell, I could hear Mama running down the long hall. She always ran.

"Mama, this is Ernest," I said, stepping back.

He put his arm around her little body and kissed her. "Mama," he said, "you have given me a wonderful present, and I thank you from the bottom of my heart." Mama's eyes filled with tears as she returned his embrace. From that moment on, he had Agnessa in the palm of his hand. Lilly and Papa were also captivated. You could not help liking Ernest. He had a way with him. Later in our marriage, he would look at me and say, "When you get silver in your hair, Schatz ('sweetheart' in German), I know what you are going to look like. You are your Mama's daughter to a 'T.'" And he was right.

We spent the whole afternoon at the Sagors'. For dinner we went to the Maases, who lived on Ninety-third Street and West End Avenue. When Ernest rang the doorbell, his brother Lester answered. He was a bespectacled intellectual, slightly shorter than Ernest and two years older, a chemical engineer with a master's degree from Columbia University. He was also, unfortunately, chicken-breasted, because in infancy a careless nurse had picked him up the wrong way and injured his spine.

Ernest introduced us, and we shook hands warmly. Also there were Ernest's youngest sister, Bert, who was my own age and unmarried, as well as his mother. Sophie Maas was a beautiful woman even in her declining years. I saw at once how much Ernest resembled her.

"Freddie, my dear daughter," she laughed girlishly. She had just the trace of a German accent. "You deserve a medal. I was beginning to think I would never get rid of him. Now I see why I have." What a lovely compliment coming from my new mother-in-law.

Ernest's family background was German. He, too, as they say in German, was "ein spatle," which roughly stated means "split down the middle"—half Orthodox Jew on his father's side, half Protestant-Lutheran on his mother's. His father's family came from a picturesque little town in the Netherlands called Maastricht, astride the Maas River as it flows south toward Belgium to become the Meuse, with the Belgian border a scant three miles west and Germany a little more than twelve miles east. His mother's people, the Salzers, came from Stuttgart, Germany, and had a connection with the famous Jantzen Mills.

Ernest's great-uncle on his father's side, Adolph Hirsch, had been a successful clothing salesman in New York, netting ten thousand a year in salary and commissions (an impressive sum in those days). He had financed his young nephew Louis's (Ernest's father) journey to America in 1889. Uncle Adolph decided that what young Louis needed was a liberal American education and some quick exposure to the English language. So, that same year, Louis was sent out West as a salesman of Stetson hats to rich cowboy ranchers who could afford them. At nightfall one evening, tired and very hungry, he entered a Tucson, Arizona, beanery. "I would want a nice sirloin steak," he ordered in his heavy German accent. The proprietor, disliking foreigners, bristled: "You'll get a chuck steak and like it! Or leave, you god-damn greenhorn kike!" Louis Maas was getting a quick, liberal American education, all right.

Louis Maas and Sophie Salzer met in a bakery-restaurant on Grand Street in the ghetto of New York. Sophie was on her knees scrubbing the linoleum floor. Louis took one look at the young beauty, fresh off the boat, and proposed. Married at the city hall—although no official records are left to prove it—they had seven children. The oldest, Lester, was born in 1889; Ernest in 1891. Other siblings followed in quick succession—Ernestine, Martha, Phillip (who died in infancy), Irving, and Berta, all born after 1893.

A year after their city hall marriage, Louis and Sophie had saved up enough money to buy the bakery-restaurant on Grand Street. They spruced it up and renamed it "Cheese Cake Louis." They hired the finest bakers they could find, bakers who were always being lured away by big hotels and exclusive restaurants like Lorbers near the old Metropolitan Opera House. The food was fantastic and offered at a price people working in the neighborhood could afford. For seventy-five cents it was a soup-to-nuts menu, and the reporters of the *New York World*, which was downtown then, made Louis's their hangout. Department stores such as Best and Lord & Taylor were also downtown then. Sophie, whether pregnant or not, officiated as cashier and also kept an eye on the kitchen help. Louis bought the food and bakery supplies. Fulton Market saw him every day at the crack of dawn. Sophie's older brother, Otto, was in charge of the baking. Emma, Sophie's pretty, younger, coquettish sister, was behind the bakery counter. She was engaged to Eugene, the headwaiter. It was pretty much a family affair.

The business prospered from day one. Sophie kept having babies. Louis joined Tammany Hall, the corrupt political machine that ran New York City at the turn of the century, and opened a big gambling casino over the restaurant. The family's living quarters, ten rooms on two floors, were over the gambling casino. They employed two housemaids, a cook, and a sterling nurse-companion named Elsie for the children. Elsie helped raise the children from infancy, never married, and effectively became a member of the family.

As he grew richer and richer, Louis Maas developed a taste for antiques. Unschooled though he was, he had an eye for the good things, rare things, real finds. When moving pictures came along, Louis Maas got the fourth picture-theater license in New York City. His nickelodeon was a gold mine, but his only interest in his little theater was the cash box. At a nickel a head, there was a nice bonus to be collected every day, money to be converted into antiques.

As the children grew older, Louis and Sophie decided they needed a better environment, so they made the jump to the posh West Side, a Riverside Drive apartment in the eighties across from the Schwab mansion. This proved a traumatic change for Ernest and Lester, who soon discovered they were not easily accepted by their aristocratic new playmates. Rejected and homesick, they would sneak downtown to the old neighborhood whenever they got the chance.

Louis and Sophie wanted the best education for their children. For Lester, it was Columbia, where he became an outstanding chemical engineer. For Ernest, it was New York University Law School. Ernest studied law because his father's heart was set on it. But his own heart was set on writing plays. Secretly he had turned out two plays, one of which was bought by the Washington Irving Square Players in Greenwich Village. While scholastically Ernest was a brilliant student and earned a Master Law Degree, he never liked the legal profession with its hypocritical pursuit of justice. He was head of a small group of students with similar opinions. Sitting in the last row of their classes, they smuggled in Eugene O'Neill plays between their legal briefs. Some of them became journalists, others found their place in Broadway productions, and a few went to work in the motion picture industry.

Suddenly the fortunes of Louis and Sophie began to deteriorate. They lost their baby, Phillip, to crib death. The casino was closed after an exposé of Tammany Hall brought about a cleanup of New York City gambling and crime. Worst of all, Louis, a weak man, allowed himself to be seduced by Sophie's predatory sister Emma, now married to Eugene, the headwaiter; heartache and bitterness came to the Maas family. When Louis came to his senses and ended the dreary affair, Sophie understood and forgave him, but his two teenage sons could not and never spoke to him again until he was on his deathbed.

Louis did all he could to prop up his sagging fortunes. He opened a new restaurant. He poured every cent he had into it and borrowed the rest. It was a palace. The finest artisans decorated the walls, the ceilings, even the marble floor. But there was one thing wrong—Louis failed to recognize that the neighborhood was changing. With the exodus of the *New York World,* Lord & Taylor, Best, and other businesses to uptown Manhattan, his restaurant failed and he was bankrupt. Borrowing again, Louis and Sophie went back to their beginnings and opened a little bakery-lunchroom. Then Louis developed incurable cancer and his rags to riches to rags story came to an end.

Ernest and Sophie carried on the business without him, the teenager working at his mother's side after school. He never forgot how exhausted they both were when they took the subway home after midnight. But Sophie was an intrepid woman, determined to hold her family together. She fretted about Ernest neglecting his studies and spending so much time helping her, but she never fretted about herself.

Ernest graduated from New York University Law School with honors. And passed the bar exam. He was about to join an outstanding law firm when one day he ran into an old classmate. "How're you making out?" his school friend inquired. He was one of the malcontents from the back row.

"I'm joining a law firm next week," Ernest replied. "What are you doing?"

"I'm working at a motion picture studio in Long Island," was the reply. "I'm a film cutter."

"What's that?" After the explanation, Ernest asked casually, "They busy out there—looking for people?"

Good-bye law forever! Hail the glamorous new world of moving pictures. Ernest took to the new medium immediately. He became involved in active production right from the start and found it to be the perfect outlet for his creativity and energy. It was his idea to combine the evening newsreel with short subject features, and it went over. He was its editor and producer. Called the "Paramount Magazine," it soon became as popular in theater fare as the feature picture.

One day Ernest received a telephone call from an independent producer named Harry Levey, who was commissioned to produce an important film for the League of Nations. He wanted Ernest to write the script. The story, called *Uncle Sam of Freedom Ridge*, was written by Margaret Prescott Montague and had appeared in *Harper's* Magazine. The studio gave Ernest permission to undertake the assignment. He was delighted and wrote a powerful story that President Wilson proclaimed to be the best to come out of the war. Its theme brought the need for a league of nations home to the people.

The premiere of the film was held at the Selwyn-Cohan and Harris Theater on Forty-second Street in New York on Sunday evening, September 26, 1920. It was a very prestigious affair. The impressive invitation listed such distinguished guests as the President and Mrs. Woodrow Wilson, then-judge Hon. Franklin D. Roosevelt, Hon. Josephus Daniels, Hon. Newton D. Baker, Hon. William G. McAdoo, Mr. Raymond V. Ingersoll, Hon. Oscar S. Strauss, Mrs. Carrie Chapman Catt, Mrs. J. Borden Harriman, Rev. Stephan S. Wose, Governor James M. Cox, Mr. Charles M. Schwab, Miss Ruth Morgan, and Hon. James W. Gerard.

The picture drew strong criticism from those opposed to the league. As a result, a bill was passed by Congress forbidding government funds to be used for propaganda of any kind. Happily, *Uncle Sam* was completed before it became law. Today the script of *Uncle Sam of Freedom Ridge* belongs to the Academy of Motion Picture Arts and Sciences, reposing in their archives.

With this achievement behind him, Ernest returned to the Long Island studio in Astoria. When the Union of American Hebrew Congregations called on Adolph Zukor, head of Famous Players–Lasky (later Paramount) to make a film that would depict the story of the emigration of Jews to America, Ernest was chosen to write and direct it. The resulting film, *The New Dawn*, was shown at the convention of the Hebrew Union. Fox studios had also made a film on the same subject, which was to be shown after *The New Dawn*. When the Famous Players picture was screened, it received a standing ovation. William Fox, president of Fox Films, standing in the back of the convention hall during the screening, realized that the cheap, inept Fox film was no match for *The New Dawn*, made by the proud little fellow everyone was congratulating. Chagrined, Fox left the convention hall before the screening of his own film; he could not face the embarrassment.

After *The New Dawn*, Ernest wrote and directed a film called *Human Dividends*, made for the Federation for the Support of Jewish Philanthropies. The film showed the welfare, medical, and educational work carried on by the institutions supported by the Federation. He was then asked to write and produce *Keep the Home Fires Burning* by The American Defense Society; this film depicted the birth of a greater America after the war. It was shown in Atlantic City on the eve of the war's end.

Ernest hoped, even as a certain story editor for Universal had hoped, that Paramount would reward his achievements by sending him to the Coast to direct and produce. But Paramount did not see fit to give him anything except an almost invisible increase in salary. So he accepted an offer from Baumer Films, which produced commercial, industrial, and educational films, to join the firm as director of production.

Under the Baumer banner, the first important picture made was for the Transit Commission. Called *Standing Room Only*, it had a cast of more than thirty. The picture covered the evolution of transportation, with scenes of cow trails winding through New Amsterdam, then continuing to the horse-car, the wood-burning locomotive, the surface car, and the elevated and subway trains.

The introduction of three movie cameras clicking in the underground at the Grand Central station at eight o'clock in the morning, during subway rush hour, caused a sensation. Three high-powered arc lights, each about five feet in diameter, flooded stairways and halls with a blinding blaze. The lights were turned off as the trains approached so that motormen would not get confused. Police, reserved from the East Fifty-first Station and under Capt. George Haerle, took charge as the crowd of subway passengers fought for a glimpse of the action. No one was hurt, but hats were ripped from women's heads, and bundles and parcels were knocked to the floor.

In all this pandemonium, the cameras cranked steadily until a few minutes before nine. Director Maas had accomplished what he had come for—an outstanding documentary showing the subway system at rush hour.

Leroy T. Harkness, commissioner, and Marie de Montalbo, executive secretary for the Commission, had this to say about the picture: "We feel that in the Transit Commission film, the Baumer Company produced a remarkable piece of work. The success of this picture has exceeded our expectations."

After a year, William Baumer, though only sixty-two, retired in order to travel and pursue his hobbies. He turned his thriving business over to Ernest, who changed the name of the company to Roycroft Productions, with impressive new offices at 1482 Broadway. Business continued to pour in.

Films Ernest produced during this period included *The Ghost in the Crucible—Down Through the Ages*, a film about the gas industry; *Under the Eagle's Wing*, an exposé of the conditions of alms houses for the elderly; and *The Valley of Fair Play*, a picture made for the Endicott-Johnson Corporation of Endicott, New York, with a story celebrating labor in the shoe industry. There was a six-reel film *Physiotherapy* made for the Government Reconstruction Hospital in Fox Hills, Staten Island, dealing with the technique of using forms of energy in the treatment of disease and disability. Another film, made for Midland Fisheries, showed the arduous business of fishing.

When the Miami Biltmore was opened, Jack Beaumont, head of the Biltmore chain of hotels, asked Ernest to come to Miami to film its launching. The hotel was far from ready, only half furnished, with workmen everywhere, painting, hammering, completing the finishing touches. Furniture was still being brought in. Only two floors were open for the invited guests, who were in the lobby with their luggage, waiting to be assigned to their rooms. It was a scene of good-natured confusion; after all, this was sunny Miami, and everyone was on holiday. Besides, the Biltmore was picking up the tab.

Since Miami was so close to Cuba, Ernest thought this a good opportunity to visit his newlywed sister, Ernestine, and her husband, Sidney Horen, who lived in Havana. Sidney had been put in charge of Fox's Cuban film office. It was his job to see that every last peso went into the Fox coffers from the exhibition of their films. On the boat from Miami to Havana, Ernest met William J. Fox.

"You look familiar, young man," Fox said,

"Perhaps you've mistaken me for my brother, Irving, Mr. Fox. He works in your foreign department."

"Yes, yes, that's right," said Fox. "You two do look very much alike. What are you reading?" Ernest handed him the book tucked under his arm. "*Why We Behave Like Human Beings,*" he read aloud, looking impressed. "Damn good book. This fellow, George Dorsey, has a good mind." He returned the book, and with that they parted.

Two days later, when Ernest went to visit his new brother-in-law in his downtown Havana office, he was pleasantly surprised to find William Fox talking with Sidney. Mr. Fox seemed equally surprised and pleased to see him.

"After you left me, young man," Fox said, "I recalled where I had seen you before. You're the fellow who put me to shame with that damned fine picture you made for Zukor—*The New . . .*" He hesitated.

"*Dawn,*" supplied Ernest.

"Damned fine film," Fox repeated. "You seem well connected with Fox Films—a brother, a brother-in-law—why don't you look us up when you get back to New York. Fox might add you to the family, too."

Ernest forgot about the invitation when he returned to New York. Just starting a new picture, he had plenty of other things on his mind. But Fox did not forget, and now Winnie Sheehan, vice president and general manager of Fox Film Corporation, was on the phone. "Mr. Fox wants to see you. How about three o'clock tomorrow at my office?"

And that's the way it happened. Ernest kept the appointment and received an offer no man in his right senses could refuse. A three-year contract to write, direct, and produce, at twelve hundred dollars a week. It was probably more money than most directors, producers, or even executives were getting, not to mention writers! But Ernest had a successful business and had to be coerced.

"I expect you to be our Irving Thalberg," Fox decreed as they shook hands on the deal. A large order, Ernest thought, but he was willing to try to fill it.

This, then, was the man I married on August 5, 1927. Talented but modest, serious but with an infectious sense of humor, creative, hardworking, sensitive, trusting, consecrated to his craft, patient, totally without malice. He restored my faith in the glamorous motion picture business, and I began to view it again with renewed hope, that effort and dedication would bring their just rewards.

I only wish they had.

Chapter 10

HONOR AMONG THIEVES

ERNEST HAD A MONTH'S REPRIEVE from Fox, and we had planned our honeymoon carefully. After a week in New York and a week spent in train travel, we had two precious weeks left after returning to Los Angeles. The first thing we did was pick up Ernest's Chrysler roadster, which Lucy Carter had taken care of in our absence. My Moon, stored in a commercial garage, caught the eye of a Rolls-Royce chauffeur who made me a good offer, and I sold it for cash. Lucy Carter had some interesting news. She was leaving the Mayfair and taking over the management of the Villa Carlotta, newly built on Franklin Avenue near Beechwood Drive. Half of her Mayfair tenants were leaving, including the Maases, and she offered to oversee moving Ernest's effects, as well as mine, which I had parked in his place while we were gone.

On a perfect day in mid-August, we took off in our maroon roadster for San Francisco. Choosing the winding scenic highway paralleling the Pacific Ocean, we passed Hearst's San Simeon Castle, where I had once been invited to stay. Big Sur, Pfeiffer State Park, was our first overnight stop. We were just in time to catch the last remnants of the setting sun as it spread over the Pacific and to tramp through the pine woods and the redwoods before darkness and supper. What a place to meditate, so quiet and serene, except for the chattering squirrels and the calls of the birds flying about us as they always do at the end of the day. Ernest and I returned many times to Big Sur in later years.

The next afternoon, we registered at the St. Francis Hotel in San Francisco and had dinner with some old friends of Ernest's. Mamie Stevens was a department store buyer of oriental art objects and jewelry. She took us to some Chinese wholesalers, and I had a ball. If I had not stopped him, I do believe my husband would have cleaned out the trays of fine gem jewelry that were put out for us to see. As it was, we purchased a set of apple-green jade ring, bracelet, and pin; a set of blood-red carnelian beads and pin to match; and a selection of loose semiprecious stones to be mounted when fancy dictated. I was enthralled with these purchases. Unlike Ona Brown, who preferred diamonds, this brunette preferred jade, carnelian, opal, amethyst—any of nature's semiprecious lovelies.

After a few days in San Francisco, we returned home by way of Highway 101, stopping first at Carmel and leaving the next day for Santa Barbara and the Miramar Hotel. There, we spent two restful, precious days walking the length of Cabrillo Boulevard skirting the blue Pacific. After stopping in Los Angeles overnight, we headed south to Laguna and La Jolla, where our honeymoon ended at Casa Mañana, a new hostelry with a series of private bungalows built around a central edifice, and furnished with fine art, tapestries, heavy oriental rugs, and two baby grand pianos. We read and walked and talked a lot, and made love moderately; our intellectual appetites were more insatiable. Today, the Casa Mañana has been converted into a home for senior citizens, in whose company, more than seventy years later, this senior citizen now includes herself—you might say she has come full circle.

Back in Los Angeles, we settled into our new home—a duplex apartment at the elegant Villa Carlotta, with a flower-painted beamed ceiling, a fireplace, and a Spanish-tiled kitchen. The Villa Carlotta was a fun place to live. Adolphe Menjou lived there, and Myron Selznick and Irwin Gelsey headed the list of tenants outstanding in the film business.

Louella Parsons, Regina Crewe and Herb Cruickshank, Dorothy Herzog, Riza Royce (after her divorce), and Frederica and Ernest Maas all lived on the third and fourth floors. We were chummy neighbors, running freely into each others' apartments borrowing this or that. We had a soup marathon going and jokingly said that we made "soup in a bathtub" because we made enough for everyone on both floors for a week. Each of us had a specialty. Ours (Ernest made it) was lentil;

Louella's was chicken; Dorothy Herzog made a mean chowder of clam, corn, or shrimp. Riza's was pea soup with frankfurters, and Regina Crewe and Herb Cruickshank made a French onion that was delicious.

Louella's apartment was across the hall from ours. Harriet, her daughter, was away at school but came home on holidays. Louella entertained a lot, and William Hearst and Marion Davies frequently attended her parties. I had never met Hearst but had seen him at the MGM studios when Marion made pictures there. It was a real shocker to talk to him because he was a huge man, but he had a tiny, shrill soprano voice. Marion Davies both adored and despised this man, who had bought her teenage favors by promoting her father to a federal judgeship. She was an exquisite girl but with absolutely no talent for projecting herself onto celluloid, despite the millions her paramour spent to elevate her to stardom. It was torture for her to act, to be funny (she was a chronic stutterer). But her Svengali was determined, so try she did. In her drunken moments, Marion railed bitterly against the man who truly loved her but could not get his wife to give him a divorce.

Marion and Hearst were in Magnin's Boutique on Hollywood Boulevard one time when I was in one of the fitting rooms having a suit altered. Hearst selected a number of gowns, and Marion went to the fitting room to try them on. As the salesladies helped her into the frocks, she opened her purse and extracted a silver flask filled with whiskey. The more she drank, the more she used the lovely words Ernest had broken me of using.

"I'm a slave, that's what. A toy poodle." And imitating a poodle, she directed, "Now doggie, turn around. That's a nice doggie. Wag your tail, doggie. Don't want to? Hell, you'd better if you know what's good for you!" It was hilariously funny to her but embarrassing to the rest of us. Yet when she reappeared before her lord and master and twirled around in her new finery, she was all smiles and laughter, and he was putty in her hands. Louella Parsons was a true friend to both of these lost souls. I think she felt compassion for her unhappy boss and his equally unhappy mistress. People trap themselves this way, and worldly goods and power do not make up for their misery.

Three years went by quickly, and Ernest grew more and more frustrated. He was not given many assignments, and it became clear that he did not belong at Fox. With his contract nearing its end, he was assigned to produce and direct a film starring the legendary Lou Tellegen. As a stage actor, Tellegen had captured many female hearts, including the heart of the great Metropolitan soprano Geraldine Farrar, who had kings and princes among her adoring suitors. Indeed, the dynamic, attractive songstress was swept off her feet enough to marry the empty matinee idol—to her regret when she came to her senses.

Sol Wurtzel had saddled Ernest with this ass, a catch-22 assignment. Lou Tellegen could not act; he could only strut. He was no longer young; in fact, he was passé. He did not know his day had come and gone. To Lou Tellegen, he was still the Great Tellegen, the magnificent actOR, with special emphasis on the "OR," and he was impossible to handle. He threw tantrums (and leading ladies) on the set every day. He would not take direction. It was his way or no way. Ernest tried coddling, appealing to his ego. When that failed, he used sterner measures and dressed him down before the entire cast and crew. "Time out," he announced. "We will suspend shooting for today until Mr. Tellegen decides whether he wants to make this picture or forfeit his salary and the rest of his contract."

In private, Ernest was terribly discouraged. "This picture is going to break my neck," he kept repeating. "It's Sol Wurtzel's revenge." When Ernest first came on the lot, he declined an invitation to join the Jewish temple in which Sol Wurtzel was very much involved and supported. If you were to be a "Wurtzel man" and admitted into his narrow circle of loyal followers, you had to be a paying member of the Temple Israel. It did not matter if you were only half Jewish. What did matter was that you were Jewish enough to embrace Sol Wurtzel's kind of Judaism. Sol held all goyem in contempt—behind their backs, of course. Outwardly, he put on a smiling face and curried their favor. Men such as Winnie Sheehan, John Ford, William Hart, and Tom Mix had to be catered to, and Sol Wurtzel was a good caterer when he had to be.

For the first year of Ernest's West Coast contract, Sol Wurtzel was careful to handle Mr. Fox's protégée with kid gloves, hiding his true feelings. William Fox had given Wurtzel to understand that he considered Ernest to be another Irving Thalberg, who would do for Fox what Thalberg was doing for MGM. Through Henry Dunn, who was in Sol's inner circle, Ernest learned that Wurtzel had remarked,

"I'm going to break that little son of a bitch's neck. Who the hell needs another Irving Thalberg? I run the studio around here. My pictures make money. We give the stinking public what it wants. What we don't need around here are Thalbergs with crappy ideas for fancy, arty stuff. This is a business. If you want art go to a museum. To hell with that highbrow, high-faluting crap!"

Sol Wurtzel, known as "The Keeper of the B's" in the industry, was held in contempt by his equals. If some of them lacked schooling and polish, they were aware of it and bought schooling and polish in the people they hired and surrounded themselves with. Not Sol Wurtzel. He held contempt for anything he did not understand or did not want to understand. Not a literate man, he hated reading so much he would never read the scripts or books or stories that were bought. Everything had to be synopsized in plain, simple English. Ben Schulberg coined the phrase that summed up the man: "From bad to Wurtzel."

Wurtzel disliked anyone hired in the East, and he was not alone. From Louis B. Mayer down, there was always the suspicion, the fear, the dread, that "this is the guy they're grooming for my job." Few, if any, writers, directors, or producers hired in the East ever got anywhere; Wurtzel was not unique in "breaking their necks." East versus West rivalry pervaded all studios. The East was where the moneymen were, whose opinion was that those "nuts out there don't know what the hell they're doing. They must think money grows on trees the way they spend it!" And the West, where the pictures were made, felt held down by budgets that were inadequate and by criticism of their integrity. They believed the Eastern potentates knew nothing about creativity, cared about nothing but dollar-and-cents figures, and did not understand the ABCs of making films.

Ernest finished the Lou Tellegen picture, but it was never released. A disaster, it supplied the perfect excuse the "Keeper of the B's" was looking for to terminate the contract of Mr. Fox's wunderkind. If we had had any sense, Ernest and I would have returned East. Ernest could easily have set himself up in business again and returned to the making of documentaries, a field in which he excelled. But, instead, he was stubbornly determined to succeed on the West Coast. Strongly believing in him, I went along.

It had been a productive year for us. In addition to our studio work, we wrote three original stories and sold all three. We worked exceedingly well together—our adrenalin flowed, our creative minds were in harmony and provided stimulus to our inventiveness. But our story sales did not lead to screenplay assignments, nor were they ever made into films. Finally I got a lucrative assignment, of sorts—and at Fox, of all places. Chandler Sprague, a writer I knew, became the story editor at Fox and hired me to write the script for an original story by Winnie Sheehan, vice president of Fox.

When Sheehan chose to come West to try his hand at becoming a Hollywood producer, Sol Wurtzel really must have prayed hard when he davened on Friday night at Temple Israel, "Break his neck!" He did not have to wait long. Winnie Sheehan broke his own neck. And I was unintentionally instrumental in helping him break it. The vehicle was *The Farmer's Daughter,* a comedy especially conceived and constructed for a young comedienne named Marjorie Beebe. Who was Marjorie Beebe? It was widely rumored that she was the secret love of Winnie Sheehan. When I first saw her, she struck me, as she struck everyone else, as a plain, unattractive, overweight ingenue at whom you wouldn't take a second look. Yet here she was, slated for stardom and top billing. I was hired at $750 a week to write the story and script for her launching. The nicest part of the assignment was working with two witty and entertaining young gag men—Harry Brand and Henry Johnson—and a third, not-so-nice but important collaborator, the great Winnie Sheehan himself. He obviously had a stake in this picture because he had it on his mind night and day. The story was the old well-tried vaudeville skit of the city slicker (played by Arthur Stone) who goes after the farmer's daughter (played by Marjorie Beebe), intent on making her with lots of tumbling in the hay. It was so bad, so corny, it was nauseating. Yet, who were we to change the brainchild of the vice president of Fox? All that Harry Brand, Henry Johnson, and I could do was spoof it up all we could. We became hysterical at the gags we concocted—gags, of course, that never went into the script.

But if we were wild, it was nothing compared with the unhinged story mind of Vice Presidnet Sheehan himself. Several times a day we received such electrifying memos as the following: "Att'n—Frederica Sagor, Harry Brand, Henry Johnson: Suggest in Scene 24, Page 18, the hero comes down the hill on his motorcycle, sees the girl and is on the make and drives into a manure pile at the bottom of the hill. The girl laughs so hard at seeing him in the manure pile up to his neck, she slips and falls into the manure pile herself. In this way he manages to get hold of her and get the kiss he has been after. Think this would make a very funny love scene." Signed, W.J. Sheehan.

From memos like this, Brand, Johnson, and I knew that nothing we could dream up would be too unfunnily funny. It had to be slapstick, pure and simple. And when we got done the early Keystone comedies had nothing on us! All three of us decided that it was the worst material we would ever work on. The really hilarious part was that the broader our comedy, the better Winnie liked it—no, he loved it!

"Terrific!" he would red pencil. "Funny as hell. Keep it up."

But in the end I got my revenge. It fell to me, as the writer of the project, to do the full script. How do you write a script about a hero who keeps falling into manure piles and a heroine who simpers like an idiot and coos like a dove in her passion for the hero? Why, you write it free verse, of course! Tongue-in-cheek, I wrote a script in free verse. It was lyrical. It sang. It was a delicious fraud and everyone on the lot, including the mail department, got a kick out of it. But I am sure Winnie was unaware of my deception.

The picture was made with Arthur Rosson directing. I received full credit for the scenario. The audience laughed, I was told, but I could not get myself into a theater to see it. "Farce comedy," the bewildered critics dubbed it, "with some brand new angles on kidding." "While this will not rate as a first rate comedy, it has a refreshingly new slant on treating a lot of the old comedy situations, for which somebody should step up and receive three hurrahs." It was certainly the last hurrah for Winnie Sheehan as a producer and for Marjorie Beebe as an actress.

About this time, most of Los Angeles was in a tizzy over the disappearance of evangelist Aimee Semple McPherson. Her followers were desolate and gathered at her tabernacle to implore the Almighty to restore their prophet to them. Harry Brand, Felix Young and his wife, and Ernest and I had all visited the tabernacle before to watch Aimee's ecclesiastic antics. Now that she had mysteriously disappeared, we returned there to observe the hold she had on these people who so fervently believed in her. It was uncomfortable to sit beside these inconsolables, to witness their despair. How sad that people like these have to attach themselves to a cult, to bond themselves to a false enchantress claiming to represent the Almighty. They had filled her coffers in the face of their own poverty. After an hour we left the tabernacle feeling uneasy at what we had witnessed. Such misguided faith. Of course the ending to this night's drama was a cynical one. Aimee was "found" safe and sound—she had escaped for several weeks of forgetfulness with some secret lover.

That night, we all ended up in our apartment at Villa Carlotta where Ernest officiated as bartender. Harry Brand entertained us with a host of wonderful stories. He was a good raconteur once he got out of his shell. Harry was a shy man, perhaps because of his lameness, of which he was extremely self-conscious. I had met Harry through Harry Wilson, and we had dated. But it was my initiative that got us started. He was too timid to ask me, for fear I would turn him down. I am sure that when he was later elevated to the post of director of publicity and advertising for Twentieth Century–Fox he must have lost some of his early sensitivity. He married a capable woman, Sybil Brand, known for her whirlwind activities for charity and good causes.

On this particular night, Harry Brand left us at eleven, but Felix and his wife stayed for one last nightcap. It soon became clear why they had lingered. Felix came out with it. "Ernie, I'm in a terrible bind. I've accumulated some gambling debts and I'm being pressed to pay up—or else."

"How much do you need, Felix?" Ernest responded.

"Five thousand dollars."

Ernest went to the desk and took out the checkbook. I was about to have a heart attack. Five thousand dollars ain't hay. "I can't lend you five thousand, Felix," he said, "but I'll give you twenty-five hundred. Of course, I expect you to pay me back when you can. But if you can't, I hope you'll pass it on someday to somebody else." With that my husband wrote out the check and handed it to Felix. I was appalled. Everyone knew the reputation of Felix Young, the well-known restaurateur and New York nightclub owner. It was said he could sweet talk a cardinal out of his red hat. He came to Hollywood because he felt the pickings would be better there. His wife and he were a clever pair of manipulators who well deserved each other. And here my husband was forking out twenty-five hundred dollars to this opportunist, this gambler, this leech.

"I thought I was a soft touch but I must say you take the cake," I remarked after the Youngs had pocketed their check and departed. "How could you give that punk twenty-five hundred, just like that?"

"I've known Felix a long time," Ernest replied. "He lived on the East Side. We went to school together, and I'm well aware of his failings. I know he'll never pay it back. I know he's a gambler, always broke, that he's a heel who borrows money wherever he can. But I feel sorry for the guy. Don't ask me why. I just do." The subject was closed, but I could not help smiling inside. The man I married was a schnook, too. Just like his wife.

Ben Schulberg, for whom I scripted *The Plastic Age*, was now vice president in charge of production at Paramount Studios (which had finally shed the Famous Players–Lasky handle). He offered me a year's contract to join the writing staff. With the full confidence of his boss, Adolph Zukor, Schulberg had a free hand to put Paramount on top. There would be none of the waste, pompousness, stalling, or posturing of studios such as MGM. Schulberg ran the show, working long hours, overseeing all aspects of production, keeping control over everything. He was a just man, sensitive and compassionate, an executive you could talk to anytime you had a problem that had to be resolved. But Ben Schulberg had changed since I first met him. He was becoming boastful and cocky, and it was obvious that the strong wine of success was going to his head.

Schulberg had an efficient and loyal secretary, Henrietta Cohn. "Henry," as her friends called her, was a homely girl, but what people remembered about her was her big heart and warm smile. She was no fool and knew studio politics and the sycophants hanging around her boss's office. She distinguished the doers from the fakers. Keenly aware of her boss's weaknesses as well as his leadership abilities, she was his best friend, and he knew it, even if the boy in him defied authority and sound advice. Henrietta and I clashed when we first met because she thought I was just one more female supplicant out to win her boss's favor. Later, when we knew each other better, she accepted me wholeheartedly as a friend not only to her boss but to herself and her younger sister Gertrude, a friendship that endured for over sixty years.

One particular day I had something important to speak to Schulberg about. Henrietta was away from her desk and could not announce me. Having formed the habit of entering his office without knocking when I was at Preferred, I barged in now. Mr. Schulberg, vice president of Paramount in charge of production, had a young starlet on his lap. I hastily withdrew, realizing I should have knocked or waited for an appointment. What a faux pas; no man likes to be caught with his pants down!

Another shocker was to find Felix Young ensconced in a plush office as a Paramount producer. He and Ben were compulsive gamblers, and gossip had it that he owed Ben so much money that Ben decided to add him to the payroll. For all his intelligence, Ben Schulberg had an ego that had to be nourished by leeches like Felix Young. He had other friends, myself included, who told him the truth, who warned him against putting his trust in the wrong people, but he wouldn't listen. He also had enemies. One was Walter Wanger, head of Paramount studios in the East, a man with excellent connections with the New York banks that had invested in Paramount Pictures. The anti-Semitic actor, Adolphe Menjou, kept Wanger advised of the mounting gambling debts of the playboy Schulberg and his minion, Felix Young. But B.P.'s successful run of moneymaking pictures, and his efficient and economical management of the studio, stymied them. So they patiently waited for an opportune moment to topple him. That moment came soon enough in the person of Sylvia Sidney. The twenty-year-old, curvaceous, Lillian Gish type, picked from the Broadway stage by Mrs. Ben Schulberg herself, proved the instrument of Ben's destruction at Paramount and the tragic breakup of his marriage. This sunset romance was Ben Schulberg's downfall. He wagered everything on it and lost.

I had been assigned to a producer named Lloyd Sheldon, a former newspaperman but with none of the pleasant outgoing qualities usually found in gentlemen of the press. Mr. Sheldon was a first-class prig, serving in the "lowly" picture business that he heartily disdained—yet at a handsome salary. Surreptitiously, he was involved with a voluptuous young woman reader in the story department fifteen years his junior. Vera (I do not recall her last name) had an aristocratic Russian background. She too had condescended to be employed in the "lowly" picture business and was quite a snob. They later married and retired to a ranch in Santa Barbara.

I worked on four stories during that year with such teasing titles as *It, Red Hair, Hula,* and *Rolled Stockings.* The first three were Clara

Bow pictures. The fourth, *Rolled Stockings*, featured the new flapper star, Louise Brooks, with James Hall, Richard Arlen, and Ed Brendel. It was a college story patterned after *The Plastic Age*, but this time two brothers vied for the cute coed, and instead of football the sport was boat racing. Louise Brooks, who was a good actress, deserved better than this inane story. Like Frederica Sagor, she too was typed for this stupid fare, which the producers thought the public wanted. Flapper triviality, but good box office.

Rose Pelswick, film critic for the *New York Journal*, was inspired enough to write a poem after seeing the picture: "Were I asked to enroll in some college / I'd choose one like those on the screen. / The film halls of letters / mean parties and sweaters / and campus parades that are keen. / The students do nothing but frolic, / one wonders what courses they took. / And what's more, they were never / (or rarely, if ever) / shown owning or reading a book!" She also had this to say about the "Rolled Stockings" title: "Perhaps the reason why the producers named it that was because, hopefully, stockings get a run. Otherwise, try as this columnist has tried, it's impossible to see any reason for it." Other reviewers were much less kind. "Thanks to the untalented inept director, Arthur Rosson, who took a trite story and made it infinitely worse by his bad taste."

But there were lines around the Paramount Theater for all matinee and evening performances, for the run of the picture—not because of the film that was being offered (my picture) but because of the superlative program the theater built around it. In 1928, for the price of forty cents for weekday matinees, seventy-five cents at night, or ninety-five cents all day or night on Saturdays and Sundays, you had three hours of solid, quality entertainment before the feature went on: a full first-class orchestra and overture, a short subject about the romantic story of Robert and Clara Schumann, a magnificent organ recital, a cartoon, and the Paramount Newsreel. And to top it all, the great Charlot Revue with Gertrude Lawrence! Those were the days when cinema patrons really got their money's worth.

While I was working at Paramount I took Ernest in to meet B.P. I had the idea of Ernest joining the production staff there, where, with his background at Paramount in the East and his stint at Fox, he rightfully belonged. Ben Schulberg had expressed a keen curiosity about the man I had married. I expected it would be a constructive, healthy curiosity. But it was not. B.P. assessed him narrowly, cross-examined him, deliberately challenged him on a number of trivial points to deflate him, and seemed determined not to like him or be impressed by his background and qualifications.

I find it hard, even to this day, to forgive Ben Schulberg for that interview. Schulberg told me years later that Felix Young had talked Ernest down, said he was hard to get along with. Human nature being what it is, I suppose it would have been too much to expect gratitude for the loan/gift of $2,500!

I knew the caliber of the producers on the Paramount lot. They were an ordinary bunch then. David Selznick, a recent university graduate, was still learning the business. Buddy Lighton, the best of the bunch, was basically a lightweight. His passion was owning automobiles, and not just one or two. From the way he bragged about his acquisitions, he must have bought one every month; he could talk about little else. When I first met Buddy and his wife, Hope Loring, they were a couple of mediocre writers on the low end of the totem pole. They lived in a studio single off Sunset Boulevard and Fairfax Avenue and bused it, for they could not afford a car. But Hope Loring was a cleverer woman than I, for she succeeded in selling her husband's talent where I failed. Her tall, handsome husband, younger than she (her second marriage), looked like a producer, so Hope Loring, a manipulator and fast talker, got him elevated to play the role. Hope had a heart condition, which she played up to the hilt. It won her B.P.'s sympathy and helped her control her Buddy. She was the brains of their writing partnership. He needed her and could not afford to lose her.

With all that, I liked Buddy Lighton, and he liked me. He certainly was an improvement over the curmudgeon I was assigned to, Lloyd Sheldon. I tried my best (this time, diplomatically) to get Ben to transfer me to Buddy's unit, but it didn't work. I was stuck with Lloyd.

Ernest and I had sold a story to Fox earlier in the year. It was a sparkling, captivating little yarn about two salesmen, one male, one female, in the hosiery business competing for the same accounts. We called it *Free and Easy*. When released, Fox (typically) changed the title to *Silk Legs*. It starred Madge Bellamy. The leading man was James Hall, and the unimaginative, pedestrian director was Arthur Rosson (the same man I later worked with on *Rolled Stockings*).

At the same time that the story was presented to Fox, our agent, Ruth Collier, had submitted it to MGM. In fact, when we wrote it we had MGM's Norma Shearer in mind for the female lead. I had lunch with Sidney Franklin, a splendid director of light comedy and musicals at MGM, and told him the story. He liked it, took a copy, and said he would discuss it with Harry Rapf immediately. When Fox bid for the story, I called Harry to inform him of Fox's intention to buy it. But he did not believe me. He thought I was bluffing, pulling a well-known ploy to spark MGM's interest in the vehicle. "If Fox wants to buy it," he snapped, angered by my supposed ruse, "my advice to you is sell it to Fox."

So we did. Not too enthusiastically, I might add, and for less money than it would have brought through competitive bidding. We knew that an MGM production was bound to be superior. Their budget would be twice that of Fox, and Norma Shearer with Sidney Franklin directing was about the ultimate in production. But those are the breaks writers are faced with. Mr. Rapf's reaction gave no indication that MGM was interested in the story.

Several weeks after I had sold the story to Fox, I received a phone call from Henry Dunn, who, having left Fox, was now working at MGM as a writer. "Do you know MGM has made copies of your story, Freddie," he informed me, "and they've taken your name off. I thought I should let you know." "But we sold the story to Fox," I protested in disbelief. "I told that to Harry Rapf."

"Well, it's not your headache," he laughed. "Fox has a legal department. It's their problem now, not yours. Let Rapf and Wurtzel fight it out." I still did not fully believe it. It was beyond my ken to think of MGM having the audacity to pull anything so bizarre, so plainly dishonest. It had been in the trade papers, after all, that we'd sold the story to Fox. I believed it finally when, one day in my Paramount office, I got a phone call from a very irate Sol Wurtzel. "What's the big idea, Miss Sagor?" he asked. "Where did you get the nerve to sell a story to two companies?"

"I don't understand, Mr. Wurtzel. What do you mean?" My voice shook.

"I mean, Metro is shooting the same goddamn story with Norma

Shearer. That's what I mean!" Then I remembered what Henry Dunn had told me. "Then, Mr. Wurtzel," I replied as calmly as I could, "I think you had better have your legal department take action against MGM at once. They have stolen Fox's story. I no longer own it. Fox does."

"Then you didn't sell it to MGM?"

"Of course not, Mr. Wurtzel. It was submitted to them by my agent for consideration, but they evinced no interest, so I sold it to Fox."

"Those momsers," he exclaimed, letting forth a stream of other imprecations equally unflattering. The crude "Keeper of the B's" was so mad, he ran out of expletives and slammed the receiver down.

The irony, of course, was that MGM made a perfectly beautiful picture, far superior to the legitimate Fox production, *Silk Legs*. Madeleine Ruthvin, Harry Rapf's secretary, told me that when Wurtzel called Rapf to protest MGM's ruthless plunder, he let loose a burst of profanity that had the telephone wires sizzling. But did they sue? MGM and Fox might be competitors, rivals, hate each other's guts, but they did not sue. Remember, there is honor among thieves.

Chapter 11

THE MAASES GO
TO EUROPE

OUR DECISION AT THE END OF JUNE 1928 to go to Europe was a sudden one. Father had a younger brother in London. Uncle James, a bachelor and very, very rich (having invested heavily in African diamond mines), had been completely indifferent to the existence of his American relatives until this Frederica Alexandrina decided to change that. I wrote to him, and a lively correspondence ensued that lasted almost a year—until his solicitors in London informed us of his death and that he had willed the sum of seventy-five thousand dollars to father and me. The money would be forthcoming when the estate was settled.

Ernest and I did not have to go abroad to collect the money, but it was a perfect excuse for us to take the European holiday we had been dreaming about. Why worry about new assignments or writing contracts? What we both needed was a change. A seasoned pro like Waldemar Young, who knew the ropes, did not take long vacations from the scene of celluloid action. He knew better. But the Maases? They had yet to learn the ABCs of the Hollywood scene; in fact, constituted as they were, they never would learn. And they would eventually have to pay the piper.

We planned our itinerary carefully. We would take at least two months off. We would go to France first and then to Belgium. We would reach Germany by way of the Rhine, landing in Frankfurt. Then by train we would go to Berlin, Nuremberg, Munich. From Munich, we would go to Switzerland—Zurich, Lucerne, Lausanne, Geneva—and then back to France. Finally, we would cross the channel to London where we would collect the "booty."

In those days, one crossed the big Atlantic by ship, and we were confident that Ernest's brother Irving, in the Fox Foreign Department, could book us passage. To our dismay, there were no openings on any line sailing out of New York harbor. The best we could do was to go to Canada and sail from Quebec. Since we were determined to go, we took the train to Canada, where we boarded the chalk-white, freshly painted *Montnairn.* She was a trophy that Great Britain had acquired from Germany—she had been the *Prince Friedrich Wilhelm.* We discovered this original name on the copper faucets in our cabin.

After two and a half heavenly days, the *Montnairn* slipped out of the calm waters of the St. Lawrence and into the cold, treacherous Atlantic. The rest of the voyage was especially rough and bitterly cold. The ship slowly inched its way through a channel of towering icebergs. It was eerie. Our breath was steamy in the cold air. The captain was on watch night and day. Foghorns blasted incessantly. In our stateroom we could hear the groans and feel the agony of the sturdy "little" ship as she plowed through the treacherous waters. Rumor had it that the ship carried the wrong kind of cargo, which shifted instead of rolled (or was it the other way around?). It mattered little to the seasick Maases. Finally, we entered warmer and safer waters, leaving the icebergs behind. What a relief it was to see the green and yellow mustard fields of the French countryside! At last Cherbourg! Terra Firma!

We had new and, of course, too much luggage: an expensive hand trunk, a museum piece now, but considered very "in" then; two valises each, one made of genuine crocodile and weighing a ton empty; and several smaller bags. To our mortification, we watched our luggage receive its official baptism as the ship handlers tossed it indifferently from the ship to the dock below.

It was dark when the train from Cherbourg finally puffed into the Gare du Nord in Paris. We taxied to the Hotel Laetitia, which Riza and Joe von Sternberg had touted so highly. It was named after the mother of Napoleon Bonaparte. I can still see the big "L" embroidered on the purple satin bedspreads on the twin beds and emblazoned on almost everything—including the bidet, which was a complete mystery to us Americans. After we had washed and unpacked a little, we repaired to the dining room downstairs. It was empty at that late hour. We dined regally with the waiters and maitre d' hovering over us. Having consumed more than enough champagne, we were high in spirits when we set out to discover Paris on foot. I remember our first sighting of the Louvre in the full light of the moon. We ran up and down its steps, touching the building reverently. We ended up at the Café de la Paix, sitting there until nearly daybreak smiling and waving drunkenly to the French going by. We were in Paris! In Paris!

It was not a conventional European tour we made. Rather than continue from city to city, we found ourselves returning to Paris again and again—we spent two months in Paris alone. Paris was a sorcerer that kept calling us back. Paris! The city of absurdities and contradictions! Where else would beauty operators use ether to shampoo ladies' hair? And where else could you create an international incident over a pair of men's pajamas that were cotton and not silk, as the hotel manager insisted when it came time to pay a laundry bill? "My husband does not wear silk," I told the manager. Finally Ernest was victorious in the pajama dispute when a neutral old gentleman called in as a referee decided in his favor. The manager was crushed. Eighteen francs were deducted from the grand total of the "doit" of 162.10 francs. Fini la guerre!

I had family in Paris: Aunt Lisa, my mother's sister, and some interesting cousins. They were part of the large colony of White Russians who had fled the Red Revolution of 1917. Uncle Simon Schiffrin had been known as the "Oil King of Baku," operating the wells together with French and British interests. After he died of a heart attack on the streets of Paris, his wife and children continued to live in the extravagant style to which they had been accustomed—until their sables, diamonds, and money ran out. Then they rolled up their sleeves and went to work. My cousin Senia became a movie producer; cousin Yasha, who had been a concert cellist, joined Brentano's and ran their fine arts department. Cousins Helene and Eugenia became successful designers. Helene had a salon in Place Vendome. Her trade name was "Lyolene," and she sold to all the luxury shops in big cities.

It was through the cultivated eyes of these emigres that we saw

Paris. They guided us through museums, cathedrals, and theaters. We ate in a White Russian restaurant where the entertainment consisted of a wizened accordion player—reputedly the late czar's favorite—and a group of gypsy singers who had sung and danced in Russian courts. We had dinner one night at the Bois de Boulogne park with a former Russian prince who worked as a taxi driver six days a week, only to blow each week's earnings on one night in the park's luxurious surroundings. And on Bastille Day we danced in the streets until dawn.

One morning we were enjoying our hot chocolate and brioche breakfast at a sidewalk table outside the Hotel Laetitia when we heard sirens, the hoarse blasting horns of fire engines. We were astonished to see the familiar figures of Harry Brand, my writing partner on *The Farmer's Daughter,* and roly-poly director Dave Butler in one fire truck, followed by two cameramen on the second, cameras grinding away. Fox was shooting a picture—street scenes—in Paris! They went by so fast they did not see us. With the help of the hotel manager, we tracked them down to the Ritz Carlton, where they were staying, and left a message. They called back later, and we arranged to go out on the town with them the following evening.

As might have been expected, this Fox crew was interested in the seamy side of Paris. They had coveted addresses, all houses of "assignation." Although normally women were not included in these kinds of bawdy forays, Ernest insisted that I come along. The first was known as the House of All Nations and was most luxurious. Since we were a group of puerile American tourists, and not customers, for a modest fee we were given a specially conducted tour. The place was lavishly furnished with oriental rugs, Chinese tapestries, and some good art on the walls—nudes, of course. Outstanding in my memory were the long corridors on the two floors above the reception salons, where customers waited to choose their lady-of-the-evening from the collections of beauties the madame of the brothel brought forth. Doors . . . doors . . . each bearing the name of a different nation. Some open, some closed, mysteriously occupied. Scantily clad women—Oriental, Caucasian, African—carefully picked for youth and pulchritude, would appear and disappear. The *piece de resistance* of the tour was the room that contained a massive chair especially built for the avoirdupois Prince Edward Albert (later King Edward VII), the playboy eldest son of Queen Victoria, so that he might more comfortably engage in his frivolities.

Another was the extravagant bathroom, with a solid-gold bathtub, for King Leopold of Bavaria, in which he caroused with his lady friends.

The second address we visited, on the Left Bank, was very different. Here the women were older, more shopworn. They imbibed heavily of absinthe and vermouth. The highlight of the evening here proved to be feeding the lost creatures endless silver dollars that they skillfully picked up off the corner of the table with their private parts, a trick they artfully accomplished. One of the girls, taking a liking to Ernest, insisted on sitting in his lap, much to his discomfort and embarrassment. He kept pointing to me and telling her in his limited French that I was his wife.

"Votre espouse?" she repeated again and again. "Votre femme? Quelle belle! Quelle belle!" all the while gently stroking the gray fox shawl collar of my silver lamé evening wrap and then caressing my cheek. It was *triste*—so touching, I could have wept.

The Maases were secretly relieved that their Fox companions were returning to the States the next day. One such night on the town was enough. If we had told our sophisticated Russian cousins about it, they would have been shocked. And rightly so.

At the end of July, after visiting Brussels, Bruges, and Antwerp, we took the Rhine trip, our introduction to Germany. The verdant hills, romantic castles, neat rows of vineyards, and the boats carrying freight down the muddy river Rhine did not distract us from the fact that the Germans had no love for Americans. Or Jews. When we had lunch aboard our ship, the table to the right was occupied by a group of pretty American college girls touring Europe. At the table to our left was an elderly, well-dressed Jewish couple. All of us at these three tables placed our orders and then waited, and waited, and waited. Our waiter filled the orders at all the other tables around us—but ignored us. We could feel the dislike and contempt held for Americans who had helped defeat the kaiser and the German war machine in 1918. And the Jews? Well, they were disliked because they were Jews and were blamed for the country's sick economy. Hitler's rise to power in 1933 was only five years away.

Finally Ernest, sizing up the situation, decided it was time to take action. "Kellner, what is the meaning of this conduct?" he barked in his best German. "We have been waiting long enough. What is going on?"

A typical German, the waiter recognized the voice of authority. "Mein Herr," he purred, clicking his heels and bowing servilely. "No offense intended, I assure you, mein Herr. You will be served at once. At once!"

This was only the first of many such incidents. Again and again we experienced similar evidence of hatred and resentment. In Cologne, at a Turnverein of lady Amazons with long plaited braids and abbreviated shorts, Ernest was spat upon when he smiled at one of the lady gymnasts. Similar incidents occurred in Frankfurt, Heidelberg, Berlin, and Munich. It was not our imagination. It was real. It was the way the surly clerk at the hotel desk handed us our room key, the rudeness of the taxi driver, the nasty manner of the chambermaid, and the jostling from pedestrians in the streets. The Maases were not comfortable in the Weimar Republic.

Switzerland, after Germany, was pure heaven. Gone was the uptight feeling of hatred, contempt, and insidious plotting to regain a rightful place in the sun. In Switzerland, the air was clean, unpolluted; the clover fields so tidy not even the barnyard animals were permitted to desecrate them—their fodder was brought to the barn.

After a week in the banking city of Zurich, the train took us to Lucerne. It was nearing sunset when we emerged from our hotel on the lake, where a steamboat moored at the door was taking on passengers. We knew not where it was going, but board it we did to find that it served those who lived or summered in the many little towns along the lake in this enchanting William Tell country. Having discharged all its passengers, the boat headed back, and we were the only passengers left. Dark had fallen, and we had neither coats or sweaters. The chill of the water and mountain air had us huddled together in a deck chair struggling to keep warm, when we were rescued by the captain. The captain's quarters were snug and warm, and he had a bottle of good cognac, which we helped finish. We wound up, the three of us, in a little restaurant Josef von Sternberg had told us about. It was here that Richard Wagner, on the run from irate husbands, creditors, and politicians, used to come nightly while he was completing his "Meistersinger" masterpiece.

Lucerne was the cradle of the Swiss Confederation and heart of historic Switzerland. We spent a bundle in Lucerne on carved wooden pipes, ivory, and bone cutlery. But the Atelier de Soeurs Gubser Et Al, Alpemstrasse 9, remains most memorable. In front of the gaily painted shop sat three women in mountain regalia, working away, spinning, making lace, and weaving. They were a perfect invitation to step inside and look around. The place was a repository of fine lace, fine embroidery, and fine weavings of the most intricate patterns—superb workmanship. The Gubser Soeurs were maiden ladies who were carrying on the traditions of their parents, grandparents, and great-grandparents. Once they realized how appreciative we were, they opened the safe and treated us to their prize museum pieces. We came away with an especially beautiful lace centerpiece for which we paid fifty dollars in American money, a fortune then; and a two-hundred-dollar order for embroidered dinner and luncheon cloths, bureau scarves, and initialed handkerchiefs—to be mailed (when ready) to everyone in the family, our friends, and ourselves. Only recently I had the prized lace centerpiece—tucked away all these years—framed to hang on my wall beside other treasures. In today's inflated economy, it cost two hundred dollars just to have it framed! Times have changed, Ernest.

It was a hot night and we had an early train to Lausanne in the morning, so we returned to the hotel. It was not quite ten o'clock when we put out the light over our twin beds, ready for slumber. But I could not sleep. This was our wedding anniversary, and all day long I had waited patiently for my husband to acknowledge the occasion. Nary a word. Not a hint that he knew or cared. I was hurt, and the more I thought about it—as I lay there atop my featherbed, waiting, thinking—the more horrendous his neglect and indifference became. Tears began to trickle down my nose as I felt sorrier and sorrier for myself. I was a neglected wife!

"Are you crying?" came a voice from the matching twin.

"Yes. I'm crying," I sobbed. "Why wouldn't I be? This is our wedding anniversary and you have completely forgotten."

He got up and came over to my bed. I expected he would take me in his arms and tell me how sorry he was to have forgotten. Instead he grasped the featherbed I was lying on and pulled it and me onto the floor. "There," he said disgustedly as he dumped me, "that will give you something to cry about. Every day of this trip is a celebration for me. The trouble with you is you're a spoiled brat. Now stop crying and get some sleep. Good night."

I lay there on the floor atop the featherbed, too shocked to reply. Then it came to me how right he was. He had not even mentioned the day's fantastic shopping spree at the Atelier de Soeurs Gubser. What a droll, incomparable fellow I had married. How lucky I was to have him.

Lausanne, Berne, Geneva. During a week in "League of Nations" Geneva, we tour-bused it to Mount Blanc to have a look at the famous Mer de Glace glacier, whose yawning crevasses absolutely terrified me. I still have sprays of edelweiss as a remembrance of that day. The journey was nearly over. We had followed our hastily planned itinerary faithfully. Only one city remained—the focus of our trip: London. Money awaited us at the offices of Uncle James's solicitors. Father had written me that he thought the money should be divided to include all his daughters, and I readily agreed. However, that would wait for our return. I was to collect the full amount.

Brown and Brown and Brown had their offices downtown near Fleet Street, not in an office building but in a vintage frame house going back a century or two, sandwiched between two tall, modern buildings. The offices were musty and dark, but young Mr. Brown was warm and friendly to the American relatives of his deceased client. While the bank draft was being drawn up, we enjoyed high tea and delicious crumpets. Magnanimously, we were offered a car and chauffeur—the better to get around London. But unfortunately, that was not to be. When we returned to our hotel, we found a cable from Ernest's sister, Martha, and her husband, Harry Oyen. Would we meet them in Paris? Harry, an advertising artist, had just received a fabulous promotion. He had been put in charge of the European offices of the H.K. McCann Advertising Company, with headquarters in Berlin, Germany. We had planned to stay in London a full month; there was so much to see and do in this city, which Joseph Pennell had etched so lovingly for posterity. We consoled ourselves that we would make it up on our next European holiday. What we didn't know was that there was never to be a next European trip . . . that we would make together.

We returned to Paris once again. We met the Oyens at the Gare du Nord and deposited them at the Hotel Laetitia. They had a three-year-old daughter, and we promptly engaged a French nanny to care for her.

The nanny wore a bonnet with flowing ribbons and a caped navy blue uniform. Little Marylin also had a *voiture d'enfant*–roughly translated, a princely baby carriage.

Ernest and I were staying at a modest hotel called The Rochester. It was on the Right Bank, off the Champs Elysées. In addition to the luxurious Laetitia, we had stayed at the ultra chic George V and a hotel on the Left Bank called Hotel Royal. All were premiere and expensive. But The Rochester topped them all. It was spanking new—you could smell fresh paint. Our beds had never been slept in. Fresh fruit and a bottle of *vin ordinaire* stood on our bedtable. It was a steal at only six dollars a night. And we were given a souvenir to take home, compliments of the management—a wooden peppermill that I still use.

The high point of our rendezvous with Martha and Harry was a trip we made by train to Château Thierry. My brother-in-law Harry had been an infantry soldier who fought in France during World War I. The train station was deserted, or so it seemed, until we came upon a dilapidated automobile parked nearby. The driver, eyeing us hopefully, wore a washed-out blue smock and a tattered straw hat. He looked as if he could use a few francs. "Wanna see the battlefield?" To our astonishment he spoke perfectly good American English without a trace of an accent. "Hop in," he invited, opening the only door of the Chevrolet sedan that worked; the other was tied shut with a rope. It was a Chevy, all right; the remaining hubcap attested to that. Martha, Ernest, and I sat in the back seat, its upholstery oozing out. Harry sat up front with the driver. The floorboard under the driver's seat was missing. The poor wreck choked and sputtered but pluckily took off. Evidently it had no brakes, but the driver pushed it to its limits, stirring up clouds of dust and pebbles, which leaped through the hole in the floor and peppered us helter-skelter. All the while, the driver talked and talked and talked. It was as if he were trying to convince himself that he had not forgotten his native tongue. We learned that he was a G.I. who had been stuck in Château Thierry at the end of the war, had messed with a French girl, and voila! a shotgun marriage. An all-too-familiar story. He came from Chicago. Did we know Chicago? The greatest city in the U.S.A. In the world!

"But I'll never get back," he sighed heavily. "Not a chance. I'll never see Chicago again. I'm stuck with seven kids. Seven! And she's pregnant again. You don't know what it's like living with these frogs. I'll never get used to it. Never. And my kids? I try to teach them to talk American, but they laugh and answer in French. I help work on the farm. A helluva way for a guy to wind up, ain't it? I'm askin' you."

We commiserated with his sad plight. But now we had come to a fork in the road. "Take the road to the left," directed Harry.

"Naw," contradicted the driver, veering to the right. "This way's shorter."

"I said left," commanded Harry sternly. "I ought to know. I've driven this road enough times." We went left.

Throughout the drive Harry remained silent, strangely withdrawn, as if he were reliving buried memories now coming back into focus. When we reached the scene of the battle, we left the car. Our driver, to whom visiting the battlefield was old hat and only worth the few francs it would bring him to buy tobacco for his long clay pipe, remained.

Harry walked ahead like a zombie in a hurry. He pointed to a well: "My pal Mac was killed here. Never knew what hit him. There were dead lying all around and some wounded calling for help. Then I got shot in the leg. I crawled to that tree . . . it's still here." He ran his hand over the trunk. "Imagine, still here." He went on, "My leg was hurting and bleeding. I tried to stop the blood, but couldn't. 'I'm going to die,' I thought, 'bleed to death!' Then I smelled something funny. It made me sick to my stomach. 'Gas! They're using gas, those damned Heinies!' And I had lost my gas mask. There was a guy lying beside me. I didn't know if he was alive or dead. Anyway—he was unconscious. So I took his gas mask and put it on, then I lost consciousness myself. When I came to, I was in an ambulance and the medic was saying, 'You'll be all right, buddy! Just some shrapnel in your leg. Nothing broken.'"

All this while, two old men, one with a flowing white beard, the other wearing smocks like our driver, were seated against the remaining wall of a bombshelled house. They had been watching Harry—for they could tell from his behavior that he had seen action on this field. Now as we walked slowly down the hill back to the car, they came over.

"Soldat, soldat," they repeated again and again, pumping Harry's hand, tears in their red-rimmed eyes. "Merci, merci! Merci beaucoup, soldat. Merci!" This seemed to bring Harry out of his trance. He laughed and embraced the old men.

"Don't mention it," was his modest reply. Fortunately, he was still young and in good health, off to a great new job. Years later, his lungs collapsed and he was invalided to an army hospital—a victim of mustard gas after all.

After a final week in Paris, our four-month vacation was at an end. Before we left, Ernest insisted on returning to a dusty antique shop near the Universite de Paris, where we had rummaged and bought other trinkets. There was one item we had admired but had not purchased—an exquisite, miniature sixteenth-century cameo, a real classic of perfection and beauty. This time, however, it left the shop with us. "It's 'you,'" my husband said softly. "I could have kicked myself for not buying it for you when we saw it the first time." What better remembrance could I possibly have of our beloved city on the Seine?

We sailed from Le Havre on the "De Grasse," a new French liner. I was reminded of the maiden voyage I had missed, years earlier, of another French liner, when Universal Pictures and their unhappy story editor parted company. Was this compensation? I wondered. The ocean was a sea of glass all the way—and dolphins kept us company.

Chapter 12

"Swell Fish"

UPON OUR RETURN FROM EUROPE in September 1928, we expected to return to the West Coast. But that plan was altered when Ernest was offered a one-year contract at the Astoria Studios of Paramount to direct a feature film in the East. Walter Wanger was eager to challenge his West Coast adversary, Ben Schulberg, and expedite his takeover of the West Coast studios.

To be in New York again meant that I could see more of my family, especially my mother. We attended daytime concerts together, attended matinees at the opera, and visited art galleries. We loved Central Park, where I had spent so much time from babyhood until I was nine years old. It was an opportunity for me to get to know my mother better and for her to tell me about her girlhood, her early struggles in America, how much she missed her native Russia and her family, and about her life now that she was getting old and rheumatic. Her children were grown and gone, with the exception of one daughter, Lillian, who lived at home and was unmarried.

Sorrowfully, Mama admitted that Lilly did not understand her and she did not understand Lilly. Lilly blamed Mama for her celibate state. In justice to Lilly, Mama had much to answer for. She was an obstinate, imperious matron with fierce principles of right and wrong from which one could not deviate. I was the maverick, the only one who refused to be tamed or intimidated. For this I owed a vote of thanks to my sister Lilly, who always took my side in my differences with Mama and fought my battles for me. Mama had been adamantly against my using any makeup for my high school graduation, even powder, claiming only women of ill repute painted their faces. Lilly stood up for me. When I fled the house to go where I wanted to go and do as I wished, Lilly would remain at home and brave Mama's wrath. Time and experience mellowed me, and I was able to forgive my mother, but Lilly could not forget or forgive. This was a great pity because it soured her life and her years with Mama. They had no rapprochement, no communication. Lilly took off every summer and all the holidays during her school vacations. There wasn't a country in the world she did not visit at least once. This was her escape. She was running away from Mama.

Ernest and I lived at the Hotel Victoria on Seventh Avenue near Fifty-seventh Street for a while after we returned from Europe. It was new then. It was there that I lost my cherished jade ring and my white chiffon bridal nightgown and negligée, which Irene had sewn for me by hand and given me as a wedding gift. The ring disappeared when a window washer came to clean the hotel windows one morning. I had taken the ring off while washing my hands and left it in the bathroom on the washstand. My guess is that the beautiful green of the jade stone was more than he could resist, and he filched it as a gift for his colleen. Anyway, it vanished that day, and I have missed it ever since. It was a trinket I prized as a memento of our honeymoon. The trousseau items were also a sentimental loss. But Ernest and I both agreed that it was my carelessness that was to blame and not the pretty young chambermaid we suspected of taking them. It taught me to be more careful. I have never lost anything valuable in hotel rooms since, I am happy to say.

We were glad to quit the Victoria. Though centrally located in New York City, it was not the best of hotels. Through a friend, we were able to sublet a tiny two-bedroom, furnished apartment on Fifty-fourth Street between Sixth and Seventh Avenues. It belonged to the first violinist of Toscanini's NBC Symphony Orchestra, Josef Stopak. He and his wife were going to live in Europe for six months. It was a break for us.

I found only two faults with that apartment, and one was partially my fault. The electric stove in the windowless kitchen, so typical of older New York apartments, had three burners on top plus a baking oven and broiler below. Simpleton that I was, I could never learn that if all three burners were going on top and you wanted to broil or bake, you would create a short. A short meant summoning the superintendent and having him replace the fuse. This inevitably occurred when I had dinner guests. Disaster! Black-out! How I loathed that electrical contraption that caused me so much embarrassment.

The other fault, however, I bore no responsibility for. On the first floor of our building there was a vocal teacher, and every morning at about eleven I would be treated to the most awful demonstration of a feminine voice vocalizing, attempting operatic arias. It was so terrible I had to close my windows. Also, around this time in the morning, I noticed a vintage brougham limousine, in mint condition, with liveried chauffeur waiting outside and wondered to whom it might belong. One day I caught a glimpse of its occupants as they emerged from the car and disappeared into the vocal studio on the ground floor. I recognized Hope Hampton at once from her newspaper photographs and assumed that the elegant fedora-ed gentleman at her side, who was old enough to be her father, was none other than Jules Brulatour, a millionaire and her distinguished sponsor. She had come for her voice lesson.

But voice or no voice, flat or not, Ms. Hampton did make it to the Metropolitan, in the opera *Mignon*. Ernest and I attended its one performance—an incredible evening. Hisses and catcalls came from the top balcony; patrons left after the first act. The critics next morning delivered the full *coup de grace* that ended Miss Hampton's brief operatic career. Their assessment of her talents and performance were summed up in one word: awful!

Another dividend of our stay in New York was my mother-in-law, Sophie Maas. When this dear lady learned I could not cook, did not even know how to read a cookbook intelligently, she offered her services. And teach me she did, bless her generous heart. For a whole month, rain or shine, that dear lady came over every morning. First we went grocery shopping. Then we would take our purchases home to my apartment and cook the dinner. She took it step by step, from the kitchen-kindergarten to the graduating-chef level, and I was emancipated from my phobia that I would never master kitchen abracadabra. After lunch, except in inclement weather, we would walk to Central Park and sit on a bench within view of the Plaza Hotel on Fifty-ninth Street. Sophie would dictate the recipes, and I would take them down in shorthand exactly as she spoke them, typing them later on index cards. If I am a good cook today, I can thank my wonderful mother-in-law.

My long hair had been, ever since I was knee-high to a grasshopper, my mother's pride and joy. Mama gave me raw-egg shampoos and vinegar rinses, and she brushed it and brushed it. Long hair certainly added to my popularity and lent me distinction, I thought, especially now that everyone was bobbing their hair. I was certain I would never bob my tresses, especially since I did not care for short hair, the new look. But the trend was mounting. Short hair was "in." Everyone urged me to crop my locks, including Ernest.

"I'd like to see what you'd look like. I'll bet you'd look interesting," he urged.

So, taking courage, I made an appointment at Saks Fifth Avenue. I was there at nine on a rainy Monday morning and placed myself in the hands of Pierre, a Paris import considered the best in the business. "Has Madam a preferred style in mind?" he asked.

No, "Madam" had no preference. "I leave it entirely up to you, Pierre," I said confidently. "Cut it the way you think would suit me."

"Madam has a delicate face and very beautiful hair," he told me, studying my head and countenance from all angles. Then, coming to a decision, he began his surgery.

Snip, snip, snip went the scissors. The hair rained to the floor, gobs of it, around the barber chair. I could not look. I closed my eyes and prayed. The snipping continued until I was sure I would be baldheaded. Finally the shearing was over. I opened my eyes, took one look, and burst into tears. This was not me in the mirror. This was some insipid nobody I wanted nothing to do with. He had given me the Louise Brooks-flapper look, down to the last bang on the forehead. On her it looked good. On me, monstrous. What had I done? This had to be the most terrible day of my life!

Pierre handed me a package. "Your hair, Madam. It will make a fine switch for you someday." I could see he was crushed at my disappointment in his artistry. In all good conscience, I could hardly fault him. I had left it up to him.

I called Ernest at the Astoria Studio from a booth at Saks. I did not want to wait to spring the surprise on him, as I had intended. I had to let him know at once what had befallen me.

"I cut my hair," I wailed. "It's the biggest mistake of my life. You'll hate it. Everybody will hate it. I hate it!"

"Now, now, Schatz," he comforted me over the phone. "If you

don't like it, just let it grow back. It isn't the end of the world."

I still have the small box containing the dark-brown, beautiful locks of my youth, so brutally shorn that day. Ernest, of course, was right. It wasn't the end of the world. In three months my hair was long enough to twist into a fair bun, never again to be cropped. Too bad I am gray now, or I might be tempted to use those lovely locks for a switch.

In November, Ernest was interviewed by *The Exhibitor Tribune*. I quote the article in its entirety because it indicates how Ernest and I both felt about the introduction of sound into motion pictures:

"SOUND IN PICTURES A LOGICAL STEP" SAYS MAAS
Ernest Maas, who recently completed a contract with the Fox Film Corporation as assistant to Sol Wurtzel in the West Coast studios, and who has just returned from several months' stay in Europe, is greatly elated over sound and talking pictures. Prior to his entry in motion picture production, Mr. Maas was engaged in legitimate stage work.

"No one can gainsay that the one certain sign of vitality in any art form is the energy with which it fights its limitations and seeks to realize the dreams and visions of those who work in that form," Mr. Maas said in a recent interview. "This being so, we have here a sufficient reason for the advent of sound to the screen."

Mr. Maas further stated that the whole history of motion pictures has been one of innovation after innovation, always a striving after the more perfect illusion and the greater appeal to the imagination. In short, more than any other modern art form, and despite its obvious shortcomings, the motion picture has refused to stay fixed and put. And therein has resided its hold on the public, and therein will always reside the salvation.

"The agitation, therefore, in some quarters that sound is a step in the wrong direction, that it is an intrusion having no place on the screen, that at best it is only a passing fancy limited to effects, and so on, is quite useless and absurd when dispassionately analyzed," Mr. Maas believes.

"The public, all these years, has been waiting for those images and shadows and phantoms to come to a more per-

fect semblance of life. And that is what sound, with the aid
of that scientific magician known as a microphone, 'mike'
for short, is bringing to the screen," he said.

This was about a year after Al Jolson's Warner Brothers picture *The
Jazz Singer,* had exploded on the picture industry and the world—the
first sound picture. It was a fantastic time to be a writer in motion
pictures and realize that you could now give your characters a real
dimension in dialogue, instead of trying to match stilted film emotions
to crippling, inadequate titles.

We were more than ready and eager to meet the challenge. Our
contribution was *Slums of Heaven,* a fully dialogued story, really a
play. Wanger purchased it for Paramount as a vehicle that would demonstrate his abilities as a producer. He was very keen about the story,
after the stage success of Molnar's *Liliom.* It was a story of a twenty-
year-old delinquent in New York City whose brief career ends in a
miserable holdup that nets him just ten dollars and results in the murder of a watchman. In fleeing, he seeks refuge on a rooftop, where he
encounters a desperate teenage girl who had come to that roof to com-
mit suicide. He convinces her that life is worth living, and, in this one
good act of his misspent life, he is awakened to the realization that life
is a very precious gift. But it is too late. The police surround the building, and he is captured. Convicted for the murder he has committed, he
ends up on death row awaiting the day of his execution. His only visitor
is the girl he saved on the roof. The main body of the story deals with
his reveries, as he fantasizes about what his life could have been . . . a
wife, children, grandchildren. His whole life passes before him as it
might have been. Only the girl he saved waits in the rain outside the
prison at the hour of his execution. Only she mourns his passing.

It was a fine, sensitive story and would have been our first talking
picture. But it was never made. Wanger, thwarted by his superiors in
his ambition to dislodge Schulberg, lost interest. And he had other
plans for Ernest Maas.

On March 28, 1929, the trade paper, *The Daily Review,* ran this
item: "MAAS, EDIT'L SUPERVISOR PARAMOUNT SHORTS IN N.Y. Ernest Maas,
who returned from an extensive trip abroad several months ago, has
been appointed editorial supervisor of sound short subjects at
Paramount's Eastern studio. Maas will make Paramount's initial exte-

riors with its newly-acquired Movietone truck, probably the first of a sound-recording fleet. The subject will be golf course excitement." Thus it was that, instead of directing our first talking picture, Ernest found himself allocated to directing sound shorts and also making tests of new hopefuls, actors and actresses either already cast or about to be cast in films.

There were many illustrious names among them. One was Jeanne Eagels, the fine actress who had starred in the play *Rain,* based on the short story "Sadie Thompson" by Somerset Maugham. Alas, the great Jeanne Eagels ended a heroin addict, a complete physical wreck who had lost all sensibility and control. When she needed to urinate, for instance, she simply pulled up her skirt and squatted—she wore no pants—and relieved herself before everyone on the set, much to their chagrin and embarrassment. Yet another actress fallen from grace, whose memorable performances still linger with those of us still around to remember her.

Six months had gone by since our arrival in New York. Josef Stopak and his wife returned from Europe, and the Maases had to move from their apartment. Since we could not find another sublet for less than a year's lease, we moved to the New West Hotel on Madison Avenue near Forty-eighth Street. It has since been demolished to make room for a high-rise office building. It was a ten-story edifice filled with affluent residents who preferred hotel living to housekeeping. We had a bedroom and living room with French decor. It was expensive, but we had no choice. The worst part was having to eat all our meals in restaurants, even breakfast. At first it was a novelty to eat in a different place every day, but we soon tired of the game, "where to eat." So we simplified our lives by choosing the Longchamps restaurant right across the street from our hotel. It was nice to be handed a familiar menu and to be served by waiters you knew. During the twenties, Longchamps was considered one of the finest French restaurants in New York. It was deluxe. Everything *a la carte.* Not cheap by any means. Yet I recall their specialty, *Roast Beef au Jus,* was only $1.10! Good old days . . .

Our friends in New York included Mike and Mary Simmons, and Marie and Maurice "Red" Kann. Mike was a publicist; Red was editor of *Motion Picture Daily.* Our friendship went back to the days when I worked at Universal in New York; we were all single then, and tramped the Palisades and Catskills together. Now I also met Marie. She was my age, a handsome Ashkinazei Jewess born in the U.S.A. I loved that girl. She was warm, generous, a delight to be with. We lunched at the Algonquin, walked the lengths of Fifth Avenue, Madison Avenue, Park Avenue, Broadway. Ernest and I, with Marie and Red, saw pictures at the Rivoli, Strand, Roxy—sound pictures now. We attended the premiere showing of *Spring Is Here*, that heartwarming musical by Rodgers and Hart, and liked it so much that we saw it three times! They were our best friends in New York.

Marie's weakness was antique shops, especially Spanish antiques. Their apartment was Spanish-Moorish in style, heavy ecclesiastical pieces too somber for my taste.

Marie and Red rented a primitive cottage in Maine for the summer, and we spent weekends there. We cooked over a wood stove, drew water out of a well, picked berries, cherries, apples, and other fruits as they ripened. Then came the last weekend over Labor Day. We had planned to spend it with Marie and Red but had to cancel because Ernest had an impacted tooth. Everyone was disappointed.

When they were returning home after the weekend, it was raining, a torrential downpour. Marie and Red owned a Plymouth roadster with a rumble seat, where Ernest and I usually sat. A friend of Red's was driving, his wife beside him. They were our substitutes. Marie and Red were in the rumble seat under a tarpaulin to protect them from the rain. It was impossible to see anything on the road ahead clearly. There was a stalled milk truck, and they ran into it. Red was lucky. He escaped with a bump on his forehead, but poor Marie was thrown upwards by the impact and, as she came down, hit an iron rod on the rumble seat—it ruptured her liver. Only twenty-nine, she died on the way to the hospital. If Ernest had not had a toothache, I would surely have been sitting in that rumble seat. Instead, I lost my best friend. Life's ironies constantly confront us.

One of the side effects of being in the movie business was the "shirttail friends" and relations who wanted to use us as a springboard into pictures. One such movie hopeful was Max Stein, a druggist who had attended high school with Ernest and now lived on Ninety-sixth Street, near Broadway. Ernest and I ran into him repeatedly on our evening walks, and it took us awhile to realize that these supposedly chance encounters were not so chance at all. Max claimed to be the proud possessor of a dog so remarkable that New York University had studied him as a case in canine extrasensory perception. Max was certain that his dog, Wolf, would prove the most exciting find of the century and insisted we come up to his apartment to see for ourselves.

Finally, we agreed to check out this canine wonder. We were, of course, totally skeptical about the fantastic claims of his owner, and we were even more skeptical when, at a whistle from Max, he made his appearance—an undersized, ill behaved, unkempt, listless puppy. Then Max began to put him through his paces.

"Wolf," he directed, pointing to Ernest's necktie, "tell me the color of this man's tie."

Wolf barked three times. R-E-D. Ernest's tie was a dark red knit.

"Wolf," directed Max again, "add two and two and subtract one."

And Wolf barked the answer—three short barks.

This was only the beginning. There were more complicated sums of addition and subtraction, even multiplication and division. The dog never erred. What was the key to this remarkable performance? The capper came when Max ordered the dog to go into the next room. Then he asked Ernest and me to write a word on a slip of paper—any word. But no more than five letters, so as not to unduly stress the dog's barking. Ernest wrote the word "money" and handed the folded paper back to Max.

"Wolf," called Max, "you can come back into the room now." But Wolf did not show, so Max whistled and called out "Wolf" again more sternly. Wolf ran in eagerly, playing with an old tennis ball. "Wolf!" called his master. But Wolf was more interested in playing with the ball than performing. "Wolf," scolded Max, "put down that ball and come here!" Wolf recognized the ring of authority in his master's voice this time and obeyed.

"Wolf," said Max, holding up the folded paper Ernest had given him, "what is the word written on this paper?" Max had not opened the paper, so even he did not know the word Ernest had written. Yet Wolf barked five times: M-O-N-E-Y. He went through the same procedure with me. My word earned four barks: L-O-V-E.

We had entered Max's apartment about nine that evening. It was after midnight when we left. Walking back to the New West, we tried to figure out how Wolf's stunt worked. We had detected no trickery, no signals from master to dog. What then was the explanation? No wonder New York University was studying the animal. It certainly appeared that the dog was psychic, a mind reader. This dog, this mongrel, had followed Max home one cold, rainy February night, shivering and hungry, looking for a home. Right from the start, Max's wife, Sylvia, did not take kindly to the animal. She already had a cat, and one pet was enough. She insisted that Wolf, so named because he wolfed down his food so ravenously, be sent to the pound "where he belonged."

Finally she delivered her ultimatum. "Either the dog goes or I do. You've gone crazy, Max. Completely bonkers. Neglecting your business and me, and all over a lousy dog. You can't make me believe there's anything special about that skinny, ugly mutt. Max," she repeated, "it's me or the dog!"

Max chose . . . the dog! He gave up his business, closed his pharmacy, and lost his wife. Unfortunately, the Maases could do nothing to promote Wolf for stardom on the screen. Rin Tin Tin and Lassie might not know how to count or spell, but they were photogenic. Poor Wolf, so incongruously named, was not.

Not all such stories turned out so miserably. One evening we received a telephone call from Alexander Dubinsky, the brother of old friends of my family. Dubinsky, a cellist, had learned that Ernest was connected with Paramount Studios. Could Ernest put in a good word for him? He needed a job.

We were privileged to spend an evening at the Dubinskys' Upper Riverside Drive apartment. He was not just a cellist—he was an artist. Without notes, without accompaniment, he played excerpts from cello concertos and encores—Elgar, Brahms, Dvorak, Bach, Saint Saens, Falla. And, finally, Bruch's "Kol Nidrei." Unfortunately, there was little hope for employment at the Astoria Studios. However, we promised to speak to Josef Stopak, the violinist with the NBC symphony whose apartment we had rented. Miraculously, it worked. Dubinsky was given an audition. Maestro Toscanini hired him on the spot. In gratitude, Dubinsky visited the Sagor family domicile and played for Mama again and again. Our favor was well repaid.

One day when Ernest came home from the studio, I could tell from the moment he came in the door that something was amiss. After dinner, he came out with it.

"I ran into Jack Bachman today," he began casually.

"Did you?" I returned, only mildly interested. "What brings him East?"

"He's producing a picture with Emil Jannings, the German actor, and they are planning to shoot some of it in New York."

"What's the picture?" I asked.

"*Beefsteak Joe*," he said, delivering the bombshell as quietly as he could.

"Our *Beefsteak Joe!*" I repeated, incredulous. *Beefsteak Joe* was a story Ernest and I had written in Los Angeles before embarking on our European trip.

"Only, they are calling it *The Way of All Flesh*, like that novel by Samuel Butler, and they've changed some of our story around. Instead of a restaurateur, Jannings plays a small-town bank teller."

"I don't believe it," I cried out.

"It's true, Schatz," he said putting his arm around me. "I got hold of the script. It's our story all right—rewritten, but our story. I knew there was something wrong when I ran into him. He looked at me as though I was a ghost. He actually turned pale and stuttered, 'I di-di-didn't know you were working at Paramount, Ernest. . . . ' When I returned to my office, I sent for a copy of the script, and I had the answer."

"What are we going to do? We'll sue!" I proclaimed. "Paramount can't do this to us. We'll sue!"

"I'll talk to John about it tomorrow," was his calm reply. John Butler was in charge of Astoria Studios. He was the righthand man to Zukor, Lasky, Wanger—a studio manager in high standing. More importantly, he was a staunch friend and champion of Ernest. He knew Ernest's early work and held him in high esteem.

Beefsteak Joe was a work of love, based on the life of Ernest's father: the story of a successful restaurateur, a devoted family man with a wife and children. He loses everything when his wife's younger sister comes from Germany and turns his head, causing him to go completely downhill until he becomes a derelict. Returning home on Christmas Eve, he cannot bring himself to go inside. He watches the festivities, the trimming of the tree, from the outside. There is a photograph of him on the mantel in a black frame and, because of the frame, he realizes that they believe him dead. He recalls the newspaper story of a man killed on the railroad tracks, the man who had stolen his identification papers from him. So he goes away, never to return. It was a powerful story, fully developed in 150 pages. Regina Crewe's sister, proficient in German, translated the script so that we could give it to Jannings to read. We also told the story to Jack Bachman and left him a copy to read. Both scripts, English and German, were returned to our agent, Ruth Collier, without comment, rejected by Bachman. We swallowed our disappointment and forgot about it in the excitement and diversion of travel.

Now, once again, a story of ours had been appropriated. True, there were changes, but the essence of the character, the central idea, was the same and so was the ending in its entirety. The culprit clearly was Jack Bachman, our friend, the man we had socialized with, the man we had come to respect for his appreciation of good literature—above all, a man we trusted. When in later years I told Ben Schulberg what had happened, he was genuinely shaken. "Why didn't you let me know?" he repeated again and again. "Why didn't you let me know?"

"After the way you treated Ernest, I didn't think you'd care," I told him.

"The phony bastard. The phony, pretentious bastard." He shook his head in disgust. "I always knew he was an intellectual phony. He and Josef von Sternberg, with their pompous airs of superiority and knowledge." Phony or not, Bachman had stolen our brainchild for his own ends. He never dreamed that Ernest would turn up at the same studio and that they would meet face to face.

The next day, John Butler took the matter up with Walter Wanger. Wanger called Jack Bachman in, delighted to have this producer from the West Coast, this ally of Schulberg, put on the spot. Never batting an eye, Bachman stood his ground and denied ever having seen or heard of our story. Jannings, he said, had given him the story idea, and he had consulted Schulberg, who assigned writers to do the treatment. They were told to write a story patterned after Jannings's successful picture, *The Last Laugh.*

"That measly Schulberg stooge is a bloody liar," concluded Wanger after Bachman left the office and he was alone with Johnny Butler. "What are we going to do about Maas?" asked Butler, keeping Ernest as his primary concern.

"Not a thing," snapped Wanger, almost angrily. "It's his word against Bachman's. And Bachman's a producer now—I'm not messing with the West Coast on this one!"

"But they can't just take a story like that." Johnny Butler spoke angrily in Ernest's defense.

"Can't they? They do it all the time," laughed the big Eastern executive. He could have said "we."

"Maas could sue," returned Johnny Butler.

"Let him," returned Wanger, "and see how much good it'll do him. He'll be through at Paramount and every other studio when the word gets around."

The Maases did not sue. The industry did not look fondly on writers who had the temerity to challenge the theft of their creative wares. Smarter writers, with "ins" to the front office, reduced their ideas to a one-page synopsis and received commissions to develop the yarns on studio payrolls. In that way, at least, you got some money out of it. Your legal contract says in fine print that the story idea belongs to the company. In other words, if after X number of weeks the story did not jell and you got canned, the story idea would revert to the studio. They knew how to protect themselves. The writers end up the patsies.

The irony of our case was that *The Way of All Flesh,* scripted by Jules Furthman and Lajos Biros, turned out to be a famous film. It won for Jannings the first "Best Actor Award" from the Academy of Motion Picture Arts and Sciences. It should have been our triumph. But as we writers say, "Those are the breaks."

I did not take Mr. Wanger's callous dismissal of the theft of our story lightly. "Let's get out of this business," I pleaded.

"Schatz," returned my husband patiently, "you have to take your lumps if you want to work in motion pictures."

"We could open an antique shop," I persisted. "I don't care if we have to live in the back. You know the antique business. I could learn."

He was adamant. His heart was in the picture business, and I tagged along. He had so much to offer, and I had to believe he would succeed. Surely the break would come. I no longer cared about furthering my own career. Nothing mattered but helping my husband further his.

Frederica and Ernest's brave but futile answer to the Motion Picture Industry was a parody they composed, years later, based on

Gertrude Stein's musical play *Four Saints in Three Acts.* Theirs, titled *Four Complaints in Three Acts,* was a memorial to all the "Swell Fish" they had parented—scripts that never saw the light of day. The parody was full of clever industry in-jokes such as naming the high and mighty "aficianados" of the industry "Saints." If it was too esoteric for most, well . . . people didn't understand Gertrude Stein either.

The parody was printed on March 19, 1934, in the *Hollywood Reporter.* It won for its writers much flattering comment but, alas, no assignments. Foolish Maases.

"Four Complaints in Three Acts"
Wrapped in Cellophane
By Frederica Sagor and Ernest Maas
(After Gertrude Stein)

PRELUDE: A Narrative of Prepare for the Worst.

ACT I: Swell Fish half indoors and half out of doors.

ACT II: Might it be Hollywood if there were no Swell Fish.

ACT III: Hollywood: Its Saints and why they are so.

ACT IV: The Saints reassembled and re-enacting why they do do like they do do.

PRELUDE

To love to love to love them so.
They make Swell Fish.
Swell Fish.
Swell Fish at least. Oh at least.
Swell Fish.
Aboriginals and sub.
Suboriginals and ab.
Ab sub sub ab.
Ab.
Sub.
And digga digga doo.
You write them.
Fish
Swell indeedy.
So what.
Or you don't so what.
So what you don't.
Or don't you.
So what what what so what so what so what what.
But Swell Fish they make.
Swell indeedy.
Saints love to be teased.

ACT ONE

About Swell Fish.
How would you like to be fried half indoors and half out of doors? Year in and year in and in and out and in?
Indoors and out of. Fried half and half.
Like Swell Fish.
Or versa vice and not profoundly around the other way or behind the beyond the beyond of it either. They make the grandest bouillabaisse.
Which Saints are fond of.
Or should be.
Or would be.
Or may can must might would should and could be.
But.
But toasted Susie is their ice cream. Toasted Susie is their ice cream.
Their ice cream.
You're telling us.
The answer is phfui.

ACT TWO

Money money money money money money money.
Beautiful word. Burb of a burb Money.
But not for Swell Fish.
Positively not.
It would be unsaintly.
To say nothing of heterodoxical unorthodoxy.

Putting it quaintly.

So always remember to forget it if you like to remember to forget it if you like to forget to remember to forget to remember to forget it that ice cream is their toasted Susie. Hey hey.

Ice cream is their toasted Susie.

Toasted Susie is their ice cream.

Their ice cream.

Hey hey.

Some fun eh kid.

Hey hey.

And what hey hey hey hey hey hey would become of Hollywood if hey hey there were no Swell Fish to fry year in and in and out and out half indoors and half of doors or to put it more clearly and less plain what would become of it.

Become become become of it.

Become of it.

Become.

Hey hey hey hey hey hey hey what would of it become

This is getting too coherent.

That's apparent.

Could four acts be three.

Don't ask foolish questions.

For Art's sake.

All Saints wear Brown Derbies.

ACT THREE

Saints and why they are saints no one can tell you because no one can and if one could one wouldn't wood won. Yet the Saints of Hollywood are Saints because they are not and producers is just a lovy dovy nickname for them. Although associate producers and producer associates are also that way. Only more so. Oh much.

Swell Fish have no grievance with the Saints but the FOUR COMPLAINTS IN THREE ACTS which will be four before we get through and after all four complaints in four acts which are as yet only three is little enough about Swell Fish for that matter or any other.

But this is getting too coherent again. Like some pictures.

And getting like some pictures too coherent again is not getting that incoherence which is so essential to nothing at all and destroys that unity never intended in the first place. We refer of course to Swell Fish.

Swell Fish.

Deliciously Swell Fish.

ACT FOUR

Skol Saints. Skal skol skol skol. Skol.

Scene 1

Saint B.P.   How do you do.

Saint Louis M.   The same to you.

Scene 2

Saint Irving.   How do you do.

Saint David.   The same to you.

Saint Walter.   How do you do.

Saint Harry.   How do you do.

Saint Hunt.   The same to you.

Scene 3

Saint Winfield.   HOW DO YOU DO

Saint Sol.   THE SAME TO YOU

Saint Jesse.   The same to you.

Scene 4

Saint Carl Jr.   Hello.

Saint Carl Sr.   Wie gehts.

Scene 5

Saint Darryl.   How do you do.

Scene 6

Saint Jack.   The same to you.

Saint Hal.   Wal how do you do.

Scene 7

Saint Samuel.   How do you do.

Scene 8

Saint Merian.   How do you do.

Saint Pandro.   How do you do.

Blessed blessed blessed all.
And blimey.

It looks like.

A.

Great.

Year.

For Swell Fish.

Sooooo.

Let Lucy Lily Lily Lucy and let
Lily Lucy Lily.

Who cares.

Which is a fact Gertie.

THE END

Chapter 13

THE DEPRESSION YEARS

WE HAD OUR TICKETS BACK to California in hand, our goodbyes said to family and friends, our bags checked at the station. We were ready to board the Twentieth Century Limited at 8:45 A.M. With a few minutes to spare before our train left for Chicago, we stopped at a kiosk to buy a paper. They were sold out. Hefty deliverymen appeared carrying high stacks of yet another edition. Almost before the stacks were put on the stands, frenzied travelers snatched the papers. We managed to buy a copy of the *New York Times*. Its headlines reported WALL STREET STOCKS CRASH!! BROKERS JUMPING OUT OF WINDOWS! FINANCIAL PANIC!

The date was October 29, 1929.

Once aboard the train, in our compartment en route to Chicago, we found our tongues. "I guess we can kiss our ten thousand dollars goodbye, Mrs. Maas." My husband was trying to cover up how upset he really was. "I guess we can, Mr. Maas," I returned, equally upset.

The year before, back in California in June of 1928, Ernest had come home from the Fox studios with a letter signed by Winnie Sheehan. The letter was addressed to the employees of Fox studios. It informed us that the board of directors would issue a new block of stock, and Mr. Fox felt that this was a rare opportunity for the people who worked for Fox studios to invest and double their money. Aimed primarily at producers, directors, writers, and players under studio contract, the letter was virtually a mandate to "invest or else." Each investor was expected to invest at least 20 percent of his yearly salary.

180

Ernest and I, on that long-ago summer evening, stood on the balcony of our Villa Carlotta apartment and pondered our decision. Should we or shouldn't we? We refused to be intimidated entirely. We would toss a coin: heads, yes; tails, no. We lost.

Now, ten thousand dollars was gone with the wind. "Los Angeles, here we come," sang the wheels of the train. A fine homecoming!

We had lost in other ways as well, although we did not realize it at the time. Waldemar Young had warned me not to leave the Hollywood scene for too long because it was too easy to be forgotten in the film ratrace. Not only did we embark on a reckless four-month pleasure holiday, but we added to the perilous absence and further alienated ourselves from the West Coast by staying in New York and working at the Astoria Studios. The outright theft of *Beefsteak Joe* might never have happened if we had still been an intimate part of the Hollywood grapevine. But "que será, será."

We arrived in Los Angeles expecting to stay at the Villa Carlotta again, but there were no apartments vacant. Lucy Carter was still the manager, and she arranged for us to live at the Champs Elysée apartments across from our former abode. The Champs Elysée, like the Villa Carlotta, was built and owned by Mrs. Thomas Ince. It was luxurious and the rents astronomical from the standpoint of the Maases, who were unemployed and had just kissed ten thousand dollars a fond farewell. Fortunately, Lucy also arranged for us to stay for the same rental we had been paying before. The Champs Elysée was home to Clark Gable, Carole Lombard, Humphrey Bogart, Errol Flynn, Ginger Rogers, and Eddie Robinson at one time or another. There were two doormen, and security was tight. But while the Champs Elysée had been home to the stars, it was not home to the Maases, who much preferred the friendly informality of the Villa Carlotta.

One morning, Lucy left the Villa Carlotta to do some errands. She did not expect to be hit broadside by an inebriated driver running a red light. She was killed instantly when thrown out of her vehicle. A seat belt might have saved her, but they were nonexistent then.

With Lucy gone, we decided to change our abode—and luck—and try Beverly Hills, where apartments were plentiful. We found a furnished apartment near the Beverly Hills High School. In the twenties and thirties, it was still difficult to find an apartment that was not furnished. This was still considered a transient town, with people moving in and out, to return, most likely, to the cities from which they came. If you wanted to furnish, you bought a house as proof that you were here to stay in the City of Angels. Our abode was near enough to the Beverly Hills High School for students to park their cars—and carcasses—on our street, where parking was not restricted. The "car set" attending this high school came from privileged families, where it was the norm for a teenager to have his or her own car as soon as he or she came of age to drive one. Drugs such as marijuana, cocaine, heroin, were not "in" yet, but alcohol, cigarettes, and partying all night were. Some of those students looked so bedraggled at nine o'clock in the morning, so dissipated, you wondered how they would make it through the day. That scene was the precursor of what we have today—a lost generation finding answers in escape.

Westana Carleton Nathan, her ten-year-old son, Robert, and Benjamin, their black Persian cat, had an apartment not far from us. Westana and Perry Nathan had been married the same year as Ernest and I—they in June, we in August. Perry, a contract writer, and Ernest had both done penance on the Fox lot under the mean-spirited Sol Wurtzel. Perry's antecedents matched Ernest's. Both had their American roots in the ghetto. Westana, like her name, was a true westerner of covered-wagon stock. She came from Colorado. She was a beautiful, willowy woman, stately, lovely, with wavy auburn hair and penetrating gray-blue eyes full of merriment.

Perry was away in New York, one more unemployed writer trying to earn a living so that he could send for Westana and her son. Suddenly, out of nowhere, Papa Carleton (Westana's previous husband) became very much in evidence, ardently courting his ex-wife. Westana was having difficulty meeting the rent and buying Robert's school clothes. Perry sent what little he could, but it wasn't enough to take care of the two of them. Westana's coldly practical relatives urged her to divorce Perry, out of duty to Robert. Westana was a badly mixed up, confused lady.

"I have to consider Robert," she kept saying. "What's best for him."

"Get a job," we pleaded, "and give Perry time. He'll reestablish himself and send for you and Robert. You can't go back to a man you don't love just because he fathered your son."

Ernest and I could not abide the over-genial Papa Carleton. This crude oaf was a gambler and a braggart. All he had going for him was money that, from all appearance and hearsay, was not too cleanly made. Ernest and I knew enough about Perry Nathan to feel confident that, given a little time and with his connections back East, he would be able to have the economic situation under control. Fortunately for Westana, she allowed her heart to rule her head. She got herself a job at Magnin's.

A clever woman with an outgoing personality, she succeeded right from the start. Westana, Robert, and Benjie, the cat, became family to us. We ate most of our evening meals together. We played rummy and bridge together, and we cheered up one other when we were down in the dumps. I'm happy to relate that Westana and Perry got together within the year, and we all lived to celebrate our fiftieth wedding anniversaries together in Washington, D.C., in June 1977.

Four years had passed since we'd returned to Los Angeles. Because of the worsening depression, we'd mostly sat on our hands, without work. One story we did work on was for Universal, about the Armored Car Service. We needed background material, so on March 10, 1933, Ernest made an appointment with the manager of the Armored Car Service, whose offices were located on the twelfth floor of a downtown office building on Sixth Street, near Wilshire Boulevard. At four-thirty, the hour of the appointment, Ernest arrived at the offices but, to his surprise, found them locked. Hearing voices and detecting movement inside, he knocked on the door of the office. A guard's face appeared at the grated aperture in the center of the door, which still remained securely locked.

"I have an appointment with Mr. Beaver at four-thirty. Please tell him that Ernest Maas is here to see him," Ernest told the guard.

"Mr. Beaver just stepped out of the office," he was told. "He should be back momentarily. He said for you to wait."

Ernest, thinking it strange that he was not invited into the office, waited in the corridor. He did not have long to wait before the burly figure of Mr. Beaver emerged from the elevator and approached him. He apologized for being late. They remained in the corridor to talk for a moment, when there was an incredible noise, the groaning of steel, and the building quivered as if shaken by a sudden explosion. Ernest found a loaded gun stuck into his abdomen. "Put 'em up," ordered Beaver, thinking a bomb had exploded and Ernest was part of the conspiracy. The building continued to moan and sway.

"Earthquake!" Mr. Beaver shouted, withdrawing his weapon and pulling Ernest behind him into the nearby men's restroom to seek protection beneath its doorway. When the first shocker had subsided, Ernest followed Beaver out into the hallway. The door of the Armored Car Offices was wide open now.

Inside the office were six strapping armored car guards, still not fully recovered from their fright and shock, on all-fours trying to gather up all the money they had been counting. Millions and millions of dollars, in paper money, which the national Treasury was considering issuing for the first time. Fortunately, Washington decided not to do so after all. The country would weather its financial crisis without subjecting it to the terrible remedy that Germany had experienced after World War I. We came mighty close.

Anxious to get back and see how I had survived the quake in Beverly Hills, Ernest made his speedy departure. Researching the armored car background would have to await another, calmer day. Since the building elevators had all been knocked out of commission, Ernest dashed down the twelve flights of stairs. Entering the building parking lot, he saw that his Chrysler, parked smack against the building wall, was the only car still remaining on the lot. He handed his parking ticket to the attendant. "Mister," said the shaken man, "I'm not going near that wall. If you want your god-damn car, get it yourself!"

Ernest was in a state of panic as he drove past the devastation. Everywhere there were shattered buildings, buildings fallen from their foundations, others without their facades. The screeching of fire engines and ambulance sirens added to the terror.

He need not have worried. I was unhurt. Our building in Beverly Hills withstood the tremor, but barely. I had been busy in the kitchen preparing dinner when the tremor struck. I grabbed a big steel cooking pot and held it over my head as I stood in the doorway of my kitchen. I remembered the warnings not to run out into the street and be felled by flying glass and debris. In the six-point-three intensity of the quake, I watched in horrified fascination as my living room wall bulged forward and then fell back into place, held together by chicken wire used to earthquake-proof buildings. It left a wide, three-cornered crack as evidence of what might have been if the quake had been stronger. For weeks, the aftershocks came so often that we soon paid them no mind. "Here we go again," we would laugh and then continue doing whatever we were doing. Mother Earth had done her worst and now she was settling down again. The devastated areas would be rebuilt, and life would continue as usual. Ants rebuild their sand castles when they are demolished; Man's lot in earthquake country is no more secure.

My sister Lillian, forgoing her usual foreign country excursion, decided to spend the summer with us. To conserve our resources, Ernest and I had taken an apartment with only one bedroom. This was turned over to our guest, and we slept on the sofa-bed in the living room, which was not the acme of comfort. As accustomed as we were to twin beds, Lillian's visit was a trial. Unemployed and working on originals, on pure speculation, we had to entertain my dear but helpless sister, who would go nowhere by herself, not even as far as the corner market. Our nerves frayed, our financial worries mounting, we had anything but a happy summer. Indeed, overall, it was not a happy year, nor were the two years that followed.

We had lots of good company in our misery. My friend Adele Commandini, who had been a reader for me at Universal in New York, had come to the Coast to try her luck at writing. She would later get a break and write *Three Smart Girls*, which launched Deanna Durbin as a star and Joe Pasternak as a producer. It brought Adele enough fame and fortune to buy a home in Pacific Palisades. Meanwhile, Adele was living at a small Hollywood hotel called the Mark Twain. Also staying at the Mark Twain were the writers Lorna Moon (who was to die soon after from galloping consumption) and Sara Hart (who was engaged to the editor of the *American Mercury Monthly*). All of us were on the skids, more or less, living on mounds of spaghetti and meatballs at cheap little Italian restaurants and winding up, nightly, in Beverly Hills at the home of the Maases. There, over coffee or tea, we read our works to each other—Lorna, the dark, Scottish beauty, recited her gossamer poetry, her defiant cry to a life slipping away; the more staid, plain Sara read her poignant stories of the South; Adele Commandini and Frederica Maas read their poor, rejected offerings to the sacred altar of filmdom.

During those years the Maases subscribed to and faithfully read *The Daily People's World*, a far-left Socialist daily. It was noised about that this was a Communist newspaper, backed by Moscow, when in reality it was not only *not* backed by Moscow but very nearly not backed by anyone in those Depression years. It was never out of the red—although, ironically, it was accused of being "Red"—and had to struggle to keep the presses going from issue to issue.

The Maases also subscribed to a publication that was the predecessor of *Soviet Life*, a reciprocal magazine our country exchanges with the Russians—ours printed in the Soviet Union in Russian and theirs published in English and distributed in the United States. What a publication this was, when so little was known about what was transpiring over there! I especially recall the coverage of the war years—the graphic pictures, the articles, the poignant and detailed descriptions of the battles, the destruction of the great cities, the partisans, the siege of Leningrad, the hand-to-hand fighting in bombed-out buildings in Stalingrad—very little of which could be found in our own newspapers.

One of the premier Soviet journalists of that period was Ilya Ehrenberg. He chronicled it all: the sacrificial war to save the motherland that began June 12, 1941, when Nazi Germany launched its attack on the Soviet Union; the war that ended May 8, 1945, with the surrender of the vanquished Germans; the terrible war the Russians fought almost singlehanded as a nation until the Allied armies joined them, with a second front, at the eleventh hour. The Germans were stopped practically at the threshold of the Kremlin's Red Square. Three encroaching armies that Stalin mustered from the north, south, and west forced the Germans back into retreat and into the trap of the oncoming Russian winter. Years later I visited Moscow, and as I stood in Red Square, cold shivers ran down my spine to think how close, how very close, the Germans came, and what the world owed the Russians for pushing them back.

Madeleine Ruthvin no longer served as Harry Rapf's Girl Friday and was retired now and married to a county public official who shared her political views. It was through her that I met John Howard Lawson, a screenwriter who had several Broadway plays to his credit. One meets many people in the course of a lifetime, and mine spans over ninety years, but I met only one John Howard Lawson. He was American through and through, with the kind of Americanism our founding fathers must have had. His liberalism was not cosmetic. It was genuine, Jeffersonian logic, and he lived it. He, as well as Ernest and I, had read

Marx, Engels, and Lenin. We shared the conviction that capitalism was outliving its usefulness as an economic system, that it was devouring itself in insatiable expansions and mergers, internationally as well as nationally. But our beliefs did not lead Ernest and me to join the Communist Party.

The naive, simplistic visionaries, for the most part, who belonged to the Communist Party in this country were far removed from hard reality and would easily come apart when faced with the real problems of change. Whether Lawson belonged to the Communist Party, I could not say. Nor did it bother us whether he was a card-carrying Communist or not. What did matter was that he was a decent, fine man of quiet intelligence looking for constructive answers, even as we were (and I still am). John Lawson would one day be crucified as part of "The Hollywood Ten" by the infamous Sen. Joseph McCarthy.

By the fall of 1934, it was plain that we were not a big success in Hollywood. In these five years we only found work doing short studio assignments—cleaning up other people's scripts—and had failed to sell our own original stories. We were both confused, completely at sea, about our situation. Ernest had not made the contacts necessary to break back in as a producer; he also lacked the initiative to start a new career. Because we had no answers or plans to extricate ourselves from our dilemma, we decided to go back to New York. So, in November, we sold the Chrysler roadster to our friends, Mike and Mary Simmons. Mike had come to the Coast to work on an original story he sold to Columbia. The story, we later found out, had actually been written by a female fellow publicist he had worked with back East, a collaborator whom he "forgot" all about when he arrived. Writers . . . writers . . . beware! We are a breed of brain pickers—even the best of us—not to be trusted.

The Chrysler disposed of, we stored what few possessions remained in a friend's garage and returned to New York again. We both were ready to put Hollywood behind us. Ernest was determined to gather up the pieces of his original documentary business and start over. But nearly ten years had elapsed and there were no pieces, even scraps, to pick up. For this was the Age of Sound. Others were in the saddle now, handling what meager business there was. These were the deep Depression years, and big business was still in a state of shock. The Depression in New York was different from Los Angeles. All around you, you saw scenes of poverty—people selling apples on Fifth Avenue, building fires in ashbins in Greenwich Village; people sleeping in doorways, in subways; people lost, discarded like the garbage they scavenged when their bellies were empty enough. Los Angeles had its influx of dustbowl victims—Okies were pouring in—but if you didn't get downtown you didn't see them. In New York City, the Depression permeated every corner of daily life; you couldn't escape it.

We took a lease on a studio apartment in the Rhoerich Museum apartment building at 310 Riverside Drive, and we lived there several years. It was so called because the large basement had been turned into a public museum exhibiting the paintings of Russian artist Nicolas Rhoerich, a good artist if not a great one. Some of his American relatives had put up the building and had hit upon the ingenious idea of opening a public museum in it to avoid paying taxes, since public buildings were free of taxation. It did not matter that the public was largely unaware of and indifferent to the museum. The resourceful builders and owners of 310 Riverside Drive put it over.

The Rhoerich was more properly a residential hotel rather than an apartment building. The units consisted of one very large room with a daybed, a desk, and comfortable chairs; a large walk-in closet with plenty of storage space; and an enclosed "efficiency" kitchen, with room for pots and pans and a two-burner gas stove. Living this way, you quickly appreciated collapsible chairs—collapsible anything—that could be stored away in the closet and brought out when needed. It was wonderful how you could manage when you had to. I entertained our families and friends in that one-room apartment, serving full-course dinners, efficiently planned and cooked over several days and stored in the tiny icebox—another part of the "efficiency" kitchen. I was a good cook by this time, and nothing stumped me. We often had five or six to dinner; and with plenty of large cushions to supplement the chairs, we served buffet style—pot to plate. Good food makes up for festive tables and fancy menus anytime.

I liked the Rhoerich. It was different, intimate, arty. Nearly all its tenants were connected with the arts and had to be thoroughly Bohemian, you may be sure, to put up with living in a one-room enclosed efficiency-kitchen apartment.

An early riser all my life, I liked to leave Ernest asleep in a snug warm bed and walk uptown to Child's Restaurant. There, at six in the morning, I would partake of bacon and eggs and plenty of good hot coffee, always with a copy of the good old *New York Times*. I defied the elements, be it rain, shine, or zero weather. Sometimes the wind from the Hudson River was so strong I had to hold onto a railing near the building or be blown by the force of the wind into the river. An exaggeration, of course. But those were mighty strong, blasty gusts, I can tell you.

Our sixth-floor apartment overlooked the Hudson River. In winter, the upper Hudson froze, and in spring the ice broke up and floated down the river in big slabs, making one think of Eliza in *Uncle Tom's Cabin* fleeing across the ice.

One evening, as we were eating our dinner, we saw the *Hindenburg* blimp heading toward New Jersey. I don't remember the time, but it was still light out. We were tremendously impressed and surprised to see this great big thing pass by our window. As we sat at the kitchen table, we just had time to raise our hands to wave and to see a few hands wave back. It wasn't much later that we heard on the radio of the horrible explosion that befell it when it tried to land. It was May 6, 1937.

Almost directly facing our windows, we could see and watch a colony of homeless springing up along the banks of the river. Shelters were constructed out of huge cardboard packing boxes lined inside with newspapers. Some were able to get their hands on wooden boards that they nailed together and covered with a roof made out of tin. Some even managed to find slabs of aluminum siding—anything and everything was ingeniously thrown together to make a home. There they lived, whole families with children, some with grandparents. It was a veritable commune. Those who were able to find a day's work contributed almost all their wages to the enterprise. They sought donations. With this money they bought food at wholesalers in large quantities as cheaply as they could. There was one common kitchen, three large butane stoves. A good nourishing soup was the mainstay. Sometimes there was meat, even chicken on Sunday. Mostly it was soup, potatoes, vegetables, and apples, oranges, bananas, all discards from markets and restaurants. It kept them alive.

These were not beggars. These were decent people with families, out of work. They were proud of their community and kept it clean and orderly. Everything was shared equally and fairly—food, chores, work. They built fires to keep warm. A few lucky ones had coal stoves. The ingenuity of the have-nots was amazing. Nothing went to waste.

Ernest and I visited the camps often. We made friends with the organizers. Before I knew it, I was involved, helping to raise money for the enterprise. I contracted with restaurants and big markets to give us their discards. I even prevailed upon two local doctors to visit the camp when needed, especially when the children or older campers took sick. At Christmastime every home had a tree, collected from the leftovers that had not been sold by Christmas Eve; decorations were either hand-made or discards. There were Christmas presents for the kids from stores and private families. A group of twenty of us women got to-gether and provided automobile transportation for the children who had to go to school in inclement weather. We did everything we could to help these gallant people, clinging desperately to dignity, to hope and trust in their country. To them, Franklin D. Roosevelt was the Messiah. Somehow he would restore this promised land again. They believed this. And so did we.

Then it happened. Without warning, city workers burned the shan-ties right down to the ground. They just came in one bitter cold wintry day and did it.

Ernest and I, bewildered and devastated ourselves, tried to offer words of encouragement, but no one said a word. Nobody cared any-more. A man can be pushed so far and no further. They were numb. This was the end of the road for them. After these people had drifted away, God knows where, we drew up petitions of protest, appealed to the mayor, to the governor, but to no avail. The powerful had spoken. The owners of the big apartment houses lining the river claimed that their tenants had complained, that the dwellings of these vagabonds were an eyesore, desecrating their view of the beautiful Hudson River, its golden sunsets spreading across the sky. Or, was their conscience unable to face how the other half lives?

Chapter 14

MARRIAGE IN CRISIS

WHEN WE FIRST MOVED BACK TO NEW YORK, Ernest had looked up a good friend in charge of the New York office of the *Hollywood Reporter*. His name was Abe Bernstein. Abe had been Ernest's secretary when he founded his documentary company, Roycroft Productions. In the fall of 1934, Abe engaged the Maases to cover openings of the most promising plays on Broadway. The less promising plays were assigned to others on his staff. Thus it happened that Ernest and I had the best seats for the best plays for all the opening nights on "The Great White Way" during the 1934-37 seasons.

It was a challenge to write play reviews emulating such eminent critics as Brooks Atkinson, John Mason Brown, Alexander Wolcott, and John Corbin. It took a lot of hard work to match their brilliance and competence, but what a privilege it was to try. I was exposed to good music as child and, as a young woman, I had been exposed to the theater as well. Practically without interruption, I attended the New York theater from 1920 to 1937, years I consider the richest in New York stage history. It started, of course, with my apprenticeship at Universal as secretary and assistant to John Brownell and Robert Rodin, and climaxed in the year I became story editor, covering all the plays, good, bad, and indifferent in Boston, Philadelphia, and Atlantic City. Now, Ernest and I were reviewing "The Best" with the best of critical traditions. When I look back, I can scarcely believe it. For a five-dollar bill (scalper's profit included), you had yourself an orchestra seat on opening night. In those highly significant years of the theater, with such eminent playwrights as Eugene O'Neill, Zona Gale, John Galsworthy, and Bernard Shaw, I must have seen well over a hundred plays and musicals.

The saddest experience Ernest and I had during this period was seeing two plays written by my old friend, John Brownell. John was now retired, living comfortably in Mamaroneck and enjoying his boat, but he wanted to make a brave stab at leaving his mark on the theater. Of course Ernest and I wanted to see John's plays and support his efforts. Unfortunately, they were bad. Really bad. *Her Majesty, The Widow* ran thirty-two performances after it opened at the Ritz Theater on June 18, 1934. *A Woman of the Soil* opened March 23, 1935, at the Forty-ninth Street Theater and ran twenty-four performances. We met John in the lobby and bravely offered our hypocritical congratulations, as all his other friends were doing. We all loved John and wanted to be kind.

The critics, however, were under no such compunction. They told it like it was: "Amateurish!" "Banal plot!" The well-known actress Pauline Frederick had staged one of the plays, proving once again that players are seldom good judges of what constitutes a good play. Most actors or actresses, left to their own devices, will pick a lemon every time. Or, even worse, write one. Their egos get in the way of their recognizing a good play for a good part. They believe they can make the play, but no player can make a bad play into a good play—and even the best thespians have had to learn this lesson the hard way. Dear John was a player at heart. "The play's the thing," wrote William Shakespeare, and he knew a thing or two about the theater.

We celebrated New Year's Eve 1935 with my family. My sister Vera came in from Chicago. It was our last time together, a sad occasion; my father was dying of lung cancer. Yet, still in good spirits, he participated in his favorite game of pinochle with Mama and his son-in-law, Joe, the doctor. Papa was always so proud to have achieved a doctor in the family. Mama was not a good card player. She played mostly to please Papa, who always won—unless, in order to humor her, he let her win.

This marriage of Arnold Sagor and Agnessa Litvinoff was a unique one. It was a happy marriage despite the differences in their backgrounds. My mother was a university graduate, spoke several languages, and was highly cultured. When they were apart, she'd had to learn Yiddish because my father couldn't write or read Russian; I doubt whether my father had any education at all outside of Hebrew school. Yet they were happy, in part because they shared the same political views—they were early anarchists. But most of all, Papa respected Mama, looked up to her, and deferred to her in everything. And she loved him because he was handsome, faithful, hardworking, and honest.

Papa had been sleeping in a chair for about a year because he could not lie down, yet Mama would not hear of calling in a nurse or putting him into a nursing home. A cigar smoker most of his life, in 1928, on doctor's orders, he switched to a pipe. Ernest and I brought two beautiful pipes back for him from Switzerland. Never having smoked a pipe before, he burned holes in both pipe bowls. Finally he learned how to puff and draw properly. Damage to his lungs was the result of his long-standing indulgence. He accepted the sentence gallantly, especially with Mama to look after him. Sick as he was, it delighted him to receive all the attention she was lavishing on him.

One thing bothered him, one of life's riddles he could not resolve. It had to do with his old crony, Willie Williams. Willie was a Wall Street tailor Papa had met during the years he was in the wool business, a business that proved very profitable for him during the first world war, when Papa had cornered the market on khaki, which he then sold to the army for uniforms.

I was alone with Papa this afternoon. Mama had taken off for a couple of hours and gone to a local movie house. She loved movies but complained that there were too many cowboy pictures. Again she had no choice but to watch yet another cowboy picture. Papa had requested an omelet for lunch. I prepared it with loving care and set it before him, but he would not eat more than a bite or two. Too late, I remembered that Mama used milk in her omelets. I did not, and mine was too dry for him. I felt so guilty to have forgotten. This could be the last omelet I make for Papa, I thought.

Then Papa began to talk about Willie Williams. Through the years, he and Papa had an enduring friendship that was frowned upon by my mother. Willie was Papa's nemesis, Mama claimed. He had introduced Papa to the racetrack, and Papa had become hooked on the ponies. Willie frequently visited now that Papa was ill, and Mama grudgingly let him come in. She knew how much Papa enjoyed his company.

"You take Willie Williams," Papa began, out of a clear blue sky. "All his life he has run around with women. He drinks. He gambles, loses his shirt at poker. And is he sick? No, he's fit as a fiddle. And look at me—all played out. I never ran around with women. I never drank. I never gambled."

And here he hesitated. "Well," he conceded reluctantly, "I liked to bet on the ponies once in awhile."

"You don't have to worry about that now, Papa," I said. "That's all water over the dam."

Still, he went on. "I know I shouldn't have done it. It made your Mama angry. Your Mama has a terrible temper. She's a Litvinoff, and she takes after her Papa. When that red-bearded fellow roared, everybody ran and hid. Everybody but your Mama. She was never afraid of him." I laughed. I had heard those stories before about my fierce, red-bearded grandfather and his oldest daughter Agnessa.

"I lost a lot of money," he went on, as if to ease the guilt feelings. "Rent money. Food money. Your Mama was right to scold, to lose her temper. But I never got mad at your Mama. She blows up and then it's all over. You mustn't get mad at your Mama either."

"Why worry about all of that now, Papa?" I said. "I could never get mad at Mama. Papa, I'm like you. I understand her."

A smile covered his face, and there was a twinkle in the eyes behind his spectacles. He took my hand in his, bent over and whispered as if my mother were nearby and he did not want her to hear what he was about to confess: "But do you know, daughter, if your Mama hadn't been after me—if she had left me alone—I know I would have come out ahead. I would have made a clean-up. I would have won. Won . . . beaten the system."

What a delightful confession to come from an old man destined soon to meet his Maker. Dear, dear Papa! Yes, all of us have vices we hate to part with even to the bitter end. He died peacefully during the night of January 31, 1936, sitting in his chair, where Mama found him in the morning.

We had a simple funeral for him. Old family friends showed up, whom we had not seen in years and had almost forgotten: Mrs. Siebel, a garrulous, chain-smoking reminder of our Madison Avenue days; Mr. and Mrs. Sturm, the grocers Mama had dealt with. All came to mourn with us. Mr. Steng, who had the millinery shop below our flat on Southern Boulevard in the Bronx, came to pay his respects. The big surprise was Mrs. Shisgall, with whom the family had summered at the Deaner Farmhouse in the Catskills as far back as 1905. I remembered the Shisgalls because they had a pony and cart for their two small sons, and they let me ride with them. You could hardly forget something like that. Mrs. Shisgall, now divorced and proudly self-supporting as a trained nurse, brought pictures of her sons, now grown. One of them was married and a father of three; the other was a writer of fiction whose stories were published in good magazines like the *Atlantic Monthly*. Why is it that people you have almost forgotten turn up at funerals? Is it nostalgia or curiosity? A little of both, I guess.

Before they closed the casket, my nephew Eddie and I said our last goodbye to Papa together. We placed a pack of pinochle cards under his head. Dear, dear Papa.

After the funeral, Mama and I went to Atlantic City for a week. It was midwinter, but we both loved the cold—it was the Russian in us! We bundled up and strode the boardwalk every day, arriving back at our hotel tingling, with red noses and cold toes but inwardly warm and refreshed. Mama was nearly eighty then, but still agile and spry. Her mind was like a steel trap. She was interested in everything going on. She read the newspapers carefully. She listened to the news on the radio. Her favorite American magazines were *The Nation* and *Harpers*. Everyone at the hotel fell in love with her spirit. Mama claimed she felt young when she was with me. She said it was my birth when she was in her forties that kept her from becoming an old lady too soon.

Mama was unaccustomed to hotels and restaurants, so this holiday was a lark for her. Everything was new and exciting, and she was easy to please. She particularly enjoyed the cup of bouillon she had with her dinner one night and ordered it again for lunch, and even for breakfast. She took it for granted that the consommé was made as she made it, from scratch, especially when anyone was sick. She simmered lean beef, marrowbone, and knuckle of veal together with chicken stock, carrots, celery, onions, and turnips. Then, after several hours of cooking, she removed the fat and strained it. She never suspected that the bouillon she relished came from a dehydrated cube, and I did not have the heart to tell her. She would not buy anything canned, believing

firmly that something in the canning process—in the cans themselves—
was an agent of cancer. Mama had her own theories, and some of
them made very good sense.

It was about this time that Ernestine, Ernest's oldest sister, came back
to the States from Spain with her two young sons, Peter and Michael.
They had had to flee Barcelona at the outbreak of the Civil War—it had
been a harrowing experience for them. Ernestine was a matron who
more rightly belonged in Suburbia, U.S.A. She was not cut out to be
the wife of a foreign representative of a film company, whose job it was
to roam the world. She had experienced revolution in Cuba and now
again when fascist and communist forces locked in mortal combat for
the soul of Spain.

In Spain, Ernestine, her husband Sidney, and the children had
been staying the weekend at the villa of some friends, twenty miles
outside of Barcelona. Their holiday was interrupted by an SOS call
from the American Embassy, ordering them to return to Barcelona at
once: It was unsafe for Americans to remain in Spain any longer. The
democratic revolutionary forces were clashing with the fascist Franco
and his army. An American battleship was standing by to take all
Americans out of Spain.

Those twenty miles back to Barcelona were a nightmare. Their
car was stopped again and again by revolutionaries waving red flags
and nervously carrying firearms with which they were not yet comfortable. Finally, five miles outside of Barcelona, they were ordered to
leave their car and enter a nearby hotel. They were searched and questioned. Fortunately, my brother-in-law, Sidney, a man of all nations,
spoke fluent Spanish. He offered to treat everyone to wine and whatever food was available. When the men had been served and were in a
better mood, he arose and said he would like to make a speech if they
would permit him to do so. They lifted him up on the table so he could
be better seen and heard.

"Ladies and Gentlemen—Comrades," he addressed them. "These
are serious times we are living in. You have been oppressed, ill-treated,
duped by Fascist forces. Now you want democracy, your freedom for
which you will have to fight. But remember this, comrades, the eyes of
the world are on Spain now, on each and every one of you. How you
behave as true revolutionaries will tell the world how civilized you are,

how worthy you are to be victorious in your cause. We are Americans. My family and I are entirely at your mercy. Yet I have no fear. I have complete faith in you, comrades. You are ladies and gentlemen. You will give us safe escort to our home. The American Embassy is evacuating us so we do not interfere with your progress. Long live the Revolution, Comrades!"

The speech, aimed at appealing to the best in their volatile natures, won them a special escort for the remainder of their journey back to Barcelona. Red flags flying, they were not stopped again, but waved right through. Contacting the Embassy, they were ordered to pack a few bags and leave at once for the battleship. My poor sister-in-law rebelled. Even if she had to face a firing-squad, she could not, would not make that battleship that day. They were told the battleship would leave without them but there would be an English freighter that would pick them up the next day—but there could be no more delays. Next morning, they left their nine-room apartment in Barcelona, with all their silverware, clothes, and other fine things in the hands of their servants, and boarded the freighter. My brother-in-law left his family when they reached a French port. He had to remain in Europe to protect the interests of the Fox Company. Somehow, in the raging civil war, he won the goodwill of both sides, Fascist and Revolutionary, and continued to go back and forth, managing to get Fox's profits out intact, using the Vatican and the influence of the Catholic church when necessary. Capitalism always finds a way.

My sister-in-law steeled herself to the assumption that she would never see her possessions again, but she was wrong. A year later she had everything back, down to items like washcloths and dust rags. Everything came carefully packed, so nothing was broken. The honesty and loyalty of those Spanish servants restored one's faith in human nature. My sister-in-law wept tears of gratitude. After the revolution was over—the Franco forces victorious—she sought out those servants and rewarded them all.

In addition to covering plays, both Ernest and I continued to work on motion picture projects. One of the ideas Ernest had been working on was a game, a new form of movie entertainment, called "U-Spot-It." To play the game, moviegoers would receive little cards as they entered the theater. The cards, which were all different, bore "identifications" that could be words, numbers, symbols, bits of dialogue, music, action, props, or sound effects. The moviegoer was to watch the film carefully, waiting for his particular identification to appear in the natural course of the action. All of the cards except one were dummies—that is, the identification designated on them would never appear in the movie at all.

At the end of the film, a master of ceremonies would mount the stage and ask who in the audience had spotted their identification. The lucky moviegoer, in order to receive his prize, was then required to join the master of ceremonies on stage and answer a few simple questions about where and when he "spotted it."

Several companies and exhibitors were interested right from the start. There was a packet of money in it if it could be put over. Because of the Depression, attendance at theaters had fallen off dramatically, and companies were desperately looking for enticements beyond the feature pictures to lure people into their theaters. A prospectus was developed and written. Ernest had tied in with a fellow named Eddie Spitz, the young scion of a wealthy Paterson, New Jersey, family. Spitz was looking for an opportunity to get into the entertainment business. He was the money man.

U-Spot-It was Ernest's baby. I had no part in it. I felt the time had come for each of us to go our own separate ways, career wise—that we each would do better if left to our own devices.

During this period, I was immersed in writing an original drawing-room comedy for someone like Katharine Hepburn. She had had a big success on stage in *Holiday,* Philip Barry's fine play of 1928. I admired the play greatly and felt the story I had in mind would lend itself to the same kind of treatment.

My blue-blooded heroine was a maverick who had gone into business for herself, scandalizing her family. She opened a bridal salon that took care of nuptial details, from the invitations to the showering of rice and the honeymoon. It was titled *Hail the Bride* and revolved around a wedding she was planning for her cousin, the bride-to-be. The cousin refused to send an invitation to the aunt and uncle of her fiancé because of the humble lineage of the simple farm couple from Nebraska. She felt that they did not belong at her wedding.

This aunt and uncle had raised her fiancé from early childhood, were very dear to him, and had given him every advantage—they sent him to college at great sacrifice to themselves. He was not about to cast them blithely aside. A self-made millionaire, he was not interested in limited acceptance into the "400 Set" to which his bride-to-be belonged. And so she loses him to the cousin handling her wedding, who does appreciate this man for what he is. In trying to waken the bride-to-be to the seriousness of the problem she is creating, our heroine ends up falling in love with the prospective bridegroom, and he with her. The planned wedding ends in their elopement.

The Leland Hayward Agency, a well-known and powerful agency, handled my manuscript, but it never got off the ground. We had a few nibbles, even one scheduled production, and then I packed it away with our other rejects—one more addition to our list of Swell Fish.

It was May 1937, and the time had come for Ernest and me to come to some basic decisions. Our lease at the Rhoerich was up. We were just about broke. U-Spot-It was being seriously considered by Metro-Goldwyn-Mayer. Nicholas Schenck had liked it and sent it West for reaction out there. I decided to go back to Hollywood, alone, to get our things out of storage. I needed to think about what I wanted to do. I was unhappy and confused. Ernest was vehemently opposed to my going and delivered an ultimatum—that if I went it could mean a final separation.

Ultimatum or not, I could not pass up an opportunity for free transportation. Wilfred Rothschild, who had worked at the Astoria Studios with Ernest, had a new Buick he was driving to California. I borrowed money from my sisters to tide me over and left; Ernest moved in with Ernestine and the boys, now living in an apartment in Forest Hills, Long Island.

The trip back to Tinsel Town remains a painful blur. Wilfred Rothschild, a rich, good-looking bachelor about my own age (and distantly related to the moneyed Rothschilds) was a difficult traveling companion. He was a fussbudget, meticulous in everything. He was also an extremely boring conversationalist.

We took Route 66, the main highway from the East to West Coast. The scenery that made up the three thousand miles between New York and Los Angeles vanished in the exhaust of the engine. Seven hundred miles a day was our mileage, day after exhausting day, and then to a hotel or motel for two bedrooms for the night. I insisted on paying my way for lodging and meals.

Wilfred's short-legged, wiry, black-brindled Scottie, Mr. Winston, reluctantly shared the front seat with me. He did not favor sitting in the back of the car alone. He liked company and always did whatever he wanted to do. He was a handsome animal, but he had no brains.

Whenever Wilfred stopped to attend the gas, I would walk Mr. Winston on a leash. I was amazed at how much curiosity he engendered, especially in the South, where we were stopped again and again, by children and grownups. "What kinda dog is that?" they would ask, circling him and looking him over. "Never seen the likes of him before."

The most intelligence Mr. Winston exhibited on the trip occurred in Phoenix, Arizona, where they were having a locust plague. The biggest, most voracious grasshoppers I had ever seen scared me half to death—landing in my hair, crawling over my face, creeping inside my clothes. My room was full of them. In desperation, I borrowed Mr. Winston. "He really goes for grasshoppers," Wilfred assured me. And Mr. Winston really did. That carnivorous Scottie made short shrift of the pests. He killed every last one and had a fine time doing it. I vowed never again to resent his crowding me in the front seat.

I had to be up and ready by six—Wilfred was a stickler for getting an early start. We always breakfasted later on the way, not that I wanted breakfast. I had developed a case of heartburn that only Tums could deal with, and I was carsick, too.

Every mile of that wretched highway was taking me farther from my husband, whom I dearly loved and who I knew loved me just as dearly. What did the future hold for us? Today old Highway 66 is a neglected, forgotten highway, but I am not nostalgic about it; it was heartbreak road for me.

We crossed the Texas Panhandle in the worst electric storm I have ever been in. Great bolts of lightning fell on the empty plains around our Buick. If we were struck by lightning, I thought to myself, I would have nothing more to have to resolve, no problems to confront, nothing to fear. "You needn't be worried about that lightning," Wilfred assured me. "It won't strike us. We're safe. Our rubber tires will protect us." He did not suspect my dark, private thoughts!

On arrival, I holed up in the Lido Apartments in Hollywood. They were located in familiar territory, across the way from the Mayfair Apartments where Ernest had lived before we were married. My rent at the Lido was only forty dollars per month for a studio apartment, utilities included. Instead of the dreaded wall-bed, I slept on a studio couch. I had no car; I had to take the bus. It took nearly half a day to get to Beverly Hills—three buses with interminable waits between.

Entering the Lido elevator one Saturday morning, I found myself in the company of a worn, fourtyish woman whom I barely recognized as Mae Murray. With her was a young boy, whom I judged to be eight or nine, in uniform, obviously home for the weekend from a military school. They presented an awkward picture of a mother and son trapped in an uncomfortable relationship. The boy was the offspring of Mae's unfortunate marriage to Prince Midvani, who, as everyone knew, helped rid her of her fortune and deserted her. She was wearing a faded silk dress and carried a frayed tan coat, patched not too neatly at the elbows. She looked haggard and lost. We all got off at my floor; their apartment was only three doors down the hall from mine.

It was hard to imagine that this sad creature was once a pampered movie star. On the MGM lot, I had often caught glimpses of Mae Murray climbing into her canary-yellow Pierce Arrow or Rolls Royce, with liveried chauffeur and a handsome Russian Borzoi dog on the front seat. MGM was the heyday of Mae Murray's career. Von Stroheim's *The Merry Widow*, in which she starred, was a box-office smash. Bob Leonard, for whom I scripted *Dance Madness*, was Mae's first husband. He felt bitter toward her because he spent many years promoting her career and neglecting his own, yet she put him through the wringer when they divorced. "She'll end up in the poorhouse," Bob Leonard had prophesied. "She can't handle money and she thinks she'll be young forever. Now she's stuck on some prince who is probably after her money." How right he was. Ten years later, here she was occupying a tacky studio apartment, same as mine. She too had no car.

I made no attempt, in the beginning, to talk to the former queen for fear it might embarrass her. A few weeks later I did invite the little soldier in, when I found him roving the corridor, and treated him to milk and a piece of chocolate cake. I could see he was hungry.

"I wish I didn't have to come home weekends," he confessed. "They feed me at the school." After that I made it my business to knock on the Murray apartment on weekends with offerings from my larder.

"I'm called out of town . . . I'm going away for the weekend . . . I don't want the food to spoil," were some of my excuses. The food was always graciously accepted, if diffidently. "You shouldn't really," she would say. "You're too kind."

A few days later there was a timid knock on my door. It was Mae Murray. Her eyes were red. She had been crying. "Could you lend me fifty dollars, Mrs. Maas," she faltered. "I'm behind in paying rent and they are pressing me for payment." I gave her the money even though it depleted my own meager funds. Next month, she and the boy were gone. For a long time I wondered what had become of her. Then the *Los Angeles Times* ran this item about her: "Mae Murray arrested for vagrancy when discovered sleeping on a bench in New York's Central Park." What a sad ending for a goddess!

I was low in spirits and looked to others for comfort and advice. Adele Commandini and Riza Royce were the two people I saw most frequently. I saw others: Hilda Stone, wife of John Stone (Sol Wurtzel's right-hand man at Fox); Bill Conselman; Malvina and Henry Dunn; Mary and Mike Simmons. Mary and Mike had bought themselves a house on Rodeo Drive in Beverly Hills. He was scripting B pictures and doing quite well at it.

One thing I quickly learned—do not rely on the advice of others when you are down, or uncertain about yourself or where you are heading. Without exception, these friends sought to widen the separation between Ernest and myself. They hinted, and even urged, that I dump him. It was advice that came from the tops of their heads. Not one of them really cared; they all had their own woes and concerns. My dear mother used to say that if each of us put our bundle of troubles before our front door and were given the option to choose between our own bundle and someone else's, we would most likely choose our own again. It was up to me to fight my own battles and make my own decisions.

I was attending a preview with some friends when I ran into Leonard Fields, story editor for Republic Pictures. Leonard had succeeded the Japanese lady who had stepped into my shoes as story editor at Universal. He was glad to see me and urged me to drop in at the studio. "I might put you on the payroll," he kidded. But it was no laughing matter to me, for I needed a job badly. I had yet to pay back my obligations to my sisters. I borrowed a car to take me into the valley where Republic was operating, and I brought the manuscript of *Hail the Bride* with me.

"It's a great story," Fields conceded when I had finished outlining it to him. He meant it, too. "I wish I could buy it," he added. "But it's too sophisticated for Republic. It's MGM stuff. We're not in their class."

I could not agree more. Then before I realized it, I pulled an Eddie Goulding trick. I outlined an idea I had been flirting with but had not yet committed to paper. I called it *A Bill of Goods*. The difference between Goulding and me was that I had a definite story in mind, not an idea born out of the blue, concocted on the spot.

My characters were a department store buyer, a successful head of a children's department in Topeka, Kansas, and a young salesman rapidly making headway in his New York firm, which manufactured a line of children's apparel. Its theme dealt with the rampant bribery and casual sex that existed among the male manufacturing salesmen and the female department store buyers. These women, in addition to being wined and dined, also extracted their pound of flesh with every bill of goods they bought. Hence the title: *A Bill of Goods*. Leonard liked the story line and the story's box-office possibilities, so he hired me to develop it, at a modest three hundred dollars a week.

There was only one drawback. The man in the front office who was responsible for the contract was none other than Manny Goldstein, the former office manager for Universal in the East when I was story editor. He was no friend of mine then, and we had many run-ins. Too many times I had had to combat his penny-ante tactics. Now, loathsome Manny was all smiles, and so was I. I asked to be allowed to take the contract to my office and study it. I found that the contract stated boldly that all rights to my story idea reverted to the studio after a trial period of two weeks. So, despite a flurry of memos from Goldstein reminding me to affix my John Hancock to the contract, it remained in my new office, unsigned, while I worked.

At the end of two weeks, I had a fair outline of *A Bill of Goods* completed. Carefully, I placed that outline and other pertinent papers in my briefcase, and just as carefully I made sure there wasn't even a remnant of a scrap of paper left to give a clue to what I had been working on.

Briefcase in hand, and with my chapeau perched jauntily on my head, I let Manny Goldstein's secretary usher me into his sanctum sanctorum. I handed him the contract. "It isn't signed," he noted, unable to conceal his displeasure.

"No, Mr. Goldstein," I replied, "it isn't. What's more, Mr. Goldstein,

I have no intention of signing it. What guarantee do I have that Republic will not hand me my walking papers after I have committed my idea to paper? Under this contract, Republic could acquire my brainchild for six hundred dollars, just two weeks' salary." The situation was almost too much for him to handle. His blood pressure was rising.

"Does that mean you are walking out on us—just like that?"

"Just like that, I'm afraid, Mr. Goldstein, and with the story right here in my briefcase. You still have the option of changing the contract and acquiring the rights on my terms," I smiled, keeping my self-control.

He pushed the contract over to my side of the desk. "Take it or leave it," was his reply. I left it.

Leonard Fields, understandably, was very put out with me. My brazen collection of two weeks' salary did not endear him to Manny Goldstein or his other superiors in the front office. For once, a writer had bested them at their own game. For once, these industry pirates, these wily crooks, had nothing to steal; the story was securely tucked away in my briefcase. It was a hollow victory at best. If you were to say that I had grown paranoid about the integrity of the motion picture industry, you would be right. But then who could fault me after the bitter experiences Ernest and I had had at its hands?

I did have six hundred dollars to add to my bank checking account. That was better than nothing. I could manage easily on a hundred dollars a month. After my forty-dollar rent expenditure, I had sixty left for food and incidentals. It was a time when leg of lamb was seventeen cents a pound, lamb breast ten cents. A five-pound chicken could be had for under a dollar, swordfish and fresh salmon for twenty-five cents a pound, milk twelve cents a quart, eggs twenty-five cents a dozen. I had learned how to cut corners. I could dream up a casserole dish for about forty cents that would last a week.

My biggest expenditure was postage, special delivery and regular letter, and telegrams. Ernest and I were in daily communication. Long-distance phone service was not yet in existence. We used the mails and Western Union.

Ernest had inveigled me into a cross-continent collaboration. Ironically titled *Are You Married?*, it was an idea we had discussed and mulled over in the months before our separation but never developed. Ernest was now committing it to paper. As he did not type, he wrote in longhand. I would type what he sent me, adding my changes, and mail it back to him in New York.

But my heart was not in it. The Republic debacle had exacted its price on my deflated ego. I was chagrined to have to write home about yet another fiasco. Ernest and my family had been so elated when I had wired the initial news of the Republic assignment. Then, to have to write that the deal had fallen through was a bit much.

The Lido had a solarium atop its roof. On sunny days, I took my portable typewriter, paper, and pencils, and stretched out on a beach towel or opened a beach chair and worked there. That is, I tried to. Tears would splash down on the handwritten pages of my beloved who was trying so hard and doing such a good writing job. But I was in no condition to appreciate it, even to read it. I felt physically ill at the thought of trying to write again.

"What's the use?" I kept asking myself. "Another disappointment? Haven't we had enough Swell Fish?"

I was not the only frustrated soul on that roof. There were other Lido denizens who came there to sunbathe and while away the heavy hours, waiting between calls from Central Casting: pretty young starlet-aspirants not yet on company payrolls and handsome young male hopefuls looking for that bit part that would change their lives, that crumb of opportunity to be noticed on the silver screen. Between waits, there was always extra work for them. That money paid the rent and bought the hamburgers.

Now that we were apart, I felt closer to Ernest than ever before. On July 6, my thirty-seventh birthday, I received thirty yellow roses (my favorite) and one extra white rose "to grow on." On August 5, our tenth wedding anniversary, Best's Fifth Avenue in New York sent me a handsome blue leather pocketbook with five crisp ten-dollar bills inside, and the florist delivered ten yellow roses. Absence makes the heart grow fonder, it is said. And husbands do change and remember anniversaries.

One night I ran into B.P. Schulberg at Lucey's, a restaurant on Melrose Avenue near the Paramount Studios. It was another popular rendezvous spot for Hollywood filmdom. He was seated alone at a corner table and was genuinely glad to see an old friend. Despite all past feelings of hurt and resentment, my heart instantly went out to him. He had become just another lost soul in the Hollywood scene.

Gone was the charismatic, ambitious executive who had engaged me to script *The Plastic Age* for his newly founded company, Preferred Pictures. The man before me had aged. His normally pink complexion was ashen, his face flabby, loose-jowled, his eyes bloodshot and circled, his flaxen hair snow white. His hands shook as he put down his high-ball glass and rose to greet me.

We made a date for lunch. It was to be the forerunner of a number of luncheon dates at Lucey's, all at the same corner table. You might say this table was now B.P. Schulberg's unofficial office. The measure of this man, what made him different and outstanding in the industry, was his compassion. I felt free to unload my feelings on him. Most endearing were his words of comfort and advice about my separation from Ernest. Unlike others, he told me how lucky I was to have someone I really cared for and who cared for me. He counseled me to hold on to my marriage, no matter what. His big regret was that he had married young, before sowing his wild oats, before he was ready for the responsibilities of being a husband and a father. Sorrowfully, he admitted that Ad, his wife, still cared for him and would take him back despite everything. But he could not face a reconciliation. He no longer loved her. In fact, she and the whole Jaffe family to which she belonged were anathema to him. He had a deep-seated animus that he could not overcome when it came to them.

I did not know Ad Schulberg, had never met her, so I could not combat him on that score. I thought, what a contradiction this man was. At heart, he was an old-fashioned Jew, with old-fashioned values that he had violated and could not reconcile with his conscience. He revered the institution of marriage and felt guilty for having failed both at marriage and being a father.

He told me about his fall from grace at Paramount, his unhappy love affair with Sylvia Sidney (now over), the stormy dissolution of his marriage. He talked about the shock of discovering that he had been reduced to a nonentity in the industry, a marked man; that he was practically ostracized, that all doors were closed to him.

"I couldn't get a job as a dogcatcher," he summed up balefully.

But most of all, he talked about his kids, Budd, Sonya, and Stuart. He felt he had let them down. There had been bitter quarrels between Ad and himself, quarrels about Sylvia Sidney, about money, about his gambling and drinking, his addiction to buddies-in-pleasure like Felix Young.

He was proudest of the fact that he had instilled in his kids an appreciation of the classics by reading aloud to them on weekends when he was at home. Musicians, he was sure they would never become. Ad had tried to force the harp on Sonya and the saxophone on Budd. It did not take in either case. But when it came to books, he was sure all three would turn out to be literary geniuses, particularly Budd, who he said was sensitive and idealistic.

"He wants to write a novel blasting the film industry."

How proud he was when, not too many years later, the novel *What Makes Sammy Run* became a bestseller. It blasted the film industry, all right, and exposed it like the emperor without clothes. I remember his telling me that Stuart had feared Budd's success would go to his head and he would succumb to the God of Mammon. "Not a chance," B.P. laughed, as he flipped the ash from his familiar cigar. "He's not like his dad."

In his wallet, he carried snapshots of his children when they were small. He also carried a poem his daughter Sonya had written. They were a bit worn from handling. Of his three progeny he had the highest hopes for Stuart. "He's brilliant," he kept repeating. "Brilliant. He'll hit the top." What top he didn't say, but I strongly suspect it was the industry that he still loved passionately and to which he had devoted so much of his life.

Ben and I cried a lot on each other's shoulders. "I should have signed Ernest to a Paramount contract," he frankly confessed. "We big guys behind our big desks aren't always smart. I figured he was a Walter Wanger man. It was Wanger who helped bring me down. All he needed was the opportunity, and the opportunity was Sylvia. I guess I asked for it," he ended ruefully. What he was not to know was that Walter Wanger would have his own debacle, years later. He would marry the lovely Joan Bennett and then, in a jealous, drunken rage, shoot one of her lovers, causing his own exodus from the Hollywood scene.

The industry had still another shock in store for Ernest and me. He sent me an urgent telegram: "Be sure get copy todays Film Daily. Rotten news re U-Spot-It." The *Film Daily* item read: "MGM plans error pix for contests on Bank Night plan. Suggested by the Bank Night idea, MGM will produce a short containing errors in history and characterization, to be used by exhibitors as a contest, giving prizes to those in the audience picking out the most mistakes. The first short, to be used as a trial for the scheme, will be based on Christopher Columbus. To be titled 'Flicker Flaws,' it will be handled by Pete Smith. The script is being written by George Drumgold, for Dave Miller's direction and Jack Chertok's supervision. If the idea works out, the contest short will be developed into a series."

Grand larceny again!

Despite letters and telegrams from Ernest urging me to keep my chin up and not to take it too seriously, I fell into a funk that offered no escape. I wrote suicidal messages to Ernest. To my family. In the face of its gross inequities, life had become unbearable and no longer worth living.

I turned on my gas oven. As the sweet, nauseating vapors were taking effect and putting me under, I returned to my senses. I realized what a selfish, inconsiderate thing I was doing. I was punishing my husband, my mother, my sisters. They, not I, would be the real victims of my escape from reality, my inability to deal with disappointment and defeat.

I turned off the gas and closed the oven door. In the years to come and under different circumstances, there would be one other time when Ernest and I together would contemplate ending our lives, yet come to the same conclusion. Suicide is a copout. The real victims are those who are left behind to harbor guilt and grief. No one worth their salt has the right to inflict such punishment on the ones they love.

Next day, the Western Union wires carried this message to Forest Hills, Long Island: "Darling. Please return to Los Angeles without further ado. I need you. Schatz."

It was a bright, sunny day when, at eleven in the morning, Riza von Sternberg (Wright) drove me to Pasadena and deposited me in front of the old vine-covered Presbyterian church on Colorado Boulevard a few blocks from the post office. That was to be the tryst Ernest and I had arranged through our daily interchange of Western Union telegrams. The last had come from Barstow, California. It read: "Closer now. Hallelujah! Meet you at church in Pasadena around noon."

Ernest had had a piece of luck. He was able to buy a Plymouth roadster, with less than a thousand miles of use, for just one hundred

dollars. He also found a passenger to share expenses, if not the driving. So Ernest had company coming across on Highway 66.

My heart pounded wildly, my myopic eyes strained and scanned
every car coming from the east, looking for a black Plymouth roadster
with two men in the front seat. Suddenly it appeared, a black Plymouth
with a rumble seat and two men in the front! It came to an impatient,
grinding halt at the curb in front of the church. Out leaped Ernest, who
enveloped me in an embrace. He needed a shave. He was thin, haggard from the long drive. Three thousand miles in four days! But, oh,
how good he looked to me!

Chapter 15

MOTION PICTURE PEDDLER

THE LAST POST I EVER EXPECTED TO FILL was as a motion picture peddler. But that was what happened to me next. Arthur Landau, when dealing with literary material for the Edward Small Agency years back in New York, had handled the sale of Rex Beach's *The Goose Woman*. That deal netted him a handsome commission and earned for me an expensive beaded handbag for purchasing the story for Universal.

Now Arthur Landau was in business for himself and Edward Small, having transferred his operations to the West Coast, was looking for someone to run his story department. The job was offered to me. Two hundred a week plus commission on writers I placed and any material I sold.

I soon discovered that what Edward Small, the pioneer agent who puffed big cigars into sensitive ladies' faces, had hired me to do was to dispose of the mountainous stack of Octavus Roy Cohen detective stories that had been serialized in *Argosy Magazine* through the years and were now piled in my office awaiting some form of treatment for the screen. Octavus Roy Cohen's detective, Jim Harvey, although entertaining (I suppose), was a fat, commonplace semi-illiterate who knew and befriended all the crooks in Christendom. In my opinion, then and now, the Jim Harvey stories were positively the worst magazine fiction ever published, despite their following among *Argosy* readers.

One thing was sure. The Octavus Roy Cohen material was not suitable for the screen. Cherishing what little standing I had left as a

210

judge of material, I could not in good conscience offer them for sale. Edward Small, my deluded boss, had acquired this collection for a song at an auction and was convinced he had a tidy fortune tied up in Octavus Roy Cohen.

He had to be humored and so, to hold my job, I humored him. "I think we have some interest at Columbia Pictures," I invented. "Universal is considering a series based on this material." I kept this up for nearly a year in the daily written reports I was required to submit.

I hated being an agent. Even if I had had a roster of good writers and a desk covered with good material, I think I would have hated it anyway. I disliked selling. I had been trained to buy material, not sell it. That made me something of a literary snob, you might say. Be that as it may, I couldn't sell material I would not buy. Unfortunately, Mr. Small's stable, exemplified by his conviction that Octavus Roy Cohen was the greatest writer who had ever lived, was all that kind of material. Therefore I could not sell it.

I had to cover every studio every day with my wares, rain or shine. Universal, Warner Brothers, and Republic studios were located in the San Fernando Valley, MGM in Culver City (a good thirty miles away), Twentieth Century–Fox in Beverly Hills, and Paramount and Columbia in Hollywood. Our Plymouth roadster piled up plenty of mileage and wore out a set of tires. Our gas mileage was about twelve miles to the gallon. Fortunately, the gas wars in those years sometimes brought the price down as low as fourteen cents a gallon.

I discovered an aspect that made my job tolerable: I made friends with interesting individuals at the various studios. I appreciated the opportunity to meet and talk to personalities I respected and admired for their achievements. I did not have to sell them anything but conversation.

One of my favorite "parking" places was with John Huston at Warner Brothers. Only twenty-seven, he was already showing indications of the brilliant writer-director he was to become. John was a writer-in-training, working on such scripts as *Dr. Erlich, Pasteur,* and *Freud.* It was pure heaven to while away an hour or two talking to him. And how I envied him those assignments.

Then there was Dalton Trumbo at Paramount. He was a reader then, a searching young fellow. We found we were attuned in our literary appreciation and, more important, on the political outlook of where our great country was headed. Like John Howard Lawson, Trumbo was a solid American seeking only the best for our country. And like Lawson, he too would be crucified as one of the infamous "Ten," targets of McCarthyism.

Claudine West at MGM was always a stop I looked forward to. Claudine was the alter ego of director Sidney Franklin, and she wrote most of his scripts. He depended on her, and she never let him down. They were a good team.

I also met Irving Berlin at MGM. One afternoon, the modest, prolific composer played some tunes for me on an upright piano he had had specially built to enable him to compose in one key. They were "Isn't It a Lovely Day" and "Cheek to Cheek" from the motion picture *Top Hat*, and "Let's Face the Music" from *Follow the Fleet*, both with Ginger Rogers and Fred Astaire. I told him about Hugh Herbert and Coronado, and how, as a result of Herbert's singing his tunes night and day, I had become allergic to Irving Berlin. He got a big kick out of that.

I especially liked to talk to S.J. Perelman, a brilliant satirist, a pearl of an intellect to match his name, and a solid human being besides. So many times brilliant people are not nice inside. S.J. Perelman was. He was collecting a huge salary check at MGM that he assured me he was not earning. They had hired him at twenty-five hundred dollars a week but apparently had forgotten he existed, for after six months he had yet to have a story conference.

"I'm salting it away," he joyfully confided. "Once in a lifetime. Who knows when I'll have another bonanza like this?"

One day, in my office at the Small Agency, I had an unexpected visitor. It was none other than Josef von Sternberg. Edward Small ushered him in and introduced us, assuming we did not know each other.

"Mr. von Sternberg and I are old friends," I told my boss.

"Yes, I am well acquainted with Miss Sagor," Joe acknowledged, not too happily.

I could not say which of us was more uncomfortable when Eddie Small left us alone. I was sure Joe must have been dismayed to discover that I was part of the Small Agency. Here he was, hat in hand, looking for a job, and I would be the one who represented him.

Adversity had had a salutary effect on his personality. I found him chastened, affable. Gone was that air of superiority he affected to diminish others, that air which, in the end, helped topple him. He was almost humble now, eager to please.

He had written a treatment of the Zola novel *Germinal,* a working-class story that he hoped might win him a directorial assignment. It had some of the same ingredients as *Salvation Hunters,* his calling card to the industry. I could almost read his mind. He was wondering if now that I had the chance I would exercise the dislike for him I had never tried to conceal. He had little choice. He too was *persona non grata* in the industry. No first-class agent would represent him.

He was right. I must admit I did not break my neck to place him. The outline of his proposed treatment for *Germinal* was adequate. But it was a heavy, sociological story. When I sampled the hostility everywhere at the mere mention of his name, I did not push him or his story. Agents have to keep that welcome mat out for themselves so that they can return again and again. You sell only what the buyer wants to buy, and as an agent, I followed the rule.

With beginner's luck, the very first week with Eddie Small I was able to place Charles Edwin Markham on a six-month contract with the director-producer John Stahl at a thousand dollars a week. To this day, it still baffles me why John Stahl engaged this elderly man (in his seventies) to write a script for him. Markham was a fine poet but knew nothing about screenwriting. It could not have happened to a sweeter, nicer fellow. He was living alone in a small cottage in Whitley Heights back of the Hollywood Bowl. I had to help him write his screenplay. I didn't mind. He was such an interesting old gentleman. Besides, he paid me under the table.

I placed one other writer in the year I was an agent for Edward Small. In fact, they were the only two writers Eddie Small had on his writer roster. This built up high hopes for me. My boss thought he had hired a winner for his story department. This other writer was Gordon Kahn.

Dear Gordon was an ex-newspaperman, a feisty little man who wore a monocle, which did not become him and which raised the eyebrows of many a producer and prejudiced them. "What kind of oddball is he?" asked John Stone at Fox when I offered him the services of my client. Universal Pictures proved more tolerant and hired him for a cops-and-robbers picture. Gordon was an awful hack as a film writer. As a person he was a plucky fighter who was another of the "Ten" who had to face the McCarthy interrogators.

My year's contract with Eddie Small was coming to an end. I did not expect it would be renewed nor did I want it to be renewed. I'd had my fill of the nightmare of agenting with nothing to sell. My conscience bothered me for faking it as I had and drawing my salary. I knew what a keen disappointment I had turned out to be after placing a thousand-dollar-a-week writer under contract, just like that.

Before Small and I parted company, I felt it incumbent to enlighten Eddie Small so that he could share part of the blame for my turning out to such a dud. "Don't waste your money, Eddie," I told him. "Don't replace me. You'll only be throwing good money away. You made your big success in this business as a talent agent. You were one of the very first, beginning with the big bands."

"But I had a great story department in New York," he countered. "You bought *The Goose Woman* through our agency."

"Through Arthur Landau," I corrected. "Arthur had magazine and publisher connections. He's in business now by himself and making money. He has something to sell. You haven't, Eddie. You can't have a story department unless you have something to sell. Stick to talent, Eddie. There's where you shine." Gratuitous advice, I thought, because he did not seem to appreciate it in the least. But do you know? He took it.

There was another task I longed to accomplish before I severed my connection with the agency business. I made up my harebrained mind that I was going to place Ben Schulberg on the MGM producer payroll. Louis B. Mayer had elevated the inadequate, lightweight Walter Wanger, from Paramount, to that status. Why not Ben Schulberg?

Now that I look back, I was sticking my head into the lion's den. The roaring MGM lion. Perhaps I was so brave because I knew that the lion used in the MGM screen emblem was harmless; he was defanged and toothless. Nonetheless, I felt like Miss David stoning Goliath. I spoke to David Selznick several times about hiring Schulberg. The first time was when he was still working at MGM under his father-in-law's protection, and I spoke to him again when he ventured out for himself, in defiance of Louis B. His answers were always velvety, complimentary of Schulberg's talents and all he owed him for giving him his initial chance at Paramount. "I'd love to have him on my staff," he would say, "but I don't have a place for him."

Next, I went to Al Lichtman. Al was now a full-fledged producer at MGM, an honorary post because he never did produce a single picture while he held it.

"Al," I pleaded, "you've got to help Ben Schulberg. I know—and you know it, too—if you were in his shoes, he'd help you. We've got to talk to Mayer about him. Ben made money for Paramount. He'll make money for MGM. He belongs on this lot. If Mayer can hire a nincompoop like Walter Wanger . . ."

He shook his head and interrupted: "Mayer won't have him."

"Louis B. Mayer is human. If we go to him, Al, he'll listen. I know he will. It's not right Schulberg should be out of a job. Everybody in the industry knows why and is talking about it. Mayer is supposed to hold some kind of grudge against Ben dating back to the time they were partners. Mayer can't be that heartless. Let's try to reach him, Al. I'll speak to Louis Lighton. I'm sure he'll join us. He knows better than anyone else the worth of his ex-boss at Paramount. Schulberg gave him his chance, made him a producer. He owes him that much. He knows B.P.'s record as a star maker, how efficiently B.P. ran the Paramount studio, his ability to make outstanding pictures at a fraction of the cost of other studios."

Al Lichtman was not what you would call a compassionate man, and he was not an easy man to convince. This time he weakened.

That same day, I spoke to Louis Lighton, who also was a producer on the MGM lot. He readily agreed to accompany Lichtman and me. "You know, Frederica, I would do anything I could to help Ben. You're so right. I owe him a lot."

An appointment was set up. When the day came, however, the cautious Lighton chickened out. He became conveniently indisposed and was absent from the studio. I guess, after talking it over with his wife and mentor, Hope, he got cold feet; Hope Loring was not a woman to take unnecessary chances with her husband's career. So Al Lichtman and I faced the MGM Goliath alone.

The poet Alexander Pope wrote wisely in his "Essay on Criticism": "Fools rush in where angels fear to tread." Or, as William Shakespeare put it: "Wrens make prey where eagles dare not perch." You can take your choice. Either one applies.

I could enter into a long diatribe about what took place that disappointing afternoon. It shatters me to this day to have to recall it. Louis B. Mayer may have held a big job in the motion picture industry, the biggest there was at MGM. Big job notwithstanding, Louis B. Mayer was not a big man. He was a petty man, a crafty man; above all, he was a very fearful, insecure man, unsure of his exalted post and prepared to protect it with all the canniness he could command. It was very plain. Louis B. Mayer was afraid of B.P. Schulberg.

"I told you so," Al Lichtman glumly commented as we left. He felt diminished by what was probably the one decent act in his life—to put in a good word for a fallen comrade. He looked at me, and I could see he was trying to figure out why he had permitted himself to be put into this doltish position that could not help but weaken him in Mayer's eyes, to say nothing of offending the king by pushing into his private domain of likes and dislikes. As for this foolish wren who had dared to rush in, she was outraged at the exhibition of ruthless power she had witnessed.

Ernest did not fault me for what I had done. He understood completely. "At least you tried, Schatz, to repay a favor." He was always there with the right words when I needed him.

On August 31, 1988—almost fifty years later—I wrote a letter to Budd Schulberg describing that meeting on behalf of his father:

> Dear Budd Schulberg:
>
> You want to know more about that meeting with Louis B. Mayer.
>
> Louis B. was a pompous, power-mad insensitive hypocrite. I think he actually relished his position, anointed potentate that he was, sitting there listening to an appeal for a colleague he could make or break at will. He was over-lavish in his praise of Ben, as I recall. And so outwardly compassionate.
>
> Oh, he would do everything he could, of course . . . But at the moment . . . You know the phraseology of the polite let-down . . .
>
> However, one thing may have come out of it. Shortly thereafter, David Selznick offered Ben a job. I always wondered if there was a connection. If there was, then I am sure it must have been with this proviso from father-in-law to son-in-law:

"Give him a desk and let him rot!" For that Samaritan gesture was only one more humiliation for Ben Schulberg.

Incidentally, your dad never knew I interceded in his behalf. He was a proud man and I felt he didn't need to know. If something good had materialized, I might have confessed. As it was, it led to nothing. . . .

I visited Ben several times at the Culver City Studios, which Selznick International Pictures had taken over in 1937. It became the home of that epic picture *Gone with the Wind*. RKO had been the studios' previous tenant. RKO had followed Pathé. And before that, Cecil B. DeMille had made pictures there. The studios had been built in 1919 and were occupied by Thomas Ince until his death. They are still in operation today and have seen a lot of motion picture history through the years.

When Ben Schulberg first went to work for David Selznick, he was elated, a happy man. There was a splendid office with his name on the door in gold letters: B.P. Schulberg, Producer. His desk was full of reading material. He anticipated the good things to come.

"David told me he couldn't love me more if I was his father. He says I taught him practically everything he knows. He came to Paramount, fresh out of college. David's smart. Going places. And without his father-in-law's help. He told me Mayer was mad as hell when he wanted to hit the top by himself. He'll do it, too."

But the good things Ben anticipated did not materialize. When days went into weeks, and weeks went into months and he was still given nothing to do, he began to sense that he had been hired out of kindness. David Selznick kept kidding him along and giving him more material to read.

"We've got to find the right vehicle for you, Ben," he kept saying.

"Freddie," Ben finally confided to me, "I'm getting a runaround. I don't need a desk, a weekly salary. I want a picture to produce, and I'm not going to get one. I'm quitting tonight. I'm going to tell David where he can go. Who the hell do they think I am? I don't need charity. Before I get through I'll show this industry a thing or two."

I never saw or talked to B.P. Schulberg again. Ernest and I were too entangled in our own brew of woes, worries, and problems. Plus, there was nothing more I could do for him. At least I had tried. I hate to see good talent wasted, and he had plenty of that. The motion picture industry relegated the once-important kingpin executive with the big cigar, in charge of Paramount Production, to oblivion, throwing him on the ash heap of forgotten men. He was never able to extricate himself from the abyss. Some of the blame should be put where it belongs, on the man himself. For all his professional strengths, he had too many personal weaknesses. His name would appear now and again in the papers. He married again, some young chick, and fathered a child—one last manifestation of his ego asserting itself. He died young, sick at heart, I am sure, that he had failed as a father to his Budd, Sonia, and Stuart. How he loved his kids.

Chapter 16

WORLD WAR II

USING THE EXPERIENCE I HAD GATHERED as an agent, I was able to procure writing contracts at Paramount for Ernest and myself. Paramount had acquired a mass of story material that needed culling, and we were hired for the job at an inflated salary I was able to arrange. With this money we were able to acquire a house in the new Westwood Village.

Westwood Village was a Jans Real Estate development. It was an acreage of wide, open fields begging for real estate ravishment. Its perimeters were the city of Beverly Hills on the east and the city of Santa Monica on the west, Sunset Boulevard on the north and Pico Boulevard on the south. Wilshire Boulevard ran through its center, with the Beverly Hills Golf Course at one end and the Veteran's Hospital and Cemetery at the other. To gain absolute control of the territory, Jans donated some of the land for a state university. It was a large, beautiful parcel, now completely occupied by university buildings and an outstanding university hospital, dormitories, and parking lots.

The idea was to build an attractive residential community around the university, and the concept lived up to its name. It was a charming little village in every sense of the word. Architects such as Richard Neutra and Frank Lloyd Wright lent their modernistic talents to construct individual homes and apartment dwellings as well as commercial buildings. Everything harmonized. The stores, banks, food shops, office buildings—no higher than two stories—were built around open courtyards and patios, each building with its own design and decoration. The meadows and hills became a beehive of construction activity. Houses, houses, houses everywhere. One- and two-story homes, some Monterey, others New England; European chalets, English country cottages. There was so much land that no section appeared crowded.

Today there is not an empty lot remaining. High-rise apartment buildings, high-rise condominiums, and high-rise office buildings line Wilshire Boulevard from one end to the other, completely overwhelming the sleepy little village that once was.

One of the early charms of Westwood, before the village came into being, was a sylvan hideaway, a wooded copse that was later included in the land allocated for the university. One could escape—and right in the middle of the city—to an untrampled paradise where foxes and raccoons roamed and even an occasional deer could be seen. Here was a verdant Garden of Eden, unspoiled, perfumed by pines and sage bushes, wild oak and berry bushes. Songbirds abounded. Roadrunners scuttled across one's path. Rabbits, chipmunks, and squirrels were at home here. A botanist would have reveled in the variety of its wildflowers. The Maases had discovered this miniature Little Red Riding Hood forest long before the Jans's building spree. While living in Beverly Hills, we would frequently pack a lunch and wander into the woods for a picnic. There we would walk and talk and work on story ideas. A-lack-a-day! Our hideaway now has been brutally sacrificed to student dorms and parking lots. Not a vestige left.

Everyone, it seemed, was moving to Westwood, including the Maases. It was Ernest who really set his heart on buying a house. I remembered my mother's aversion to owning property. When Papa had an opportunity to buy an apartment house, she discouraged him by assuring him that she would never evict someone for nonpayment of rent. When I first came to Hollywood, fresh from the canyon city of New York, I played with the idea of buying a house and very nearly bought one high in the hills with a view. The George Elkin real estate agency also tried to sell me on a Spanish hacienda on the corner of Wilshire Boulevard, two blocks east of Fairfax. It was surrounded by empty lots then. The May Company Department Store, two blocks away, was not yet built or even thought of. The Miracle Mile was not in existence. Wilshire Boulevard, from La Brea on to the blue Pacific in Santa Monica, was still a dirt road. This purblind MGM writer, who had scorned buying desert land in Palm Springs when it was a nickel an acre, turned down the Wilshire steal—the price was under fifteen thousand dollars—because she preferred that adorable house with a view high in the Hollywood Hills. As everyone knows, that particular corner would today be worth a cool million or two. Or more. This lady knows nothing of real estate values, then or now. In the end, I bought neither house.

So, it was a Monterey-style house we bought in Westwood. On Homedale Avenue, off Sepulveda Boulevard. Homedale was a hilly street. It had one house at the top, and one—ours—at the bottom, with empty lots in between. Our slate-gray house had yellow and white trim, and had a red-tiled roof with wisteria creeping all over it. Recessed and shaded by a huge spreading walnut tree, there were also orange, lemon, and apricot trees in front. It had a fine lawn, and all around the front of the house was a border of yellow and white flowers. The garage was unobtrusively positioned on the side toward the back of the house. Being a Monterey type, the house had a balcony in front. Upstairs there were three large bedrooms, bathrooms, and dressing rooms. Downstairs, there was a large kitchen and pantry, a sunroom and dining room, a large living room, and a library—all leading onto a terraced backyard. Seven terraces, all beautifully planted.

It was May when we bought the house. We spent the better part of the summer furnishing it. We invested in oriental rugs, fine antique French furniture, and a Steinway baby grand. We also had our own antiques to display—those that Ernest had inherited. And we had good art on the walls. It was a little band-box. My delight was two large Japanese lamps, converted from two fine old Japanese vases, placed at either end of a sofa in the living room. At the base of each lamp was an aquarium filled with tropical fish. It was especially attractive when the lamps were lit, but it was an absorbing distraction at any hour.

There was only one drawback. It was an expensive house to run. We had to engage two fulltime gardeners. After the rains each year, we had to completely replant our terraces in the back. All seven of them! How were we to know that the water would cascade down the hillside like Niagara Falls and inundate our property, overflowing into the house itself, ruining carpets, hardwood floors, and furniture? What a head-ache it was, that first storm! I could do nothing but wring my hands and weep, and rue the day we had bought the place. We woefully learned the hard way, and it cost a small fortune to install a proper drainage system. But both Ernest and I were working and earning beautiful salary checks, so we resignedly paid the piper.

That house soon became the focus of neighborhood activity. We had good times in that house and also some interesting and profound experiences. At our musical evenings, classical and jazz musicians appeared: Pete Seeger, Oscar Levant, Yip Harburg, and Jakob Gimpel, a concert pianist of renown hibernating with the MGM orchestra. German refugees and writers who lived in Beverly Hills and Pacific Palisades nearby frequently came over to read us their manuscripts. Everyone who crossed our threshold was strongly anti-Nazi and anti-fascist.

We raised money to help those escapees who were biding time in Mexico, South America, or Portugal, awaiting entrance to the U.S. whenever quotas and some influential politicking permitted it. The war in Europe was escalating, as Hitler multiplied his conquests, country after country. It was anybody's guess when the Germans would be fighting the Russians. Certainly this was the fervent prayer of the anti-German governments, egging Germany to take on Russia. "Let them devour each other" was the sentiment. When Stalin made his pact with Nazi Germany, there was great confusion in liberal circles. Many Russian supporters fell away, unable to understand that the Russians were desperately buying time so that they could build war factories in Siberia to prepare for the inevitable. The Bolsheviks were lumped with Fascist Germany and Fascist Italy. There were many heated arguments, with people insulting each other. The Maases lost many friends that way, sad to say.

On December 7, 1941, the Japanese made the mistake of attacking Pearl Harbor, and Franklin Roosevelt declared war against them. Our gardeners were Japanese. We knew them to be hardworking family men with large families, eager to educate their children, most of whom were born in the United States and attended public schools. But all Japanese instantly became innocent victims of the conflict. Our firsthand experience was with our neighbors who employed these same gardeners. Nothing could convince them that these men who grew their flowers and trimmed their lawns were not spies, ready to murder them in their beds. What was worse, the government also feared them. Our gardeners, all Japanese, were sent to internment camps to protect the rest of us. They never interned the Germans and Italians among us. But with the Japanese it was something else.

Ernest and I felt particularly sorry for one Japanese family we got to know quite well. They had a lucrative business in Sawtelle raising flowers, and their biggest crop was poinsettias for the Christmas season. People came from all parts of Los Angeles to buy their poinsettias. They had two sons in college and a young daughter in high school; the children were all born in this country. They were citizens and good Americans. Yet they too had to sacrifice their holdings, sell their home, their furniture, their automobiles and trucks, their business—everything—for a fraction of its worth. Their only sin was that they had Japanese features. We did what we could to help them. We corresponded with them in camp and sent them packages of food and clothing. Both of the boys enlisted in the Japanese-American brigade and distinguished themselves. One never returned; the other lost an arm. After the war, the Ishiharas moved to Canada, and we lost touch.

I had four nephews of fighting age, and Ernest had two. The first two of mine, Alex and Henry Kann, served in the Pacific. Daniel Kann and Edward Smith served in Africa, Italy, and France. Louis and Richard Maas almost saw action in the Pacific near the end of the war but instead became members of the occupation forces. Fortunately, they all came home without injury. It was scary to have them all in, or near, combat. One Sunday, glued to the radio for overseas news, we heard one of the network commentators describe in great detail the miraculous escape of several soldiers from a burning tank and their possible capture by Rommel's forces on the sands of Africa. The occupants had to abandon their flaming vehicle in the desert and seek refuge with the natives in the area, who fed them, sheltered them, and helped them return to their fighting units. "And the rear gunner," said the commentator, "was a Yank from Chicago by the name of Dan Kann." Ernest and I looked at each other in disbelief. Sure enough, my nephew Dan was that gunner.

It was at this moment that I received a call from my friend Adele Commandini. When I told her what we had just heard, she opened up about the war. It was a mistake for the U.S. to become embroiled in the war, she told me, to have taken on Germany and the Italians as well as the Japanese. Mussolini and Hitler knew what they were doing in Europe, she assured me. Then she opened up on the newly formed Writers Guild. She had never become a member. "The government ought to clean out that nest of commies," she railed maliciously. That did it. I slammed down the receiver on the clever, if misguided, writer who had scripted *Three Smart Girls*. We never spoke again.

Both Ernest and I had held strong anti-fascist sentiments as far back as 1929, before the Nazi movement fully ripened. That sentiment was now strengthened by our association with the wonderful German émigrés we knew, including a group who had escaped after the war began: Heinrich Mann and his wife, Nellie; Franz and Alma Werfel; and Gola Mann, Thomas Mann's second son, who had escaped from a Vichy internment camp. It was the successful writer Leon Feuchtwanger who had financed the group's escape. This great writer, largely forgotten today, was the most successful of all the German émigré authors, his historical novels selling in millions all over the world.

This is how the escape was carried out: The escapees decided that they would have to cross the Franco-Spanish border on foot. A young American Unitarian acted as their guide. In the foothills of the Pyrenees they lost him and had to continue through the rough terrain on their own, nearly perishing from the rigor of the climb. They were finally rescued by a second guide, who led them down into Spain. There followed an exhausting fourteen-day journey—from Barcelona by train to Madrid and then a flight to Lisbon, where they boarded a Greek steamship for New York.

All of them often relived this fantastic journey to freedom. Now some of them had jobs at the studios, most notably Warners and MGM, but these were only token jobs and lasted no more than a year. Then they were on their own. They helped each other. Thomas Mann and Leon Feuchtwanger were the most successful of the group, doing the most for others who were not so fortunate as they were. Franz Werfel (author of the play *Jacobowsky and the Colonel*) and Heinrich Mann (who scripted *The Blue Angel* with Emil Jannings) had the most diffi-cult time financially until Werfel began to realize royalties from his successful Broadway play.

Thomas Mann, author of *Buddenbrooks, The Magic Mountain, Dr. Faustus,* and *Joseph and His Brothers,* was the most vocal of the group. Hounded by fascists, he was on the lecture circuit constantly, fee or no fee, talking in schools, colleges, homes—anywhere he could get his message across regarding the menace of Fascism. "The shame of the Germans as a people, their cruelty and bestiality, and the culpable negligence of the civilized world to have allowed it to happen—this is what we cannot forgive." His sentiments were our sentiments.

Immediately following the attack on Pearl Harbor and our entry into the war, a City Civilian Corps was set up under Mayor Fletcher Bowron. Generals Ulysses S. Grant III and J.L. DeWitt, Chief of Civil Protection, warned residents of Los Angeles that the West Coast was deemed extremely vulnerable to Japanese attack: "We must always remember the old military maxim—to expect the enemy to do the thing which we hope most sincerely he will not do, and the thing we most want to prevent him from doing. We can be reached by the sea and air no matter what the distance and however good the measures of defense that are taken."

In Westwood Village, close as we were to the Pacific Ocean, we took the war and our danger seriously. Everyone in the community was eager to become part of the war effort and defense. I became a regional air raid warden, with district wardens and firefighters under my command. Ernest joined the volunteer fire brigade. We were photographed and fingerprinted, and we carried identification cards with us always. Wardens had an emblem of their own, as did firefighters and members of the volunteer fire department, which were worn on bands around our right sleeve. We were equipped with helmets and gas masks and were trained in identifying bombs and what to do if they fell and did not explode. We also were instructed on how to call Control Center in case of a raid and had to become proficient in first-aid procedures, rescue efforts, and care for the injured. We set up "block mothers" in the event of an air raid during the day so that children caught in the street had some place to go. Cards were displayed on lawns and front windows of all block mothers, who received instruction on how to care for the children, feed them, amuse them, comfort them.

We set up air-raid shelters and first-aid stations in basements of banks. Houses and stores were equipped with blankets, sheets, canned goods, bandages and other first aid supplies, and candles and lanterns. We had to have a special pocketbook in readiness to be slung over our shoulder, containing such things as identification tags for the injured, report pads, whistles, and several extra bandages for immediate use.

Of course, we all had ration books for food and for gas to run our cars. We salvaged our tin cans and filled them with waste fats needed to make munitions for our fighting men. Both Ernest and I donated blood regularly. We grew vegetable gardens—beets, carrots, turnips, squash, beans, peas, parsley, lettuce, tomatoes, and watermelons. The Maases grew the smallest, sweetest, most fantastic watermelons in all the 1.5 million food-producing gardens requested by the government as "Food for Freedom."

This is all vividly brought back to me now as I review the contents of a carton labeled "Civil Defense," sealed and long hidden away in one of my closets. Sorting out the chaff from the wheat, I come across this memorandum: "To: Block Warden Elliot. From: Sector Warden Maas. Saturday at 1 P.M. at Mrs. Gray's, 471 Landfair, there is to be an important incident to be supervised by a regular Zone Army training leader. Several days after that the army is going to hold a regular incident, and we are all going to have to participate." In the same box, I found a copy of the simulated incident—basically, a war game—in which all factions set up by our Civil Defense took part. Wardens, firefighters (including volunteers), police, Red Cross personnel— we all had our duties to fulfill in case of a real attack, and we all had to know what to do.

Finally came the night when it was no longer a war game. Ernest and I were listening to the eleven o'clock news on the radio when suddenly the radio went off the air. Almost immediately our telephone rang. It was Command Headquarters sounding the Blue Alert, informing us that there were unidentified aircraft out at sea and headed for the Pacific Coast. Hurriedly, Ernest and I donned our pea jackets, put on our helmets, gas masks, and emergency pocketbook, closed the windows, drew the drapes and blinds . . . and waited.

It was chilling when it came—the Red Alert—the warning, wailing, piercing sirens screaming ominously through the stillness of the night. We left the house. Ernest jumped into his car—no lights—pecked me on the cheek with a cheery "Good Luck" and thumbs up, and disappeared into the darkness. For a moment I was paralyzed, trying to remember all the directions I had been given and what I was supposed to do next. It was dark as pitch; there was no moon. As I started my patrol, I saw a house lit up like a Christmas tree. I rang the bell but received no answer. Obviously there was no one at home. I had to cut through a screen in the kitchen window, lift myself up on an ash-can, and crawl through the window, which, fortunately, was unlocked. Putting out the lights and drawing the drapes, I resumed my patrol. My next encounter was a car with its lights on and two people hurrying home. After identifying myself, I ordered them to abandon their car and seek shelter in the closest house. The terrified old lady who lived in the house was alone and appreciated their company.

"Well, we are ready for them," I thought. "Let them come." I strained my ears but heard nothing. Then, suddenly, I picked up the whirring sound of planes, a low hum, far off. It grew louder and louder. Hundreds of planes it seemed. They were almost overhead, but the bombs were not dropping; not yet. I did what we were instructed to do. I hit the dirt in an empty lot. The din of the planes as they flew over me was terrifying. But they dropped no bombs. Instead they circled and returned to sea and vanished. These were not the enemy's planes; these were our own. This air-raid warden picked herself up. The all-clear sirens now filled the night air. What a heartwarming climax to a night of terror!

By 1944 Franklin D. Roosevelt had led us out of the Depression through three terms in office and had been commander-in-chief after the Pearl Harbor attack through another three years of war. His Fireside Chats held us together. For once our union was one big family, with the stalwart, pain-wracked, polio-crippled president our father figure. One could not have asked for a better leader in such perilous times—the great war we were waging again to save democracy and to end all wars. Now he was to try for an unprecedented fourth term in office. His running mate was Harry Truman, a little-known unheralded senator from the state of Missouri. His Republican adversary was Thomas E. Dewey, the crime-fighter prosecutor of New York, dubbed "the little man on the wedding cake" by Dorothy Parker.

Under the auspices of the Hollywood Democratic Committee, the entire entertainment world was organized with Marc Connelly as chairman. The Beverly Westwood Democratic Committee, which Ernest and I helped organize, was an offshoot of that parent organization. Contact was established with all organizations whose interests were allied with ours. Material and plans were developed to arrange personal appearances of Hollywood personalities in other cities and on radio programs, both local and national.

Many of us writers were involved. Our job was to write material for the entertainment programs and campaign material for the local candidates. National candidates were scripted out of National Democratic Headquarters.

In Beverly Hills and Westwood, our congressional candidate was Ellis J. Patterson, a seasoned politician who had served as lieutenant governor for the state of California under Republican governor Earl Warren. Always on the side of the rights and welfare of the minority, Patterson was running against Dr. Jesse Kellems, an ordained Protestant minister with a wealthy congregation in Westwood. He had been elected assemblyman and had a reputation closely parallel to that of Hamilton Fish, the well-known isolationist from New York. Kellems was in favor of the poll tax, against old-age pensions, against appropriations for nursery schools and any legislation that was socially beneficial. He was the brother of Vivian Kellems, the lady in Connecticut who became famous when she refused to pay her income tax. She was later found to be corresponding with Nazi agents in South America. Coincidentally, Dr. Kellems was married to a wealthy South American heiress.

Ernest and I threw ourselves into the campaign with everything we had to offer. We wrote speeches and pamphlets for Democratic candidates. We raised money, especially for the candidates who had no resources of their own. I became regional precinct supervisor, responsible for Santa Monica, Westwood, and Beverly Hills—and everything in between. It was a monster exercise of coordination, choosing the volunteers, appointing the right people to the right tasks, and getting out the vote. We held neighborhood rallies, principally to raise money, at the homes of wealthy citizens. Sometimes there were garden parties, with speakers like Thomas Mann. More often we held indoor events with entertainment—Gene Kelly, Burton Lane, and Yip Harburg all contributed, along with dancers like Martha Graham and folk singers like Earl Robinson, who played and sang his "Ballad for Americans."

It was a wonderful time to be involved in Democratic politics. People with money gave freely for our cause, and people without money did, too, because we believed our candidates were principled, wise, dedicated men and women. It was a high point in American politics, possibly the highest of all time since our republic was founded and George

Washington took his oath of office as our first helmsman. Our euphoria was engendered by the formidable man and his remarkable lady occupying the White House, Franklin Delano and Eleanor Roosevelt. They were the inspiring models for the nation.

The election campaign was electric. Hundreds of volunteers covered all neighborhoods, manning telephones, going door to door ringing doorbells—bringing out the vote. We also had hundreds of registrars. We brooked no excuse. If you were eligible to vote, whether white, black, Chinese, bedridden, or plain indifferent, you were registered and on election day there was a volunteer to see that you got to the polls. On November 7, 1944, the country cast its ballot and delivered its mandate: Franklin D. Roosevelt handily won a fourth term as president of these United States.

Chapter 17

THE DESECRATION OF
MISS PILGRIM'S PROGRESS

IMMEDIATELY AFTER THE WAR we sold our house on Homedale. Mother Nature had treated us to one deluge too many, which, despite our new drainage system, once again wrecked our seven terraces and ruined our rugs and furniture. Enough was enough! We sold the house with all the salvageable furnishings (including my beloved Steinway) for little more than we had paid for them, but we were deliriously happy to get rid of that headache we could not afford.

We moved into a brand-new, two-bedroom apartment on Midvale Avenue in Westwood, not far away from the university buildings and the campus grounds and gardens. It was on a hillside, and on a clear day we could see as far as Catalina Island, some forty-five miles distant. And, in those pre-smog days, nearly every day was clear unless it rained or there was a heavy fog.

Through the war effort and Roosevelt campaign, we had become friendly with a number of professors at UCLA. Florence Gilhousen, wife of a psychology professor at the university, called one morning. It seemed that our sleepy little Westwood village was about to add a branch of a major department store (Bullock's) to the mushrooming community. The problem was providing parking space for customers, and the university was about to sell a parcel of its land for that purpose. That parcel contained a garden-conservatory of rare and experimental plants, a botanical treasure. However, this parcel had been deeded to the university by the city of Santa Monica with the proviso that the people of Santa Monica reserved the right to determine its future or sale; the university needed the approval of Santa Monica to make the transfer.

We had to work fast—there was still time to thwart that dastardly ploy, but barely. The plan was to raise three thousand dollars, immediately, to send double postal cards to the citizens of Santa Monica asking them to protest (on the return card) the sacrifice of these wonderful gardens and conservatory to commercialism. We had one week to accomplish the task. In two telephone calls, I raised the money—one to the Good Samaritan Oscar Pattiz, president of the Beneficial Insurance Company, the other to Seniel Ostrow, president of the Sealy Mattress Company and brother of Lou Ostrow, whom I'd worked with at Tiffany Productions. As in the Roosevelt campaign, these two corporate executives rallied to another good cause. The response from the Santa Monica citizens was unbelievable. Over ninety percent of the cards that went out were returned protesting the venture. As a result, Bullock's Department Store changed its plans and had to settle for more costly underground parking. Chalk up one small victory for aestheticism.

Suddenly, out of the blue, the Maases found themselves without a home. New owners had bought our building and laid claim to our apartment for shelter of a relative, as they had every right to do under a new law. This would not have been so calamitous if only there had been a place to move to. But there were no apartments, houses, or anything with a roof over its structure to be had for love or money. The war had curtailed building in favor of military hardware, and there was a shortage of rentals; empty apartments were worth their weight in gold. Fortunately for the Maases, their friend, Edna Reindel, a commercial artist, was scheduled to go to New York for three months on a business trip. She generously turned her studio in Santa Monica over to us for the same rental she was paying. But three months whisked by very quickly, and when the time was up we faced the same dilemma. Again we were lucky. We met Laura Reed Fort, a former Midvale neighbor, and learned of a possible vacancy in Westwood on the street where she lived. It was a tiny studio apartment, furnished, no bedroom, and a makeshift kitchen of sorts. Rent: three hundred dollars. We grabbed it.

The landlady, Mrs. Kane, was a middle-aged widow who liked to travel. The apartment complex was her main source of income. There were four apartments: one upstairs with two bedrooms, occupied by the mother-in-law of Justin Dart, the same millionaire Dart who later gained fame as a member of Ronald Reagan's "Kitchen Cabinet"; another two-bedroom apartment was occupied by Adele Murphy, a buxom Russian émigré from Siberia, USSR, who married a ruddy Irish executive of Standard Oil. They had two sons (the reason for their living in Westwood), Dennis and John, one in high school, another a freshmen at the university. Mrs. Kane had her own one-bedroom apartment and, of course, there was our studio.

There was a Rent Control Board, but Mrs. Kane either had never heard of it or chose to ignore it. Come the first of every month, we received notice that our monthly rent was being hiked a hefty fifty dollars. By the end of six months, the Maases were paying not three hundred dollars for a studio but six hundred dollars—and the other tenants with larger apartments correspondingly more. Usury, plain and simple. Justin Dart's mother-in-law was a mousy little woman, the last creature on earth you would expect to assert herself, yet she had enough ginger to take on the pitiless Mrs. Kane, with Mrs. Murphy and the Maases joining in a lawsuit and complaint to the Rent Control Board. Praise the Lord! Hallelujah! The Rent Control Board ordered all overpaid back rent returned to the abused tenants and a heavy fine, to boot, for the landlady. Poor Mrs. Kane, I don't believe she ever fully recovered from the shock.

After my year of servitude at the Edward Small Agency, Ernest and I were not idle creatively. We were collaborating on a story about the typewriter, invented by Lathan Sholes in 1873 and exhibited at the Chicago World Fair—a machine strangely resembling a sewing machine, with a treadle to work the carriage, and printing only in capital letters. We had been seriously researching the subject and finding it had intriguing possibilities: the invention of the typewriter and its social and economic influences on the world of business.

The story that emerged, in 1941, was *Miss Pilgrim's Progress*—the tale of a young woman entering the field of business, hitherto strictly a male domain. Our heroine is hired to demonstrate the miraculous invention in the window of a New York Wall Street establishment. The historical consequence of that momentous day was the eventual disappearance of male scriveners and their tall writing desks, their office

spittoons, their exclusive occupation and domination of the clerical aspects of business. All vanished, to be replaced by tables holding the
fantastic treadle typewriter machine, magically manipulated by
pompadoured females in highnecked starched shirtwaists tucked into
full-length sweeping skirts over double petticoats. Yet the lofty male
scriveners had no one to blame but themselves. Smug in the belief that
the business terrain was securely theirs, they scorned the novelty machine and refused to learn to operate it.

It was not a trite story. In addition to the quaintness of the period
and the comedic possibilities innate in the eternal battle of the sexes, it
had deeper implications. This was a time when women had no other
means of earning a living except by hiring out as a governess, teaching
school, or, if they were less educated, working in factories or department stores at starvation wages. The invention of the typewriter
proved the emancipation of the "fairer sex" from this economic bond-
age, opening up the doors of commerce to them and, for the first
time, winning for them a living wage and limitless possibilities for
their future.

Our love story was unique, not just a standardized boy meets girl,
boy falls in love with girl, boy marries girl. Our hero does not fall in love
with our heroine at first sight. He falls in love with the typewriter she is
demonstrating. She is merely an adjunct to it. When he fails to get his
old-fashioned father to relent and try the machine in their office, he
prevails upon his brother-in-law to try the machine in his office and
hire its operator.

The hero then has the brilliant idea of combining the science of
shorthand with the typewriter. In teaching our heroine the mysteries
of shorthand, much as the Englishman in *Pygmalion* taught Eliza to
speak proper English, our hero falls in love with our heroine, and she
with him. But there are sinister forces at work that interfere with the
smooth progression of the love interest. There is an offensive male
scrivener, who seeks to foist his unwanted attentions on pretty, young
Abigail Pilgrim, an unpleasant situation that finally culminates in tragedy. Our heroine's employer, seeking one day to defend her from the
pursuit of his male clerk, loses his balance in the altercation between
them, topples down the stairway, and is killed.

Scandal! Our unfortunate heroine becomes the femme fatale in a
preposterous murder trial. The case gains front-page attention, and

the concept of women working in offices becomes a wide-open moral question, with churches, housewives, men, and women in all walks of life taking sides in the fray. The attorney for the defense turns out to be a mean-spirited lawyer who takes the case when he discovers that our heroine is the same girl who refused his advances earlier in the story when he had considered adding the typewriter and its operator to his office. He hopes to make the case a sensation that will destroy our heroine's reputation, while painting his scrivener-clerk client as lily-white and completely at the mercy of feminine wiles. You might say that womanhood is on trial in this courtroom. Susan B. Anthony and other famous suffragettes of that day attend the trial and seek to help our heroine. In the end our heroine's character is exculpated, but not before it has been dragged through the mire.

It was a good yarn. It still is. With its basic idea of women entering the workforce, it would have made a great picture and lent itself to making a play or a musical. It had the same potential as Bernard Shaw's *Pygmalion*. It had limitless, rich possibilities, and both Ernest and I knew it.

Now came the business of marketing what we had, a loathsome business at best to most good, conscientious writers. So much effort is expended on fashioning the vehicle that little energy remains for the selling, the launching of one's tour de force. A writer vaingloriously expects spontaneous response and recognition of the quality of his wares. Incorrigible optimist, he discounts the obstacles in his path. For one, there are the jaded studio readers who have to wade through so much unacceptable material and who are sometimes frustrated screenwriters in their own right. Then there are the story editors who have the task of impressing the front office with original material as opposed to successful Broadway plays or best-selling novels. The nitty-gritty of it is that writers are naive, foolish idiots to speculate, to author an original story in the first place. But both Ernest and I, early products of the fantasy screen, bred on its wonders and possibilities, were stubbornly of the opinion that the medium needed its own material, so we were never play- or fiction-oriented. We wanted to write original material for the screen.

We chose Paul Kohner as our agent. The Kohner Agency occupied a two-story office building on Sunset Boulevard, more commonly known as the "Sunset Strip." He owned his own building. Sunset Strip was littered with literary and talent agents then. You might well ask why we had chosen Paul Kohner instead of a larger, more prestigious agency. Our experience with big agents in the past had proven negative. Big agents do little for small-fry clients. What really influenced us was that Kohner had recently negotiated the sale of another period story, an original written by a friend of ours about the presidency of Andrew Johnson, who succeeded Abraham Lincoln in the White House.

Our choice was a mistake. It was obvious at once that the now highly successful Kohner still remembered his rejection as a fledgling aspirant for a job at my story department at Universal. Now I, the once assertive young story editor, was seated in his office, seeking something from him. The tables were turned. Leaving nothing to chance, I outlined the highlights of our story, sensing at once from his reaction that it was a piece of Americana beyond his comprehension or appreciation. Routinely, Mr. Kohner turned us over to the woman in charge of his story department, Irene Dickenson. We were fully of a mind not to entrust our baby to the Kohner Agency had we not found that Dickenson, unlike her boss, was at once an appreciative audience for what we had to sell. She hit the ceiling and could scarcely wait to distribute the mimeographed copies we supplied her with. After all, she was the one who would be handling the story, not Kohner. He would only come in for the kill. We trusted Dickenson.

Meanwhile, I told the story to Buddy Lighton at MGM and provided him with a copy. He evinced strong interest in the property as a vehicle for Norma Shearer, and he was slated to produce her next picture. I also promoted interest at the RKO studios through Nan Cochrane, who was head of the RKO story department. She was the niece of R.H. Cochrane, my mentor at Universal. Nan saw the story as a perfect vehicle for Ginger Rogers, for whom RKO needed a story, and turned it over to her head reader, Fay Kanin, for a detailed synopsis. She was astounded the following day when Kanin turned in her critical report. It was an outright rejection, a put-down. If I had not told Nan the story in detail, she most likely would have accepted Kanin's opinion. Fortunately, she had heard enough from what we had told her to want to take the story home and read it for herself, only to find herself in total disagreement with Ms. Kanin's judgment. Columbia Pictures, through Sidney Buchman, executive producer there, and also Michael Kraike, Columbia's story editor, were also intrigued with the story.

The stage was set—there were four studios interested in our script! Twentieth Century-Fox was the first to make a bid—fifteen thousand dollars. Not at all bad for a starter. Frederica and Ernest Maas, glued to their telephone, waited impatiently for other bids to come in. It was one of those hostile, torrid days in September for which Southern California is so famous. The temperature hit 102 degrees in the shade. Our agent, Paul Kohner, fainted from the heat but recovered by the end of the day to close with Twentieth Century-Fox, still for fifteen thousand dollars instead of the twenty-five thousand dollars or more that we were expecting under the circumstances. Why was there no competitive bidding? We were informed later on that Kohner failed to contact MGM, RKO, or Columbia to inform them of the initial bid from Twentieth Century. It could have been that the excessive heat affected his judgment. Or was it indifference? It was enough to cause Irene Dickenson to end her affiliation with his agency in disgust and mistrust.

Dickenson's contact at Twentieth Century-Fox was Kenneth Macgowan, a civilized, knowledgeable producer with firm values and aspirations. He had been impatiently waiting for a suitable vehicle assignment from Darryl Zanuck and the front office, but none to his liking had surfaced, so he lay fallow until *Miss Pilgrim's Progress* came across his desk. It was exactly the kind of story he had been looking for. In gratitude for the story, and taking into consideration her keen enthusiasm for it, he hired Dickenson, who also had a stage background, as his assistant. Ernest and Frederica Maas were to write the screenplay. This helped mitigate the disappointment of lost money from the lack of competitive bidding.

The perfect setup was not to be, was not in the cards. It was doomed. Maas luck. Kenneth Macgowan's renewal option on his contract was on the firing line. Long at odds with the domineering Zanuck, he was given his walking papers, an outcome he took with good grace. He joined the teaching staff at UCLA to establish a school to train young hopefuls in the techniques of motion pictures. Dickenson was also fired, to vanish into the continent of Europe. The Maases? They were curtly informed that their story was not set for imminent production, and so their services were curtailed.

Fortunately that was not the end of it. Abigail Pilgrim, the first female to brave the hallowed halls of business via the typewriter, was to have her day on the silver screen after all. It took nearly six years for it to happen, and by that time her creators had almost written her off. RKO and MGM had both made overtures evincing interest in acquiring the property, but for some incomprehensible reason Twentieth Century-Fox preferred to allow their acquisition to yellow and wither away in their archives. Then came the day when Darryl Zanuck was hard up for a story for their big moneymaker star, Betty Grable. Heavens to Betsy—he thought of *Miss Pilgrim's Progress* by Frederica and Ernest Maas. It was still gathering dust in the archives. At the helm of Twentieth Century-Fox, Zanuck was now operating at maximum authority. He was in his element, free to employ his creative talents as he saw fit. He not only read every script set for production on the lot, he rewrote them! It was a mania, the mania of an opinionated, powerful executive convinced that he, and he alone, had the magic formula for a box-office smash. Everything had the Zanuck stamp, the ultimate Zanuck damnation. What could one expect from this early filcher of ideas, who had no compunction about copying a printed story verbatim and claiming it as his own? This is not to denigrate the man totally or disparage his entire output in a long and successful career. He had many outstanding films to his credit, subjects that survived his meddling. For the rest . . .

You might say I had a ringside seat to observe the antics of the great magician. It so happened that I knew his firsthand assistant, Dorothy Hechtlinger. She had once been Ernest's secretary at Paramount in the East. When I was an agent for Edward Small, performing my daily rounds of the studios, Dorothy's offices, adjacent to those of Darryl Zanuck, always held out a big welcome mat to this unhappy agent. Over steaming cups of coffee brewed in her office, we exchanged confidences, impressions, and opinions about the not-so-glamorous film industry we had both been a part of for so many years. Zanuck was the manipulator, Dorothy his good Girl Friday, his right hand, the perfect foil for his diabolical creativity. She had no set working hours, and neither did he. Her time was adjusted to his time, even if it ran late into night hours and sometimes even into dawn. He was a fantastic taskmaster, an indefatigable workaholic. Dorothy's job was to take down shorthand notes for revision and to incorporate the changes into a new

Zanuck script. Hers was not to reason why. Besides, she was hand-somely rewarded for her cooperation.

As was to be expected, our story went through the Zanuck mill. The juggler of Twentieth Century–Fox completely rewrote it. The first change was our title. *Miss Pilgrim's Progress* became *The Shocking Miss Pilgrim*, more befitting Betty Grable's box-office sex appeal. The locale was also changed to staid Boston despite the fact that New York City was the mecca of finance, where the innovation of the typewriter would have the most profound impact.

A Technicolor production, this latest Betty Grable musical opened at the Roxy Theater in New York on February 11, 1947, and at Grauman's Chinese Theater in Hollywood about the same time. Frederica and Ernest Maas attended the "Chinese" gala. Betty Grable fans filled the grandstands set up for them on either side of the red carpet leading into the theater. As we left our cars and followed the red carpet, amid cheers and applause of the crowd, we felt like royalty. And for the moment we were.

The screen credit read: "Written for the Screen and Directed by George Seaton. Produced by William Perlberg. From a *novel* by Ernest and Frederica Maas. Music by George Gershwin and Lyrics by Ira Gershwin." What more could one ask for? An eminent director and an outstanding producer, with plenty of good credits behind them. And Gershwin music and Gershwin lyrics.

There were full-page advertisements in magazines such as *Colliers* and the *Saturday Evening Post* featuring the incredible treadle ma-chine and the "typewriter" girl, as female typists were called then. The publicists had a ball. The teaser "24-sheet" was a masterpiece, even if, in its pages, George Seaton stealthily tried to take credit for having conjured up the basic idea for the story. But then, from the end results, one had to question seriously whether he or William Perlberg was ever given a copy of the original story to read. In all probability, all they ever saw was Zanuck's version of a story to fit the talents of Betty Grable. Their orders were to take it from there.

The New York reviews were unanimous in praise of the basic idea. "A libretto on woman's rights," the *New Republic* called it. Bosley Crowther of the *New York Times* wrote: "Miss Grable turns in the best acting job of her career. Because of the period, her skirts were long and trailing. For once, she does not display the gams that made her famous. Therefore she has no recourse but to try to act, and surprisingly does." But while the critics praised the originality of the basic idea, they were somewhat less enthusiastic about the story's development. Perceptibly they felt the matching story was "trite, forced, conventional . . . a brilliant idea superficially executed." Short wonder! Not only had Zanuck changed the locale and the title, but the story was completely rewritten, our plot completely altered. No accidental death. No sensational trial putting womanhood on the justice block. None of those story developments that lent charm and significance to the story. They were all scrapped. What remained? Another stupid boy-meets-girl Zanuck travesty.

As for the music of the deceased George Gershwin, and the lyrics of Ira Gershwin, the critics' reaction was noticeably cool and perplexed. Small wonder again. The supposedly leftover Gershwin tunes were obviously written by studio hacks. Not even if they had scraped the very bottom of the barrel could they have come up with anything so unmelodious. Not a real "humming" tune or hit song in the banal lot. Ira Gershwin's lyrics (if they were his lyrics) reflected the uninspired music. A good lyricist depends on a good songwriter. Or vice versa. In this case, Ira's brother could not answer for himself. In what was an understatement, if there ever was one, Howard Barnes of the *New York Tribune* said, "The music is not by any means Gershwin's best . . . a musical show that has no more cohesion than a collection of tintypes mouthing trivial melodies and lyrics."

But these harsh criticisms only echoed the bitter, anguished cry of distress from Ernest and Frederica Maas, who had to bear in impotence the emasculation, the murder of their offspring. They had every right to feel that their story deserved better than this brutal disfigurement. But who were they to say? They were only the authors. They had no rights, no voice, no choice but to endure and overcome the painful disappointment.

The picture, however, was a howling box-office success. The original idea, the brilliant publicity, and the popularity of the star, Betty Grable, had the public standing in long lines to see it, not only in the big cities but in the hamlets of America as well. It played in reruns on television for years and still can be seen on cable today. Think of the payment in residuals that today are paid to writers participating in motion picture production!

But there were, and are, no residual payments to the Maases. The story was sold before the Writers Guild won that concession from the Motion Picture Industry. The Maases just had no luck. What should have been their greatest triumph in Hollywood was instead their greatest creative disappointment.

Chapter 18

CIVIL WAR STORIES ARE OUT

DESPITE WHAT HAD HAPPENED with "Miss Pilgrim's Progress," Ernest and I continued to work on original stories. We had index boxes full of ideas. We wanted to see original movies that were good enough to be made into novels and plays, reversing the industry's procedure. We felt that the effect a best-selling novel or hit play has on society, an original movie could do with film.

What was it that propelled us to pursue this folly? For my part, it was the deep affection I felt for my husband. He would not abandon the industry or seek another pursuit. While I did not believe in the industry, I believed in him—his writing ability, his agile mind, his wonderful courage. He was never down, he was always optimistic. For all our disappointments, he did not consider himself a failure, nor did I. I shared his hope, his belief that he would once again triumph and enjoy the success of being his own man.

We enjoyed working together, so much so that we blinded ourselves and pushed reality aside. But nothing that we had embarked on up to now was to assume the proportions of the folly that was yet to come.

A pleasant time for writers is browsing in bookstores. In the thirties and forties, from Westlake Park to Hill Street, along Fifth, Sixth, and Seventh Avenues in Los Angeles, there were many bookstores, such

241

as Zeitlin's, Dawson's, Parker's, and Fowler's, specializing in every subject imaginable.

One afternoon, Ernest and I wound up in the downtown store of the Salvation Army, a different kind of place to do book browsing. There was no telling what you might come up with if you had sufficient patience to rummage through the bins of uncatalogued books and magazines, discards from broken-up estates.

This time the Maases were bounteously rewarded. Our find, hidden in one of the overflowing book bins, was the 16-volume set of *A History of the Civil War,* illustrated with Matthew B. Brady's pioneering war photographs! It was a commemorative of the War Memorial Association (1912) on the fiftieth anniversary of the Great Struggle—and it was in mint condition and unpriced. We hastened to the cashier's desk, trying to hide our inner excitement and prepared to pay whatever the cost. For seven dollars—a crisp five-dollar bill and two singles—we acquired the complete set. A veritable steal. Out of this was born the idea of writing a story about Matthew B. Brady.

Brady was a big canvas, a challenging canvas. At the age of thirty-seven, he owned two elegant photo galleries, one in New York City and the larger, and more elegant, in Washington. The walls of his galleries were covered with daguerreotypes and photographs of hundreds of people who had sat for him, from Andrew Jackson to the Prince of Wales. Brady was supposed to have photographed Abraham Lincoln thirty-five times, the first time before Lincoln (without a beard) became president.

The American Civil War changed the course of Brady's life. "A Voice told me to go, and I went," he is supposed to have said, answering the call of his craft. He closed his fashionable galleries. When the War Department denied him access to the battlegrounds, he went directly to President Lincoln, who issued the famous handwritten "Pass Brady."

At considerable expense, he hired cameramen on both sides to make his records complete. The New York establishment of Anthony and Sons extended him limitless credit, confident, as Brady was, that the government would remunerate him for his efforts. After all, he had the support of President Lincoln, who was well aware of his sacrifice and who would back him to the hilt in the hallowed halls of Congress. Mark Twain, enthusiastic about Brady's work, told him, "It would make the noblest subscription book of the age."

But Lincoln's assassination punctured Brady's balloon of hope. After the war, other photographers were flourishing in New York and Washington. Brady, haunting the Capitol, found himself shunted from one legislator to another. With the election of Grant, Brady's hopes soared anew. He knew Grant well, having photographed the eighteenth president many times on the battlefield. Grant was sympathetic and really wanted to help Brady, but the times were more chaotic than ever. At Grant's insistence, Brady talked to William Belknap, the secretary of war, about his predicament and received Belknap's assurance that the government would acquire the collection for the modest sum of twenty-five thousand dollars—just enough to cover Brady's debts. In the meantime, Brady was unable to meet the bill for storage and had his negatives offered at auction. Belknap, a wily man, saw the opportunity to acquire the collection at a rock-bottom, bargain-basement price and purchased the collection at public auction for just $2,840.

The hue and cry of Brady's supporters finally reached the ears of President Grant, who hauled his secretary of war onto the carpet and properly dressed him down for his shabby behavior. Benjamin Butler, a congressman from Massachusetts, had a paragraph inserted in the Civil Appropriation Bill for twenty-five thousand dollars—"to enable the Secretary of War to acquire a full and perfect title to the Brady collection of photographs of war."

Twenty-five thousand dollars was the modest sum Brady had required but had to agonize nearly eight years to obtain. It was enough for him to open a modest gallery over the Pennsylvania Railroad ticket office near the Treasury Department. Eight years later, crippled with rheumatism and nearly blind from a shell injury at Bull Run, Brady returned to New York and his old friends. In 1896, no month or day given, the *New York Tribune* reported: "Matthew B. Brady, well known as the pioneer of photography in the United States, died at the Presbyterian Hospital in this city on Wednesday evening. Mr. Brady, who was seventy-two years old, was run over by a vehicle while crossing the street in the early evening near his hotel. Mr. Brady's body will be sent to Washington for burial."

Now Ernest and I set to work on the creation of the story of Matthew Brady. I use the word "creation" because that is what we had to do— create an original story, suitable for the screen, based on the meager facts we had gathered about him after three years of intensive research. There were no biographies, articles, or letters to tell us what manner of man he was. Was he a Northern patriot? Was he against slavery? Was he a Southern sympathizer? Nothing . . . nothing, other than the bare facts that here was a man who had a vision, a sense of history, and the temerity to risk his fortune to do a job for his country—regardless of personal cost. His photographs, his five thousand negatives, alone speak for him.

After much deliberation, we decided to expand *Photo by Brady* into a fully developed screenplay. A screenplay, we felt, would best safeguard our story, its basic values and development. To balance the more somber aspects, we decided that *Photo by Brady* had to be a love story, as tender, as gently humorous and romantic, as an old valentine.

Brady first lays eyes on Julia Handy at a Washington Ball, but before he can get to her side to find out who she is, she vanishes. To his pleasant surprise, the comely spinster of twenty-five reappears at his studio several days later, a faded daguerreotype in her hand. Brady had taken this photo of the young lady's parents fourteen years before, and it had become badly damaged in the meantime. Could Brady restore it? He can and does, demanding as payment only the opportunity to photograph the lovely young woman in return. A music box that tinkles "Drink to Me Only with Thine Eyes" and a quixotic camera-shy pigeon called Oscar help the romance to develop. The young woman and eligible bachelor fall in love and marry. There is a charming repetitive note that deals with the heroine's predilection for beautiful bonnets that vary in extravagance according to the ups and downs of the Bradys. There is a pastoral honeymoon at Gettysburg, the same Gettysburg later to become the war's bloodiest battleground, with Brady returning to photograph its grim metamorphosis.

The biggest license we took was to integrate the poet Walt Whitman into the fabric of our story, using his poetic commentaries to illuminate the screen as a series of unique photo-montages—scenes of war by Brady.

Whitman was a nurse on the battlefields. Hence, it stands to reason, although it is not so recorded, that his path must have crossed that of the flamboyant photographer and the "What-Is-It" (Brady's horse-drawn darkroom on wheels, so christened by the soldiers). It was the perfect nuptial knot: Walt Whitman, the American bard, the good gray poet, a man of the people, expressing himself in words, and Matthew B. Brady, the dauntless photographic artist, expressing himself in pictures worth a thousand words. What better men than these two kindred spirits to articulate Lincoln's passing . . . these two titans, one of whom had photographed the ugly, chiseled countenance thirty-five times, the other immortalizing him in verse:

> Oh, Captain! my Captain! our fearful trip is done;
> The ship has weather'd every rack, the prize we sought is won;
> The port is near, the bells I hear, the people all exulting,
> While follow eyes the steady keel, the vessel grim and daring:
>
> But O heart! heart! heart!
> O the bleeding drops of red,
> Where on the deck my Captain lies,
> Fallen cold and dead.

A tear-jerking scene—as the thirty-five photos of Lincoln pass before us in review with the loving enhancement of a poet's voice.

On April 9, 1945, the sun rose on one of those wonderful southern California days—eighty degrees, balmy, perfect beach weather, certainly too perfect to spend indoors. Besides, the Maases had some problems to iron out in their Brady script. We decided to talk it over while walking along the sparkling Pacific Ocean. Parking the roadster in Santa Monica, we began the walk along the boardwalk that extended from Santa Monica Beach to Venice Beach, a good mile and a half. Half a mile along the way we noticed that the flags on the buildings were being lowered to half mast, and we wondered who had died. A young Negro, about twenty-two years old, with tears coursing down his cheeks, came toward us. "What's gonna become of us? He's gone . . . gone!" he kept repeating. Before we could ask for whom he mourned, we were surrounded by other people, all weeping. That was how we learned that Franklin Delano Roosevelt—our beloved captain, four-termed, thirty-second president of these United States—was dead.

That same scene of grief continued all along the boardwalk until we reached Venice Beach. We heard on the shortwave radio: "Franklin

Delano Roosevelt, victim of a cerebral stroke, passed away this morning at Warm Springs, Georgia. . . ."

No longer would he have to carry those heavy steel braces on his
legs. No longer would he need that wheelchair—now on display at Hyde
Park, where this writer saw it and wept. For to her, that wheelchair,
more than anything else, bespoke the courage of this world leader,
crippled in body, but not in mind.

On April 12, 1865, another grieving people had mourned the
passing of their Emancipation President. "O the bleeding drops of red,
/ Where on the deck my Captain lies, / Fallen cold and dead."

After having worked two more years on our screenplay, we were en-
grossed in the launching of *Photo by Brady*. From time to time we had
given parts of our manuscript to Dorothy Rivers, a reader at one of the
studios, and she was enthusiastic about what we were doing. On a
Sunday, she invited us to a barbecue at her home in Beverly Canyon,
one of the lesser winding picturesque canyons in the ridge that divides
the San Fernando Valley from the Pacific Ocean. George Wilner, a
literary agent associated with the prestigious Nat Goldstone Agency,
was there too. He had worked in the Roosevelt campaign, but we did
not know him. Dorothy had told him about *Brady*, and he showed keen
and intelligent interest in it. It seemed clear to all of us that a story like
Brady was just what the doctor ordered, a piece of Americana, a chance
to reflect on past mistakes when rebuilding a nation after a war.

It cost two hundred smackers (which we could ill afford) to have
twenty-five copies of *Photo by Brady* run off at a secretarial service in
Westwood. Each of the copies bore the prestigious hallmark of the
Nat Goldstone Agency. George Wilner worked hard, gave it all he had,
left no stone unturned. And so did the authors. Producers, directors,
and story departments were all contacted and sales-pitched. No one
was overlooked.

At first we could not believe it, yet it was happening: rejection,
blank rejection. Studio after studio turned it down. If, here and there, a
producer or director evinced interest—and a few of them did, not the
least of them John Ford—the moguls who controlled the studio purse
strings were of one mind: the public was not interested in the Civil War
period. *Gone with the Wind?* That had Scarlett O'Hara and Rhett
Butler. Every other Civil War story, before and after, had bombed, was

a dismal flop. When it was argued that our story was more than a Civil War story, covering three presidencies and with an analogy that related to our own century and time, the answer was still the same: "Civil War stories are out!

We were in shock . . . like being immersed in polar ice. Nearly five years of work for nothing. Naive speculators that we were, like Brady, we had gambled on a dream. Writers have to have powerful egos to speculate in any medium. But to do so for the silver screen is sheer madness—you did not wager five years on an original motion picture story! After our long years of experience, we surely should have known better. Too late we awakened to our folly. Another "Swell Fish"!

The industry's blanket rejection, that there was no audience, was to be proven wrong when, many years later, Ken Burns launched his documentary *The Civil War.* For five nights running, there was a vast appreciative audience glued to the screen, absorbing every detail. The five thousand plates still reposing in our capital's archives made this graphic presentation possible.

In my living room, reclining in my easy chair, I watched on my black-and-white television screen the reenactment of the Civil War as Frederica and Ernest Maas had envisioned it fifty years before—the perfect blending of Civil War photographs and song, with ingenious narration.

This brilliant raconteur, Ken Burns, had spent more than seven years in researching and bringing the Civil War to the American public and the world. It was repeated three times and will doubtless have many more showings in the years ahead.

Who said no one was interested in the Civil War? The Maases were fifty years ahead of themselves. All they needed was television, not Scarlett O'Hara or Rhett Butler.

Licking our wounds following our failure to sell the Brady story, we had no alternative but to pick ourselves up and face reality. It was 1946, and reality was a bank account depleted to a round cipher again. We did not have the next month's rent. Putting most of our possessions in storage, we moved to South Pasadena to the home of friends, Laska and Allen Hazelton, to become part of their household.

It was a weird household. Laska Winters, now Mrs. Allen

Hazelton, was an actress who had enjoyed some recognition in exotic roles during the Rudolph Valentino days. She was a Eurasian—half Chinese, half white—and married to the scion of the steel company founded by the Hazeltons in Hazeltine, Pennsylvania. Jane, the younger of Laska's two sisters, was also living there while her husband was in the army in Korea. The other sister was in the army herself, serving in Okinawa. Laska's mother, a domineering arthritic in a wheelchair, had a suite of rooms on the second floor. A woman in her upper sixties, Mama scorned gray hair and dyed hers black. Remnants of faded beauty were still evident in her unwrinkled face. She had a southern drawl, and her grammar was atrocious. Mama claimed to have been born in New Orleans, although you couldn't be sure—she liked to romanticize her past. The Chinese gentleman who fathered her children remained a mystery. He was never mentioned.

Laska also had a son, Jimmy, by an earlier marriage. He was not quite twenty-one and had her unmistakable Chinese features. He had been picked up one night in Hollywood by the Vice Squad for "cruising and soliciting." The Maases had been called upon to testify as character witnesses on his behalf, and he was exonerated and released. Laska had never forgotten this kindness and, when she learned we were flat broke, offered us her home until we got back on our feet. It was a sanctuary for which we were grateful.

Ernest and I were to occupy two rooms on the second floor, one in which we slept and one that we used as an office, and we had full use of the extra kitchen on that floor. Ernest's brother, Irving, sent us seventy-five dollars a month, which was all we requested, and on that we had to survive. We paid Laska twenty dollars a month. She would not take more; indeed she did not want to take that, but we insisted. On the fifty-five dollars remaining, we had to buy gas for our buggy, our food, and put a few dollars aside to cover the payment on our life insurance policy which, miraculously, we had managed to hold onto through the years. We barely made it, but we managed.

We were working desperately on yet another story—fools never learn! During the five years of *Brady*, we had started working on a number of other ideas, a few of which were pretty far along in development. One story—untitled—was about Susan B. Anthony, the inspiration for which came when we were writing *Miss Pilgrim's Progress*. Another was a Western about Lotta Crabtree, the child entertainer who toured the gold camps throughout the West under the name "Little Nugget." Yet another—*Two Ate One Apple*—was a story that used the New York City blizzard of 1888 as a background. But we discarded all of these. We opted for a story we thought was a sure bet—prompted by the publicity engendered by the birth of the famous Canadian Dionne quintuplets.

Our story involved a young doctor who perpetrated a fraud by adding a waif, left on the doorstep of an expectant mother's home, to the quadruplets she eventually delivers. The original four girl babies plus a male baby made five. The doctor's reasoning was that "no one cares about one needy baby anymore. They have to come in fives to get attention." The doctor's purpose is to draw attention to the town's only hospital, which badly needs funding. Everything goes well until a female biologist, who has come to the hitherto unknown southern hamlet to study the quints, discovers that little Mister X does not fit in biologically with the genes of his four sisters.

We called the story *Lullaby in Eagleton* and entrusted it to the biggest agency of them all, Music Corporation of America, and Ned Brown, who ran their story department and was well thought of among writers. I stayed up three nights banging out ten copies for him to distribute; we had no money to have it done professionally. The Music Corporation offices were in Beverly Hills, a long drive from Pasadena when you had to save gas money. So we tried to keep in touch with Ned Brown by phone, but Ned was never in when we called. We left our name and asked that he call back. But Ned never called back. Our high hopes for a quick sale, one that would have solved our financial problems, grew dimmer and dimmer, to the point that we stopped calling the Music Corporation of America. It was a toll call. We figured if Ned Brown got bids on the story he would call us. He never did.

During these stressful weeks, we also were being harassed by the Federal Bureau of Investigation, who tracked us down. Why did we subscribe to *The Daily People's World* and *Soviet Life*? Did we know so and so? Did we know that so and so was a Communist? We were told that if we cooperated we could avoid a lot of trouble for ourselves and prove that we were not Communists or Communist sympathizers. Why wouldn't we name names? We were interrogated by three different FBI agents, three different times. Through neighbors and friends of the past ten years, we learned that the FBI had been around interviewing them about us. We were sure that none of those questioned would have given us anything but a clean bill of health. After all, there was nothing in the least subversive either in our thinking or in any of the causes we had sponsored. We were honest Americans in the tradition of Thomas Jefferson, or trying to be.

Johnny Butler, who knew Ernest from their early days at the Astoria, Long Island, studios, had joined the armed forces and was working in Washington, D.C. He held a high rank and was looking for people to make training films and documentaries for the Pentagon. Knowing Ernest's competence, he was eager for him to become a part of his organization. Yet Ernest did not get clearance and hence did not get the lucrative job we needed so badly and that might have been our salvation. In the books of the FBI we had two strikes against us, *The Daily People's World* and the *Soviet Life* magazine. That was more than enough to hang anybody in those days.

Added to this was the closing in on the Hollywood Ten, most of whom we knew. It was like being seared with a red-hot iron every time one of them took the stand and invoked the Fifth Amendment before the McCarthy inquisition. There, but for the grace of God. . . . Even our agent, George Wilner, was targeted as a suspected liberal. He escaped to Florida with his family to get away from those red-baiting local politicians, Gerald K. Smith and Jack B. Tenney.

There was a new menace, too, the "blacklist," dreamed up by the panicked studios to keep "Commies" out of their ranks. We were on that list. But then, you might ask, who was not on it? Anyone who had been in democratic politics, who opposed the fascists Gerald K. Smith, Jack B. Tenney, and Joseph R. McCarthy, was suspect. A terrible injustice was done in those years to our writing fraternity. Some of the stronger of the innocent accused would put up a magnificent defense, persevere, and survive, many of them writing under assumed names until the smoke cleared years later and they were once more in good odor. One or two of them even won Oscars for best screenplays under their assumed names, a delicious but bitter irony to the rest of us. But not everyone survived the heat. Most would be destroyed, never to make a comeback. You did not have to be one of the Ten to suffer. You had only to be a democratic activist, active in the Roosevelt campaign, or a subscriber to *The Daily People's World* . . . like the Maases.

Weighing heavily on our hearts and minds were the losses of my own dear mother and also Ernest's. We had been unable to go back home to attend their funerals because we lacked the money and were too proud to accept help from our families, who offered to pay our fare. The nightmarish atmosphere in which we were living did not help any either: bickering between siblings and Mama, and between themselves; even fistfights on occasion when too much barleycorn had been imbibed; and always the groveling, the homage that the matriarch in the wheelchair demanded not only of her own family but of her boarders as well.

We had to let our life insurance lapse. Having borrowed the maximum, we had no money to pay the next premium. I was fifty. Ernest was fifty-nine. We were washed up in the picture business. You can't easily start a second career at fifty and fifty-nine.

Small wonder that the thought of suicide should have occupied our battered minds. It was the second time for me. Ernest never knew of that other time, when I was in Hollywood without him. Now we were both sunk in a slough of despondency. We arranged our affairs, wrote appropriate letters, and picked the spot. It was an isolated hilltop in Eagle Rock where there were no houses, a favorite place where we had come often to work and to watch the spectacular sunsets. When the last rays of the red sun disappeared, we calmly rolled up the windows of our Plymouth. This was to be our last sunset. The final step was to turn on the ignition. Next thing we knew we were clutching at each other in frightened embrace and sobbing. What were we doing?! Failure, disappointments, lack of money, humiliation—none of these things mattered. We had each other, and we were alive.

But we knew beyond a shadow of a doubt that our Hollywood days were over. There would be no going back. No more "Swell Fish" . . . not this time.

EPILOGUE

IT WAS AUGUST 5, 1989, our sixty-second wedding anniversary, although our private little joke had always been to add on that extra year we had lived together in sin before we decided to make it legal.

The taxi stopped and the driver helped me alight. I parted with ten fifty-cent taxi coupons from my Senior Citizen Coupon Taxi Book. I knew now how much the fare would be, including the tip. I had made the same journey to 6667 Hollywood Boulevard in 1986, 1987, and 1988. I gently pushed the door open and entered Musso-Frank's.

It was nearing 2:00 P.M., so the lunch crowd was dwindling. I waited only a few minutes before the maitre d' showed me to the same booth I had occupied in 1926 when I lunched with my dear friend and ex-boss, John Brownell.

"A sherry, a dry sherry," I requested. Musso-Frank's had changed little over the years—the same mahogany booths, old waiters, and fresh crop of busboys waiting to replace them. Busy, busy, busy. Now, as then, the diners were mostly writers, producers, directors, technicians, or secretaries, all connected with the entertainment world. Only the way they dressed made them look different: beards and long hair for men; here and there a gold chain around the neck and a single gold earring. For women, miniskirts or slacks. Sweatshirts and faded blue jeans for both. Very casual.

My eyes strayed to the empty booth in the corner where Ernest had sat that day and, in my imagination, I placed him there. I recalled how he had ignored me when he came over to talk to John. But if he had not been interested in me that day, I soon changed that, didn't I? He never had eyes for any other woman in the nearly sixty years we were together. I felt flattered because he was a very attractive hombre to the opposite sex. But then, I was no slouch myself, and my eyes never wandered either.

I turned my attention to the empty booth again. "Do you remember the letter you wrote me when we were apart for the first time, you in New York and I in Hollywood?" I asked the little man who wasn't there, but whom I willed to be there. Now, in Musso's, I thought again of the words in that letter. They were words that defined our relationship: "My Dear Wife: Let me give you the basic secret of our happiness as I have finally come to understand it, and as you yourself have revealed in your last letter. It is this: from now on each of us shall stand on our own two feet. This is of supreme importance. It makes me happy to feel that you still have sufficient confidence in me, but start worrying about yourself for a change. This is real progress, my girl, the benefit of which you shall reap much sooner than you possibly expect. E." They were brave words, confessional words. But, alas, Ernest was a man nearing fifty then, who lacked the courage to go it alone, and I, his wife, loving him as I did, understood.

My mind returned to the night in 1950 when Ernest and I had resolved to terminate our insane careers in the motion picture business. The very next day, standing on my own two feet, I had gone downtown and applied for a job as a policy typist in an insurance office. As I worked my way up—from typist to claims adjuster, to truck underwriter and finally insurance broker, it more than paid the bills.

We moved to a two-bedroom furnished apartment near Griffith Park on prestigious Los Feliz Boulevard. The first thing we did was pay off all our debts and start squirreling money away. Ernest, in addition to playing the role of house-husband, found a reasonable source of income in ghostwriting. For a fee, he wrote articles for attorneys, physicians, physicists, and anyone else who had to stay in print to bolster his or her standing in their profession. He also began to charge for a service we had been providing free for years: the dispensing of story ideas and critiques to writing friends, especially those engaged in creating ongoing plot convolutions required by soap operas and serials.

The most difficult part of our new lifestyle was spending our workdays apart, but we compensated by spending every free moment together. On weekends, holidays, and vacations, we would take off in our olive-green Plymouth Sedan. From the north of California and its redwoods, down past San Francisco and Big Sur, all the way south to the Mexican border, we explored it all. And the best part was we did it all on a dime. We stopped in motels that provided kitchen facilities. We brought most of our own grub, picking up fresh corn, berries, or whatever the farm stands along the way had to offer.

For the first time in our turbulent lives, we had no problems.

Such happiness, however, does not last.

"Your husband has Parkinson's," Dr. Dennis O'Brian told me after Ernest had gone in for a routine checkup. Ernest was dressing in another room. I had already noticed the tremor in Ernest's hands and knew Parkinson's was fatal. I was really frightened. I waited until we got home to tell Ernest what the doctor had said.

"Parkinson's? I don't have Parkinson's," he countered, defiantly holding out his hands. They shook uncontrollably. Still he tried to make light of it. "Nonsense," he scoffed. "That Irishman is off his base."

The definition of Parkinson's in the dictionary does not begin to describe what was to become of our lives. My gentle, considerate, loyal partner would become a perfect tyrant who insisted on having his way in everything, like a petulant child. He refused to dress or undress. Every day, in the morning and again at nightfall, the same battle was reenacted. He could not remember what clothes to put on or what clothes to take off. When I tried to reason with him, he would fly into a rage and threaten me with bodily harm, going after my face with his fists. I had to hide knives, scissors, hammers. He forbade me to listen to the radio or watch television. He wanted absolute quiet. I had to sell a new Panasonic stereo my nephew Edward had sent me; I knew there would be fireworks if I played it. The newspapers he used to cull so avidly remained unopened. He turned against old friends, forbidding me to see them or talk to them by phone. Nothing interested him except three square meals a day.

Ernest grew more feeble, more confused every day. He panicked when I bathed him. He had no muscle coordination and was afraid of falling in the bathtub; I had to get into the tub to support him. Our walks became shorter and shorter, with an increasing number of rest stops. Finally, on June 11, 1985, he could no longer negotiate the stairs to our apartment. Hating the thought of what I had to do, I called an ambulance and had Ernest transported to the Skyline Convalescent Home, only eight blocks from our apartment.

I visited him every day, supplementing his meals at the rest home. I prepared soups and chicken the way he liked them. I also sometimes brought sherry and caviar to stimulate his appetite.

Ernest had a removable dental plate that he disliked. It disappeared the first day he entered the rest home. We searched his room, but it was not to be found. It turned up in the laundry room—he had hidden it in his pajamas! Several weeks later, I received a call that he had fallen out of his wheelchair, in the closet of his room. He was not hurt and the incident was forgotten. But his dental plate was missing again. Later, he complained about his shoes hurting him. So I repaired to the closet to get another pair. I found his dental plate in the toe of one shoe, where he had hidden it the day he fell, secreting it! There was no denying he was a droll hombre to the end.

On July 20, 1986, he was very lucid. It was nearing four o'clock, my departure time. He didn't talk much anymore because it was such an effort for him to find the right words, but today he had no difficulty.

"Going to be much worse for you, Schatz," he said, looking at me searchingly. He took my hand in his good right hand and brought it to his lips. He was wondering how I would get along without him.

"Oh, I'll survive," I countered with great bravado, as I kissed him lightly on the cheek.

"Not like that. A real kiss," he coaxed.

So I kissed him again, the way he wanted me to, and fled, sobbing all the way home.

Next morning, when I came to Skyline, he was in the room where they put the seriously ill. He had had a bad night, they told me. His temperature was 104. He was breathing hard and deep as one does with pneumonia; he was suffering!

I rushed to the office of the new director, Patrick Logan, who had taken his post only a few days before. I was terrified they would remove him to the hospital and string him up on one of those life-support systems. Sure enough, Mr. Logan said the home could not handle his illness and the hospital was the best answer. I hailed a taxi and fled to see Dr. O'Brian. I pleaded, "As one Irishman to another, call this man and forbid him to move Ernest." He picked up the phone and made the call.

I returned to Skyline. It was nearly three o'clock in the afternoon. Ernest's condition had worsened. I knew instinctively that he was dying. I recalled the lines of a poem I had read, by Marie Howe. They were brutal words:

"Death, The Last Visit"
Atlantic Monthly, June 1984

Hearing a low growl in your throat, you'll know that it's started. It has nothing to ask you. It has only something to say, and it will speak in your own tongue.

Locking its arm around you, it will hold you as long as you ever wanted. Only this time it will be long enough. It will not let go. Burying your face in its dark shoulder, you'll smell mud and hair and water.

You'll taste your mother's sour nipple, your favorite salty part, and swallow a word you thought you'd spit out once and be done with. Through half-closed eyes you'll see that it's shadow looks like yours,

a perfect fit. You could weep with gratefulness. It will take you as you like it best, hard and fast as a slap across your face, or so sweet and slow you'll scream give it to me give it to me until it does.

Nothing will ever reach this deep. Nothing will ever clench this hard. At last (the little girls are clapping, shouting) someone has pulled the drawstring of your gym bag closed enough and tight. At last

someone has knotted the lace of your shoe so it won't ever come undone. Even as you turn into it, even as you begin to feel yourself stop, you'll whistle with amazement between your residual teeth, oh Jesus

oh sweetheart, oh holy mother, nothing nothing nothing ever felt so good.

                                                                    Marie Howe

I sat down beside him and held his hand through the railing, the crippled hand with the clenched fingers. I massaged it gently. Was he willing himself to die? Was he saying goodbye to me the day before when he had asked me to kiss him? Knowing him as I did, I felt strongly that the answer was yes.

Ernest's breathing became harder and harder, and he quivered, quivered . . . with every breath, reminding me of Saint-Saëns' "Dying Swan," so poignantly portrayed by the ballerina Pavlova. Suddenly the crippled, tightly curled fingers straightened out. The fist unclenched. His hand dropped loosely through the railing, and I knew my swan had been released.

The appearance of the sherry on the table propelled me back into the present. "Will you order now?" the waiter asked politely. I handed him back the menu. I had no need to consult its enumeration of luncheon specials. I knew what I wanted. I would order the same as I had ordered that afternoon in 1926—the same dish I had ordered again on August 5, 1986, again in 1987, 1988, and now.

"A Mushroom Omelette Soufflé—and coffee."

I raised my glass of sherry in the direction of the empty booth in the corner, to the little man who wasn't there, but whom I willed to be there.

"To memories . . . to our offspring, the 'Swell Fish' . . . and to you," I toasted.

INDEX